FOUNDATIONS
OF
DECISION-MAKING

clp CANADIAN LIBRARY OF PHILOSOPHY

Published for the Canadian Association for Publishing in Philosophy by the
Department of Philosophy of Carleton University, Ottawa, Canada

EDITORIAL COMMITTEE
Diane E. Dubrule
John W. Leyden
R. Stephen Talmage
Bernard Wand

CHAIRMAN
J.A. Brook

FOUNDATIONS
OF DECISION-MAKING

by
Alex C. Michalos

Director, Social Indicators Research Programme
University of Guelph
Guelph, Ontario, Canada

Canadian Library of Philosophy • Ottawa
1978

Canadian Library of Philosophy
published at
Carleton University,
Ottawa
Canada

for the Canadian Association for Publishing in Philosophy

ISBN 0-919936-50-4

© Canadian Association for Publishing in Philosophy

Designed and Produced by Graphic Services, Carleton University, Ottawa, Canada

To Bobbie,

With Love

"It is difficult sometimes to determine what should be chosen at what cost, and what should be endured in return for what gain, and yet more difficult to abide by our decisions."

Aristotle (c. 330 B.C.)

"There are countless books on the techniques of decision-making. Complex logical and mathematical tools have been developed for the decision making process. But there is little concern with the essential process itself. What is a 'decision'? What are the important elements in it?"

Peter F. Drucker (1974)

TABLE OF CONTENTS

ACKNOWLEDGEMENTS

I would like to give special thanks to Myles Brand, David Braybrooke, Andrew Brook, Hugh Lehman, John W. Leyden and James E. White for reading every Chapter of the original manuscript and providing me with thought-provoking counter- proposals, illustrations and references.

The following people read and gave useful comments on from one to five Chapters: John Bruce, Peter Caws, Bernard Hodgson, William Hughes, John King-Farlow, John Leslie, Michael L. Martin, John McMurtry, Ian Mitroff, Douglas Odegard, Nicholas Rescher, Michael Ruse, Howard Sobel, Donald Stewart and Gordon Welty.

I have used parts of the manuscript in graduate seminars at the University of Guelph, University of Pittsburgh and University of Waterloo, and have read parts of it at a Canadian Philosophical Association meeting, a Philosophy of Science Association meeting, a couple of Western Division meetings of the American Philosophical Association, a meeting of the Public Choice Society, The University of Cincinnati, Cornell University, Dalhousie University, University of Delaware, University of Maryland, McMaster University, University of Winnipeg, University of Western Ontario and York University. In all these places I have received some constructive criticism from people whose names I have not recorded and, in many cases, do not even know.

It was logically impossible to follow everyone's advice, but I have tried to accommodate every insight that seemed to have any merit. At any rate, the final responsibility for this treatise must be mine, for better or worse.

Finally, I would like to thank my wife, Bobbie, for typing the manuscript, retyping the manuscript, putting up with the typing and retyping, and the reading and rereading, and the questions and answers, and the listening, listening and still more listening. In the past twenty years she has often persuaded me to scrap arguments that I have constructed with apparently unassailable logic and truly wondrous prose, by tenderly uttering those three little words: "I'm not convinced."

Alex C. Michalos

Guelph, Ontario
December, 1977.

CHAPTER I

Aims and Method

1. INTRODUCTION

As its title suggests, the purpose of this Chapter is to provide a general introduction to the objectives of the investigation and the basic methodology employed. I begin by explaining the sense in which the research is foundational. In the third Section the activity of explicating concepts is analyzed as that of proposing definitions of words, and the latter is compared to merely stipulating and discovering definitions. Four necessary conditions of adequacy and two desiderata for any proposed explication are presented in Section Four. Finally, a rapid review of the general orientation and some of the distinctive features of the study are given.

2 FOUNDATIONAL STUDIES

Since several different kinds of investigation or activity may be appropriately referred to as 'foundational', it will be worthwhile to offer some explanatory remarks concerning various alternatives and the enterprise before you. In the first place, introductions to this or that discipline, subject, field or area of concentration may be regarded as foundational in the sense that they provide

beginning students with the basic elements of the subject.
There are, for example, introductory courses in logic,
geography, sociology, political science and mathematics in
practically all colleges and universities. The primary aim
of such courses is to introduce certain areas of study with
their conceptual schemes, facts, assumptions and ways of
seeing and doing things to students with little or no prior
exposure to these areas. This is certainly an important aim
and there is no good reason that I can think of for not
referring to courses or treatises with this as their primary
aim as 'foundational'. But the treatise before you is not
foundational in this sense. Although I have tried to
analyze many of the most important ideas related to
decision-making, the analyses often presuppose some material
that would be unfamiliar to people without any previous
university-level training.

    Axiomatic systematizations of fields of knowledge
or sets of formal theses are also frequently referred to as
'foundational' studies. For example, one might
appropriately regard the axiomatization of Mendelian
genetics, Newtonian mechanics, the theory of the syllogism,
and the lower and higher predicate calculi as foundational
exercises. The primary aim of such investigations is to
systematically organize a vast amount of data by means of a
perspicuous and elegantly simple set of primitive terms,
axioms, formation and transformation rules. Again, this is
an important aim and studies that have such rigorous
systematization as their primary goal may be properly
regarded as foundational. But again the treatise before you
is not foundational in this sense.

    This investigation is foundational in the sense
that its aim is the clarification of some of the fundamental
concepts that must be employed by anyone working in the
field usually designated by 'decision theory'.
Alternatively, one could say that its aim is the explication
of some of the basic concepts in any theory of
decision-making. In still other words, its aim is to
propose a plausible set of definitions for some of the most
frequently used terms in the analysis of decision-making.

    Philosophers have spent a considerable amount of
time and energy over the past thirty years trying to explain
the logical or conceptual features of concept clarification,
explications and proposals for linguistic reform, and this
is not the place to review that effort. (An excellent
review of the issues may be found in Rorty (1967).) I shall
have more to say about my own view of the issues in the next
Section. For present purposes it is enough to notice the
distinctive foundational character of this treatise and its
close relation to rigorous axiomatization. One cannot
simply straightaway axiomatize a body of knowledge expressed
or expressible in some language without sorting out in a

more or less informal way the key concepts and propositions belonging to that body of knowledge. In the absence of such a preliminary investigation, the question of the completeness of a set of axioms is unanswerable. Roughly speaking, a set of axioms is said to be complete for a certain body of knowledge if, in accordance with a given set of formation and transformation rules, every proposition belonging to the body of knowledge is derivable from those axioms. Thus, without some prior examination of a field to be axiomatized, one of the most significant questions that one would like to raise concerning a set of axioms is logically precluded. Of course the question of completeness is not the only significant question that one would want to raise concerning an axiomatic system, and it might well be worthwhile to axiomatize one's knowledge in the interests of some other question. Nevertheless, the question of completeness must remain unanswered until some more or less informal examination of basic concepts is undertaken.

3   EXPLICATIONS AS PROPOSALS

Following a long line of logical positivists, it may be said that the task of explicating a concept consists in finding a more or less precise concept called an explicatum to replace a more or less imprecise concept called an explicandum. (Carnap (1950), Ayer (1959).) For example, the imprecise concept of warmth might be replaced by the more precise concept of temperature of a certain degree, and the rather imprecise concept of probability might be replaced by some sophisticated concept like the relative frequency of the occurrence of some event in a random sequence.

As the title of this Section suggests, I see the activity of explicating a concept as nothing more nor less than proposing definitions of words. I hasten to emphasize, however, that this is a deceptively simple-sounding account of a very complicated, subtle and serious enterprise. After all, a great deal of what one is inclined and/or able to know, believe and communicate about the world (including one's own self) depends upon what words one has at one's command and the meanings of those words. In other words, what one is inclined and/or able to think and say depends a great deal upon the language that one has at one's disposal. Thus, the careful construction of definitions of the key terms in any area of investigation should not be regarded as something like a mopping-up exercise that one engages in after the serious business of theory-building is virtually complete. On the contrary, without meaningful terms there can be no meaningful propositions and, consequently, no meaningful theories either.

By "proposing definitions" I mean to designate an activity that is in some respects similar to and in others different from stipulating definitions on the one hand and discovering definitions on the other. As one might expect, it is frequently confused with both of the latter activities. For purposes of discussion or, as we say, for the sake of argument it is frequently useful to simply stipulate that certain words shall be used in certain ways or shall have certain specific meanings. When the discussion or argument is finished, one may or may not continue to use the words in accordance with the stipulations. Whether or not one does continue to use the words with the stipulated definitions depends on several factors which need not detain us. The important point is that virtually everyone stipulates definitions sometimes, but few people recommend such definitions as linguistic reforms that should be adopted by all English-speaking people (or any other natural language-speaking people). In part, then, it is this bold implicit or explicit recommendation that a particular definition would constitute an improvement in a given natural language that distinguishes what I am calling proposals from stipulations. Proposals are like stipulations insofar as both are definitions constructed by people for their own particular purposes. But proposals are unlike stipulations insofar as they are conjectured tentatively and put forward for examination and criticism. Stipulations are made for the sake of arguments; proposals are made for the sake of improvements in ordinary ways of talking and thinking. In short, then, proposers are after much bigger fish than stipulators. That is why, as we shall see in detail shortly, proposers must be especially careful about their criteria of adequacy.

Just as proposals are not merely stipulations but are closely related to them, they are not merely discoveries either; but they are closely related to them. The basic tasks of a lexicographer are to discover and accurately report the meaning and use of words in a given language. Thus, unlike the enterprise of a mere stipulator, the enterprise of a lexicographer is fundamentally empirical. A lexicographer's entries will typically be true or false reports about the meaning and use of words, but a stipulator's definitions cannot be true or false reports because they are not reports at all.

To say that explications are proposals is to say two things, namely, that they may have the force of stipulations (in which case they cannot be true or false) and that they may have the force of reports (in which case they must be true or false). The most interesting explications are those that are not so obviously reportorial that the average lexicographer would be likely to produce them nor so obviously ad hoc that the average person would not be inclined to use them for anything but the sake of a particular argument. Most of the explications offered in this book are (naturally) intended to be interesting in the above sense.

4   CRITERIA OF ADEQUACY

Broadly speaking, adequacy criteria for proposed explicata may be divided into two kinds on the basis of their range of application. Some are supposed to apply quite generally to any explicata and others are restricted to certain specific concepts. Moreover, within each of these broad categories, one may distinguish formal from informal criteria. The Kolmogorov axioms of the probability calculus are a notable example of formal concept-specific criteria of adequacy. So-called paradigm cases of ordinary usage frequently function as informal concept-specific adequacy criteria. As one might expect, informal criteria are much more plentiful than formal criteria. I shall have more to say about concept-specific adequacy criteria as I explicate the various key concepts in decision theory. The aim of this Section, however, is the elucidation of quite general necessary conditions of adequacy for any proposed explicatum. All of the conditions shall be presented informally.

In the first place, any proposed explicatum should be internally or self-consistent. This is undoubtedly the neatest adequacy criterion one can cite, since it merely requires that any proposed definition of a word must not be self-contradictory.

Second, any proposed explicatum should be externally consistent or coherent with some generally accepted body of scientific or common sense knowledge or beliefs. Obviously this criterion is typically more complicated and problematic than the first, since it involves such notoriously difficult concepts as coherence, acceptance, science, common sense, knowledge and belief. (See, for examples, Rescher (1973a).) But for all its precariousness, it is still worth mentioning, because it immediately calls attention to the fact that explicata do not and typically are not intended to exist in isolation. They usually belong to networks of concepts of different sizes with varying degrees of complexity and systematicity, and there does not seem to be any procedure for determining a priori just how big, complex and systematic a more or less "natural network" for any given explicatum should be. The fact of the matter is that concepts are frequently explicated in clusters, packages or sets with the lines of dependency among different networks seldom delineated. Thus, although many people like to think of their particular

analyses as somehow fitting into a single conceptual network
that is rich enough to contain the sum total of human
knowledge and beliefs, there is as yet little evidence that
such a system is feasible.

It is probably worthwhile to note at this point
that the bigger the cluster the greater the problems. This
became abundantly clear to me after I began in earnest to
try to explicate the concept of a decision. I found that
the task could not be satisfactorily accomplished without
distinguishing 'choosing' and 'deciding'. But there then
seemed to be no hope of unpacking 'choosing' without
tackling 'preferring'. 'Preferring' in turn drove me to
'liking' and 'wanting', and the latter pressed me further to
'needing'. Although it is surely possible to provide some
sort of explication for any of these concepts in isolation,
the greater the isolation the easier it is to violate the
following third condition.

Any proposed explicatum should be similar enough
to its explicandum to be a credible replacement for it. To
some extent this requirement overlaps that of external
coherence, because the latter constitutes an important
respect in which an explicatum can be similar to its
explicandum. An explicatum with few or none of the
conceptual dependencies of its explicandum should be
regarded as little more than a semantic peculiarity, which
is, as a matter of fact, just about how most people do
regard such aberrations.

Fourth, any proposed explicatum should be more
precise than its corresponding explicandum. A proposed
explicatum should at least strike its proposer as clearer,
more exact or precise than its corresponding explicandum.
Whether or not anyone else will be similarly struck seems to
be largely beyond anyone's control.

Finally, there are two other requirements that
have gained widespread acceptance in the literature, but
seem to me to be of secondary importance. These are
simplicity and fruitfulness. One would hope that one's
explicata would tend to be simple rather than complex in
virtually any senses of these terms and that they would tend
to suggest further explicata or fertile areas of research.
But such hopes seem to be more appropriately characterized
as desiderata than as necessary conditions of adequacy.
Sometimes clarity can only be obtained through complexity
and explicata that are useful in one area of investigation
may fail to reveal important insights elsewhere. Hence, I
would not give simplicity and fruitfulness the same status
as the other conditions.

5   GENERAL ORIENTATION

The general orientation of this investigation follows the pattern used in most contemporary studies of decision-making. I imagine decision-makers pursuing various kinds of goals or objectives in the presence of certain restrictions and with the aid of certain resources. They will typically be required to decide what to do or to believe about their goals in the light of sets of possible decisions, states of the world and more or less beneficial or costly consequences. Above all, they would like their decisions to be rational, and they would like the processes they use to make those decisions also to be rational. This last sentence cannot be emphasized too strongly. In some sense of the term, people like to think of themselves as and believe that they ought to be rational animals. Although rationality in a human being is not everything, it is regarded as a very good thing-whatever it is.

Broadly speaking, the book is divided into three parts. Part One is subtitled "Decision-Making Elements" and consists of Chapters II to V. These Chapters deal with aspects of decision-making that tend to be more or less inherent in decision-makers. For example, Chapter II is devoted to a discussion of the problem of reducing group decisions to the decisions of individuals. In Chapter III I construct concepts of preference and indifference out of more primitive notions of liking and wanting, revealing some of the logical features of these ideas that tend to go unnoticed. Similarly, the concepts of choosing and deciding are typically regarded as primitive and synonymous, but in Chapter IV they are constructed out of more primitive terms and distinguished. In Chapter V the concept of a decision process is examined in the light of general ideas about processes in order to capture the distinctive features of the former.

Part Two is subtitled "Decision Fields" and consists of Chapters VI to VIII. These Chapters deal with aspects of decision-making that tend to set the stage or field of operation for decision-makers. Chapter VI contains an analysis of the kinds of things that can be decided or chosen. Following that, there is a Chapter (VII) suggesting alternative ways of conceptualizing possibilities, restrictions and resources. In the last Chapter in this part (VIII), there is a brief review of alternative concepts of probability and measurement theories, concepts of controllability, clarity and independence.

Part Three is subtitled "Rational Decision-Making" and consists of Chapters IX to XIII. The overriding aim of the first four of these Chapters is to vindicate a way of thinking and talking about rational decision-making. In Chapter IX I try to show that two widely held views about rationality are seriously deficient. These are the views that rationality cannot be identified with efficiency and that it must be identified with action that maximizes something. Following this preparatory excursus, in Chapter X I proceed to a consideration of a priori and a posteriori procedures for appraising the rationality of decisions and decision processes, and offer preliminary explications of the latter concepts (i.e. of rational decisions and rational decision processes). In Chapter XI I defend the view that rationality should be explicated such that decisions and processes can (logically) be rational only if (roughly speaking) the outcomes for everyone affected by them are favorable, though they need not be equally favorable for everyone. I call this view 'consensual rationality' and try to show that it is in many ways preferable to the egoistic rationality that has been assumed and promoted by a host of well-known writers. In Chapter XII some problems related to the selection of accurate and consistent estimating techniques, regions of analysis, and costs and benefits are reviewed.

The final Chapter (XIII) of the book is devoted to a defense of the thesis that cognitive decision-making is subject to moral appraisal, i.e., that there is an ethics of belief.

An earlier attempt to throw some light on problems of rational group decision-making has been included as an Appendix. Some assumptions in that article are not consistent with some of the conclusions reached in this book. However, I am confident that readers will not be misled by the earlier piece, and will find it of some interest, especially since so little is said about group decision-making in the main text.

I should perhaps add here that I have tried to write with a style and vocabulary that would facilitate inter-disciplinary exchanges. After all, decision-making is not just a problem of philosophy, sociology, management science or any other single discipline. Furthermore, researchers in different disciplines have shown different interests and produced analyses of varying degrees of sophistication and strength on different topics. So, thoroughness demands crossing disciplinary boundaries. Nevertheless, it is difficult for leopards to change their spots. So I suppose analytic philosophers will find my general approach congenial, while people trained in other disciplines will find it less so.

Part I
Decision-Making Elements

CHAPTER II

Decision – Makers

1 INTRODUCTION

The problems before us in this Chapter concern species of decision-makers. In the next Section it is argued that persons certainly are and should be regarded as decision-makers, while "dumb" things, events and forces are not, should not and probably never have to be regarded as decision-makers. This is followed by a Section elucidating the main strengths and weaknesses of the so-called individualistic and holistic views of group action in general and group decisions in particular. The conclusion finally reached is that from a logical point of view holism is justifiable, but from a moral point of view it seems better to adopt some kind of individualist position. The position accepted here is called 'pragmatic individualism'.

2 PERSONS AND EVENTS

If anything can make a decision, individual persons can. But what about "dumb" things, events and forces? One sometimes hears or utters sentences like:

(1) I will let nature decide what to do about that.
(2) Sooner or later events are going to decide for us.
(3) I will let the dice decide.
(4) I will just let my impulses decide that one.

Should we say then, that nature, events, dice and impulses should be regarded as decision-makers? There are two reasons for answering this question negatively. First "dumb" things, events and forces cannot literally do anything or perform actions in the sense of initiating activities or processes with certain intentions, goals or ends in view. At best they can only cause or be causally connected to such phenomena.(cf. Brown (1968))

Second, it is possible to provide translations of sentences like (1) - (4) that are plausible and eliminate the suggestions that "dumb" things, events and forces are decision-makers. For example, sentence (1) might be used to assert nothing more nor less than

(5)   I will let all but one of my options be eliminated by the natural course of events.

Similarly, (2) might be replaced by

(6)   Sooner or later our alternatives will be eliminated by the natural course of events.

Sentence (3) might be used to cite a reason for my decision, e.g.,

(7)   I will make my decision on the basis of the result of a toss of the dice.

Finally, (4) might be regarded as nothing more nor less than a report of my decision to refuse to deliberate about a certain issue, e.g.

(8)   I will decide that one by impulse (or impulsively).

Generalizing from cases like these then, I conclude that it is probably always possible to substitute a sentence attributing decision-making to individuals for a sentence that apparently attributes decision-making to "dumb" things, events and forces.

3   GROUP DECISIONS

Oddly enough, the questions of whether or not, in what sense or in what way groups can be decision-makers has received more attention from researchers in the field of decision-making than the analogous questions for individuals. While the idea of an individual decision has not "cried out" as it were for analysis, that of a group decision has. Puzzlement over the latter has led to such problematic concepts as the General Will, the will of all, the sense of the meeting, the spirit of the group, the general consensus, the group preference, the socially preferred item, and so on. I shall try to answer the fundamental questions without reliving too much history. Indeed, apart from the discussion in this Section and the article in the Appendix, I shall have practically nothing to say that bears directly only on group decision-making. Although most of the issues considered in this book have obvious relevance for group decision-making, my focus throughout is on individuals

The following definition of a group shall be used.

(1) $\underline{x}$ is a group $=$ $\underline{x}$ is a set of people
                            df
          with a fairly normal distribution of attributes (intelligence, motor ability, morals, etc.) who are disposed to interact socially.

The only groups of interest to us now are the kinds defined in (1). Thus, I shall have nothing to say about sets of nonhumans, ideally good or bad humans in any sense of 'good' and 'bad', skewed distributions (e.g., sets of geniuses, morons, one-legged females, etc.) or aggregates of individuals who are not even disposed to interact socially. In fact, more or less normal human beings are the only kinds of individuals considered throughout this book. Philosophical analysis is difficult enough without trying to accommodate devils, angels and all other kinds of super- or sub-human creatures.

The problems that one confronts in analysing the concept of a group decision are merely special cases of the general problems involved with the idea of group action. Hence, the problems arising here may be regarded as instances of the more general conflict between so-called holists and individualists in social science and philosophy. (For an excellent review of the central issues in this conflict see Dray (1967).) By 'holists' I mean those who hold that occasionally at least terms designating social phenomena (like revolutions) or groups (like clubs, teams, battalions, states or committees) occur essentially in descriptions or explanations of human social behaviour. I regard a term or phrase as occurring essentially in a sentence if and only if it cannot (logically) be deleted entirely or replaced by some other term without loss of descriptive accuracy. By 'individualists' I mean those who hold that such terms can always be eliminated in favor of terms designating individuals and individual action. Just as I have defended the view that sentences which apparently predicate decision-making capacities of impersonal natural forces can always be be translated into sentences predicating such capacities only of individuals, individualists would defend the view that sentences which apparently predicate decision-making capacities of groups can always be translated into sentences predicating such capacities only of individual members of groups. Holists, on the other hand, would insist that at least sometimes such translations are logically impossible. I shall examine some prima facie paradigm cases for each of these points of view.

Suppose we have a group consisting of three members Tom, Dick and Harry. They are the only members of a committee whose responsibility it is to decide which of four kinds of picnic facilities should be purchased for the town park. For brevity I shall refer to the facilities as $\underline{w}$, $\underline{x}$, $\underline{y}$ and $\underline{z}$. Suppose finally, that

(2)   The committee decided that $\underline{w}$ should be purchased.

The question is: Under what conditions, if any, could one eliminate the apparent reference to a group act, namely, the committee decision, from (2) in favor of some individual acts or decisions without giving a misleading or inaccurate description?

It might be thought that a <u>sufficient</u> condition for such a move would be that <u>every</u> member of the committee decided that $\underline{w}$ should be purchased. In that case (2) would be abandoned in favor of

(3)   Every member of the committee decided that $\underline{w}$ should be purchased.

on the ground that if (3) is true then (2) must be true too. But (3) might be true while (2) is false. Tom, Dick and Harry might each decide independently that $\underline{w}$ should be purchased long before they communicate their decisions to one another. Alternatively, they might decide that $\underline{w}$ should be purchased but fail to make a committee decision as a result of violating some procedural rule.

To cover ourselves against these possibilities, (3) should be expanded to

(4)   In accordance with all of the rules governing the activities of the committee, every member of the committee decided that $\underline{w}$ should be purchased.

Presumably the rules would include one indicating the necessity of committee members making overt decisions somewhere along the way in order for them to be counted. More importantly, the point I want to make about (4) is that it seems to me that only the most extreme holists would insist that even if (2) and (4) are <u>both</u> true, (4) is in some way a misleading or inaccurate description of the state

of affairs correctly and accurately described by (2). I
have nothing to say to persuade such holists that they are
mistaken, and I address my remarks only to the moderates.
If individualistic reduction is ever possible, as most
holists would grant, the translation of (2) into (4) would
have to count as a paradigm case. We only have three
individuals who decide severally and in accordance with
certain rules that w should be purchased. Thus, the
following sufficient‾ condition of reduction might be
posited. References to group decisions can be eliminated in
favor of references to decisions of group members without
loss of descriptive accuracy provided that:

> cl In accordance with all the rules governing
> decision-making for a group, every member makes a
> decision whose object is identical (i.e.,
> qualitatively the same) to that which is
> allegedly made by the group.

Roughly speaking, the object of a decision is
just what is decided by any decision-maker. Such objects
are examined in detail in Chapter VI. The point that should
be noticed about cl is that it is neutral as between the
holist- individualist controversy. An individualist would
assert categorically that the elimination of references to
group decisions is always possible and a holist would assert
the negation of this claim, namely, that it is not the case
that the elimination of references to group decisions is
always possible. One who affirms cl is only committed to
the hypothetical assertion that in the presence of certain
specified conditions, the elimination of references to group
decisions is always possible. This could be granted without
self-contradiction by holists and individualists. Granted
that cl provides a sufficient condition for individualistic
reduction, the question arises: Does cl also provide a
necessary condition? That is, is it the case that in order
for individualistic reduction to be possible, cl must be
satisfied? If the answer to this question is negative, then
(4), for example, might be weakened to

(5)   In accordance with all of the rules governing the
         activities of the committee, some members of the
         committee decided on behalf of the whole group
         that w should be purchased.

In (5) 'some' would usually be interpreted as a plurality,
absolute majority or perhaps two-thirds of the members of
the committee. It might also be interpreted as an elected
or appointed agent or representative of the group.
Supposing that (5) and (2) are true, my guess would be that
most holists would still be willing to grant that (5) is not
more misleading or inaccurate than (2). (5) only seems to
be a more detailed description. So I doubt that cl does
provide a necessary condition of reduction. Consider then,

$\underline{c2}$ In accordance with all the rules governing
decision-making for a group, some members make a
decision whose object is identical to that which
is allegedly made by the group.

as a possible necessary and sufficient condition of
individualistic reduction of group decisions. Again, it is
only the necessity of $\underline{c2}$ that tends to make me suspicious.
There are cases (frequently involving compromises) in which
no member of a group makes a decision whose object is
identical to that which is allegedly made by the group, and
one might still be inclined to insist that reduction is
possible.   For example , suppose our committee is using a
system of voting such that each member rank orders the kinds
of picnic facilities he decides should be purchased.   For
simplicity, let us say that a given kind of facility is
given one point for every kind it outranks, and that the one
with the most points wins. Finally, suppose the members of
the committee come up with the following rankings.

Tom	Dick	Harry
x	z	y
w	w	w
z	y	x
y	x	z

So, $\underline{w}$ makes 6 points, while $\underline{x}$, $\underline{y}$ and $\underline{z}$ each make 4. Hence
the committee decided that $\underline{w}$ should be purchased, although
no member of the committee made such a decision. That is,
no member of the group made a decision whose object is
identical to that which is allegedly made by the group. The
question is then: Should $\underline{c2}$ be modified to obtain a
necessary and sufficient condition of reduction that is weak
or broad enough to allow one to speak of the individualistic
reduction of cases like the one just presented, or should
such cases be used as paradigms in an attack on
individualism?

A possible modification of $\underline{c2}$ might run,

$\underline{c3}$ In accordance with all the rules governing
decision-making for a group, some members make
decisions on behalf of the group.

According to $\underline{c3}$, which is roughly the principle adopted by
Benn and Peters (1959), all that is required for the
individualistic reduction of a group decision is at least
one individual legitimately making a decision in behalf of
the group.   It is not required that the object of that
individual's decision must be identical to that of the

alleged decision of the group. The rules of procedure might be such that if the decision-making agent or representative decides such and such, then the group decision becomes something else, say, so and so.

Should one adopt a principle of reduction like c3 or should one draw the line against individualism with cases like those just cited? There are at least two good reasons to side with the holists and one in favor of individualism. First, it could be insisted that c3 leaves open the question of whether or not a group decision was made, while (2), for example, answers that question affirmatively. c3 tells us that some members make decisions for the group according to its rules, but it is logically possible to satisfy this condition without having a group decision made. For example, suppose Dick is the chairman of the committee and he decides that the meeting should be called to order at 1:00 p.m. instead of 1:15 p.m. because everyone is present already. This is evidently a decision made for the group in accordance with its rules, but it is not a decision of the group or a group decision. More precisely, one could say that this is a decision made for the group collectively and distributively (i.e., for the group as a whole and for each member of the group), but it is not a decision of the group collectively or distributively because the group did not even consider the question either as a whole body or individually. (Sobel (1967)) Thus, insofar as the individualist-holist controversy involves a question of logic, one has a good reason to draw the line against individualism and c3. (See also Sobel (1967).)

Second, the adoption of c3 in the face of cases like the one just cited seems to leave one with a peculiar problem concerning moral responsibility. I suppose that one of the aims of those who are inclined to individualism is to fix the responsibility for group actions on specific individuals. If, however, as in our example, no one makes the decision that is finally ascribed to the group, then who is to be held responsible? It would seem unjust to hold, say, Tom responsible for the group decision that w should be purchased when Tom decided that x should be purchased, and similarly for Dick and Harry. But if in the last analysis it is unjust to hold Tom, Dick or Harry responsible for the group decision then c3 should not be accepted, because its acceptance entails precisely this result. Thus, insofar as the individualist-holist controversy involves a question of morality, one seems to have another good reason to draw the line against individualism.

In favor of individualism, one should cite the somewhat ugly other side of the responsibility coin. If only the group (not Tom, Dick or Harry) is to be held responsible for deciding that w should be purchased, then only the group should be praised or blamed, rewarded or

punished for the decision. How do we do that? Suppose that
in one way or another it is conclusively determined that the
decision that w should be purchased is terrible. (I shall
have much more to say about evaluative criteria in Chapter
X.) How can we punish the group, that is, the abstract
entity, and only the group? If the group were treated as a
corporate person,it might be prosecuted. It could be fined
or dissolved as a corporate entity. It could not, however,
be meaningfully scolded, reprimanded, threatened, thrashed
or made to feel remorse. In many ways then, corporate
persons are nothing more than dummies and the idea that they
alone can be held responsible for anything is largely an
illusion. Similarly, all groups, from small committees to
states and empires, are to a large extent logically unsuited
to praise and blame, reward and punishment. Hence, one who
draws the line against individualism in favor of holism
opens the door for all kinds of pernicious acts on the part
of members of all kinds of groups, acts that a priori one
knows will go unpunished. (See also Chapter XI.) This
seems to be a good reason to reject holism, but that clearly
entails punishing Tom, Dick and Harry for a decision that
none of them made! Indeed, it seems probable that most of
the pernicious acts or decisions that emerge from groups may
be like the group decision that w should be purchased, i.e.,
most of them may be basically compromises that no one really
wants.

I suspect that the moral dilemma I have just
outlined is more apparent than real, because given the
decision procedure employed by Tom, Dick and Harry, what
they decided implied that w should be purchased. Consider
Harry's decision. Harry decided that y should be purchased
and, if not y, then w, then x and last of all z. Given the
decisions of the other members of the group and the voting
system employed, it was not decided that y should be
purchased. Therefore, in the presence of these facts and
Harry's decision, it follows that w should be purchased.
Analogous arguments apply to the decisions of Tom and Dick.
Each one decided that w should be purchased if something
else was not to be, and in each case the something else was
not to be. Thus, each one is indirectly responsible for the
group decision. If each of them had not decided that w
should be purchased unless some other kind of facility could
be purchased, the group decision that w should be purchased
would not have been made. Similarly, one may generalize
this argument for all compromise decisions. It is trivially
true that insofar as one opts for a compromise in the
absence of his first choice, one commits oneself to a
compromise in the absence of his first choice. Hence,
contrary to earlier appearances, such a person should be
held responsible for the compromise when it becomes the
decision of his group. Thus, there is no moral dilemma. (A
more detailed examination of some of the central issues in
group decision-making and techniques of fixing
responsibility in order to distribute benefits and costs
according to contribution may be found in the Appendix.)

On the basis of these considerations concerning the consequences of accepting c3 and individualism in general versus the consequences of drawing the line against individualism in view of compromise decisions, I conclude that the holistic position seems to be logically defensible but morally dangerous. I have been unable to find a principle that captures the necessary and sufficient conditions of individualistic reduction, but I find the prospect of holding groups (i.e. abstract entities) rather than group members responsible for group action somewhat terrifying from a moral point of view. Granted that individuals operate under several kinds of restrictions as group members and that, therefore, one ought to make some allowances, I am still inclined to adopt some kind of individualism as a working hypothesis. For ease of reference one might refer to my position as pragmatic individualism. As I see it, I have granted more to holists and less to individualists than so-called methodological individualists like Popper (1957) and Watkins (1952) would grant.

CHAPTER III

Concepts of Preference and Indifference

1 INTRODUCTION

In this Chapter explicata for what I take to be fairly ordinary concepts of preference and indifference are constructed out of several more or less primitive notions. The most primitive are those introduced in Sections Two and Three. In Section Two, the ideas of liking and disliking are examined, and in Section Three an explicatum of the ordinary concept of wanting is proposed. On the basis of these notions, two very rudimentary concepts called 'blunt preference' and 'blunt indifference' are defined in Sections Four and Five. These elementary concepts are then developed into explicata for our ordinary concepts of preference and indifference.

2 LIKING

The first point to be made about the term 'liking' is that it does not take modifiers that typically (not always and only) modify terms designating actions. One cannot, for example, like well or badly, rapidly or slowly, carefully or carelessly, efficiently or inefficiently, routinely or novelly, and so on. All of these adverbs are commonly ascribed to human actions, but not to liking. Moreover, there does not seem to be any normal sense to first person singular reports beginning "I am liking...", which is unlike verbs of action. One might say something like "I am liking what I am doing now (i.e., the kind of work I am engaged in) as much as I have ever liked anything", but this would not be taken as a report about two kinds of actions that one is performing. On the contrary it would most likely and quite properly be taken as a report about the feeling or attitude that one has about the kind of work one is engaged in now. And finally, it is quite common to speak of liking intensely, mildly, more or less, just barely, and so on. That is, adverbs that are typically applied to experiences that one undergoes or suffers rather than to actions that one performs may be sensibly ascribed to liking.

Secondly, if 'a' is a placeholder for the names or descriptions of objects, actions, persons, or states of affairs then, contrary to Baier (1963), I think that one of the things one typically intends to express and describe with sentences patterned after the schema

(1) I like a.

is that a is enjoyable or pleasing. For example, if I tell you that I like this ice cream I am now eating, I imagine that you will understand that I mean to tell you that I enjoy the particular gustatory sensations I am having while eating this ice cream. I might be suggesting a number of other things, e.g. that you would enjoy the ice cream, that you should try some, that you should buy the next round, that I probably should have bought the last round, and so on. But more often than not, I think, I would be expressing and describing my feeling about the ice cream.

If 'a' happens to be replaced by the name of a person (or even a pet) there will usually be additional modifications required, e.g., 'I like Fred' in this sense of 'like' means something like 'I enjoy being with Fred' or 'I just feel good when I'm around Fred'. Nevertheless, the main point is that locutions like (1) are often used to express and describe feelings or sensations.

There are a couple of moot points about the claims in the preceding two paragraphs that should be noted. First, I have used the phrase "express and describe" because I think sentences patterned after (1) are typically used to perform both functions. A "linguistic purist" might want to insist that such locutions are or should only be regarded as reports (necessarily either true or false) or else expressions of feelings (impossibly either true or false). But I can find no warrant for such a point of view and have therefore adopted the somewhat less pure and less extraordinary view cited above. Second, the apparently implied feeling or sensation of enjoyment or pleasure is notoriously problematic. I certainly have nothing profound

to offer to the careful analyses of these concepts provided
by Ryle (1949), Penelhum (1956) and Gosling (1969), and am
quite prepared to grant that in some ways the term
'pleasurable feeling' seems to designate some kind of
sensation and in other ways not.   I must admit, however,
that when I utter sentences like "I like this ice cream" in
certain circumstances, it is frequently because I have a
particular kind of feeling that such locutions appropriately
describe and express. In other words, I use such sentences
in the presence of or in the event that certain more or less
identifiable feelings occur, and I use them to express and
report these feelings to others. Rather than attempt to
settle the issue of the "real" nature of these feelings by
further analysis or stipulation, I shall generally simply
refer to them as 'pleasurable feelings'. Thus, the claim I
am advancing in the first place about sentences patterned
after (1) is that one frequently does use them to indicate
pleasure or enjoyment.

         Another point to be made about instantiations of
(1) is roughly Baier's (1953), i.e., such locutions cannot
always be taken as indicating enjoyment. An example of
Baier's is that of one who likes to visit his mother's grave
at least once a year. This is not the sort of action that
one normally enjoys or takes pleasure in performing. It is
done presumably out of respect for the deceased. We might
say that one who performs such actions out of respect has a
pro-attitude toward performing such actions, where the term
'pro-attitude' denotes something short of a pleasurable
feeling but beyond mere non-evaluative awareness on the
positive side. Moreover, as I shall use the term, following
Baier, one who likes in the sense of having a pro-attitude
toward something or someone is usually, but not
always,willing and prepared to offer some reason or motive
for his attitude. In this respect such liking differs from
that of liking in the sense of enjoying or finding pleasure
in something, since the latter might be accounted for by a
causal explanation but is typically not adopted for this or
that reason or with this or that motive. In sum, perhaps we
shall not be far from the mark if we regard pro-attitudes as
tendencies, inclinations or dispostions to act in certain
ways for which one is usually willing to try to give
reasons, whether or not one is actually able to give them.
The following diagram may help.

DISPOSITIONS	FEELINGS		DISPOSITIONS
CON-ATTITUDE	DISPLEASURE	PLEASURE	PRO-ATTITUDE

I am suggesting that there is roughly a center core of
feelings, some of which are good and others bad. Beyond the
core are dispositions to act in certain ways, usually as a
result of some reason or motive that one would be willing to
articulate. Occasionally, one may have pro or con attitudes

without any apparent reason, or without being willing to divulge any reason.

It might be thought that an appeal to amorphous pro- attitudes could be avoided by analysing this second sense of liking in terms of wanting. (The converse of this view is suggested by Norman (1971).) Thus, we might say that the man who says he likes to visit his mother's grave at least once a year merely wants to, and he wants to perform this action because he believes he ought to. Similarly, we might say that one wants to pay one's bills, to keep one's promises and to perform various other actions that one feels obligated to perform. In such cases use of the term 'wants' seems to have the advantage of lacking the misleading connotation of enjoyment that the term 'likes' suggests. While this is a definite advantage, I think there are two good reasons for resisting such an analysis, namely, that 'likes to' seems to imply familiarity or experience with the action described or named following 'to', and that it is possible to like something and not want it.

Taking the last point first, I like to listen to classical music, but seldom want to. More precisely, I like to listen to such music because I think that it would be a good thing for me to learn to enjoy it, but I seldom enjoy it and do not want to listen to it now because I am occupied with more interesting things. Someone might, of course, merely have conflicting wants and express his sentiments with a sentence like "I like to listen to classical music, but I do not want to." But this does not mitigate the fact that one might also use such a sentence to express a discrepancy not between wants but between what one has a pro-attitude toward and what one is inclined to do at a given moment. (For a contrary view see Edgley (1969) p. 160.)

The first point may be established by considering the peculiarity of "I like to live to a ripe old age" compared to the true sentence "I want to live to a ripe old age.". The peculiarity of the former sentence seems to arise because 'like to' implies some sort of firsthand experience or familiarity with the action or process liked, and in the case at hand I have not had such experience. 'Want to', on the other hand, does not have such an implication. We could make the sentence "I like to live to a ripe old age" sensible by turning it into a truncated hypothetical, i.e., "I would like to live to a ripe old age (if ...)", but even that is significantly different logically from the categorical "I want to live to a ripe old age." (See also Jennings (1967).)

The third point I wish to make about instantiations of (1) is that the concept of liking involved in them is essentially qualitative in the sense that these instantiations are complete in themselves. (Lest there be some misunderstanding, the concept of liking involved here is not qualitative in the perhaps more usual sense of being free of intensity or gradation, i.e., we are not bound to the two options of merely liking or not liking.) Sentences patterned after (1) are not short or elliptical for, say,

(2)   I like a more than b.

or

(3)   I like a rather than b.

A schema like (2) might be analyzed sensibly but with obvious circularity as

(4)   I like a and I like b and I like a more than b.

or without circularity but perhaps misleadingly (because (2) does not imply (5) as

(5)   I like a and I do not like b.

Like (2), the former analysis (4) again involves the connective of comparison more than while the latter (5) (which is logically incompatible with (4),) does not. Concepts which are essentially comparative do not admit of analyses like (4) or (5). For example, because the concept of preferring is essentially comparative

(6)   I prefer a to b.

cannot be sensibly analyzed as

(7)   I prefer a and I prefer b and I prefer a to b.

or as

(8)   I prefer a and I do not prefer b.

Schemata (7) and (8) are logically ill-formed in much the same way that

(9)   a is equal and b is equal and a is equal to b.

is logically ill-formed.   (I shall have more to say about comparative likings and dislikings in Sections Four and Five.   It is perhaps worthwhile to note here, however, that one distinguished contemporary philosopher seems to have completely missed the fact that there is such a concept as qualitative liking. See Hare (1963) p. 170.)

Summarizing the preceding paragraphs then, I propose the following explication. If 'a' is a placeholder for the names or descriptions of objects, actions, persons, or states of affairs and 'x' is a placeholder for the names or descriptions of individuals, then

(10)   x likes a = x is pleased by or enjoys a, or
               df
        x has a pro-attitude toward a, or both.

The main disjunction is inclusive because one might very well find pleasure in something that one also has good reasons for having a pro-attitude toward, e.g., as our dairy producers continue to   remind us, milk tastes good and it is good for you.

A general concept of disliking may be explicated from the primitive notions of displeasure or pain and having a con-attitude toward something. Thus, if 'x' and 'a' are interpreted as in (10) , then

(11)   x dislikes a = x is displeased by
                df
        a, or x has a con-attitude toward a, or both.

If one reflects on something with an aim to determine his liking or disliking for it in some appropriate sense and it turns out that one neither likes nor dislikes it, then I shall say that one is indifferent toward it. That is, if 'x' and 'a' are interpreted as in (10),

(12)   x is indifferent toward a = x reflects on a
                    df
        and, x neither likes nor dislikes a.

Two features of (12) must be emphasized. First, the conjunct of reflection is required in order to clearly distinguish the attitude of indifference toward something from the state of being entirely ignorant of something. It is one thing to hear and be indifferent toward the cries of a drowning man and quite another to simply fail to hear his cries. One's behaviour may be the same in either case; but if it is, the former situation is prima facie more anomalous from a moral point of view than the latter. Second, it should be noticed that the concept of indifference explicated in (12) is essentially qualitative rather than comparative. In this important respect it differs from the concept usually found in contemporary treatises dealing with preference and indifference. In the latter, indifference is essentially comparative like preference, i.e., one is indifferent between a and b. Here one can be indifferent toward a without considering any alternative. The logical advantage of beginning with a qualitative concept again is that it gives us some opportunity to build up a more

sophisticated   comparative concept, sone opportunity to
define a sophisticated concept in terms of a more primitive
one.   In the long run, it gives us greater insight into and
control over the <u>foundations</u> of decision-making.

3 WANTING

I have already touched upon the ordinary concept
of wanting and suggested cases that seem to demonstrate the
logical independence of this notion from that of liking.
Like the latter concept, the concept of wanting is
essentially qualitative.

(1)   <u>x</u> wants <u>a</u> more than <u>b</u>.

might be analyzed sensibly but with circularity as

(2)   <u>x</u> wants <u>a</u> <u>and</u> <u>x</u> wants <u>b</u> <u>and</u> <u>x</u> wants <u>a</u> more than <u>b</u>.

Similarly, like 'liking', 'wanting' does not designate an
action.   One wants greatly, dearly, intensely, barely or
slightly, but not skillfully, carefully, rapidly, etc.

Unlike 'liking', however, 'wanting' does not seem
to designate any sensation, even a peculiar one like a
pleasurable experience.   My evidence for this assertion is
largely introspective. Although I frequently have some sort
of sensation attending the expression of certain wants, more
often than not such sensations are entirely absent and by no
means required in order to suggest, inform of or establish
the presence of the wants. For example, I want to have a
restful sleep tonight and awaken refreshed, to wash and
shave in the morning, to eat breakfast, walk to work,
receive mail, etc. and for none of these wants can I find a
sensible correlate. While I can, if pressed, roughly assess
the comparative pleasure I obtain by having such wants
satisfied rather than thwarted, my wanting food, mail, etc.
<u>now</u> does not consist of the pleasure or displeasure I will
receive <u>later</u>. If it did, what happens later would seem to
be anticlimatic to say the least. Nor does it help matters
to suggest (as in A.I. Goldman (1970) p. 94) that my
wanting, say, to wake up tomorrow morning is constituted by
my <u>anticipated</u> pleasure of waking up. For again, I simply
do not have any feeling that could be identified as the
anticipated pleasure of waking up. But I certainly want to
wake up tomorrow!

There are a couple of <u>prima facie</u> counter
instances that always seem to arise when I present the above
view. First, there is the case of wanting to eat when one
is hungry.   Surely one does have certain uncomfortable

feelings around the abdominal region of one's body when one
is hungry.   Why should not one say that such feelings
constitute the sensible aspect of wanting to eat?
Primarily, I think, because one often wants to eat whether
or not one is having such feelings, i.e., hunger pangs.   I
want to eat at 6 p.m. this afternoon but I am not at all
hungry now. Hence, the hunger pangs experienced sometimes
when I want to eat are by no means a necessary concomitant
of such wanting.

Again, consider the uncomfortable feeling one
sometimes has when one is constipated. Given such a
feeling, one certainly wants to have a bowel movement.
Nevertheless, it is also possible and, I should imagine,
rather more typical for people to want to have bowel
movements whether or not they ever suffer from constipation.

In the light of such evidence then, it seems wise
to provide an explicatum for our ordinary concept of wanting
which is not constituted in any part by any particular kind
of sensation. Accordingly, if 'a' and 'x' are specified as
in 2(10), I propose that

(3)   x wants a = either x lacks and is inclined to
                   df
             obtain a or else x possesses and is inclined to
             resist abandoning a.

Several features of (3) merit attention. In the
first place it should be noticed that it does not involve
liking or disliking in any sense. In other words,
expressing and describing wants does not logically imply
that one is pleased or displeased, or that one has or ought
to have reasons for those wants. As Gosling (1969, p.   101)
has pointed out, expressions and descriptions of wants may
simply indicate aims or objectives without suggesting that
the aims are pleasurable or reasonable. One might also want
something on impulse as Edgley (1969, p. 158) suggests. Of
course, one might very well want something for some reason.
That is not precluded by (3). In this respect all (3) tells
us is that the provision of reasons is not logically
essential to the existence of wants.

A second notable and somewhat controversial
feature of (3) is that it makes wants basically
dispositional in character, i.e., to want something is to
have a particular kind of propensity, disposition,
inclination or tendency. Against such explicata, Goldman
has written that a

"... salient failing of a purely dispositional
approach is the difficulty it faces in accounting
for knowledge of one's own occurrent wants. If a

want consisted solely in dispositions to behave
overtly in specifiable ways, then it would seem
that the only way to tell you want x is to make
inferences from your overt behaviour. But
clearly an agent does not need to infer his wants
from his behaviour in the way that a third person
does. An agent has a sort of 'privileged access'
to his own (occurrent) wants; his reasons for
acting are knowable to him in a way that they are
not knowable to others. This fact is left
unaccounted for by a purely dispositional
analysis of wanting." (A.I. Goldman (1970 p.98)

Whether or not (3) would qualify as a "purely
dispositional analysis" in Goldman's sense in virtue of its
references to x's non- dispositional having or lacking a is
not clear to me. In any event, it is clear that his
argument rests on a confused account of our knowledge of
dispositions. Since one can certainly have knowledge of
one's own inclinations prior to acting either in accordance
with or in opposition to them, it is a mistake to assume
that dispositions must be defined behaviouristically. Once
this error is eliminated from Goldman's criticism, the
latter loses all its force. Moreover, it is worthwhile to
notice that the distinction correctly cited by A.I. Goldman
(1970, p. 86), following Alston (1967), between "occurrent
wants" and "standing wants" is not obliterated by (3). All
wants may be analyzed as dispositions or inclinations, some
of which one is aware of and perhaps acting upon or
resisting, and others of which are more or less latent and
dormant. In this respect then, wanting would be similar to
knowing insofar as one is typically only aware of and
perhaps using some of one's total knowledge at any given
time. (This seems to be behind the view of Lyons (1973).)

Third, it must be admitted that the idea of a
disposition, inclination or propensity is as problematic
here as it is anywhere else. I have not suggested any
satisfactory means of explicating dispositional concepts
because I know of none. The problems cited by Hempel (1950)
still seem to be with us. Similarly, and finally, I have
not attempted to explicate the concepts of lacking and
possessing that are appealed to in (3). Both notions must
evidently be interpreted fairly broadly in order to capture
the range of things, actions and states of affairs that may
ordinarily be spoken of as wanted. Although an analysis of
these concepts would probably be useful and interesting in
itself, I have decided not to provide it in order to push on
to more central and, hopefully, tractable issues. (Before
closing this Section, it should be mentioned that at least
one writer, Audi (1973), has claimed that no "interesting
and non-circular" definition of 'wanting' can be given.)

4   PREFERRING

The ordinary concept of preferring has already been cited as an example of an essentially comparative notion. In this Section I shall explicate this ordinary concept and define a more primitive concept that I call 'blunt preference' in terms of the concepts of liking, disliking, indifference, wanting and some new primitives. As usual I shall begin with some informal remarks about the concept of preferring and its cognates (prefers, preference, etc.) as they are used in everyday speech.

In the first place it should be noted that like 'wants' and 'likes', 'prefers' does not designate an action. Moreover, there does not seem to be any normal sense to first person singular reports beginning "I am preferring ...". On the other hand, one does speak appropriately of preferring a little, somewhat, mildly, considerably, very much, strongly, and so on. There are, of course, actions that one may perform to express and describe a preference, want or what one likes. But the actions involved in these cases are evidently those of expressing and describing, not preferring, wanting or liking. For example, if I say "I prefer a to b" I am not performing an act of preferring a to b, but of expressing and describing my preference for a over b.

Sometimes an act of expressing and describing a preference is identical to an overt act of choosing, and sometimes not. If, for example, you are in a restaurant and the waitress informs you that you may have fried or mashed potatoes, whichever you like, then you remark "I prefer fried to mashed" would normally count as an overt act of choice. You chose fried potatoes. On the other hand, if I tell you that I prefer to be a man rather than a woman, I shall not be understood as performing an overt act of choice. In one sense of the term, I do not have any choice in the latter case. That is, in the sense in which to have a choice is to have an alternative or option, I do not have a choice. Hence, expressing and describing a preference in such a case normally does not constitute making a choice. (I shall have much more to say about making and having choices in Chapters IV and VI.)

Very often "I prefer a to b" has the sense of "I like (enjoy) a more than b" as in "I prefer dancing to drinking" or "I prefer coffee with sugar to coffee without sugar". "I prefer a to b" may also have the sense of "I like (have a stronger pro-attitude toward) a than b" as in "I like to pay my taxes on time more than I like to pay them late along with a late fee". It would be a mistake, however, to think that preferring always involves liking. It might involve mere disliking as in "I prefer a headache for one hour to a headache for 'two' meaning "I dislike a two-hour headache more than a one-hour headache." In general, I think, one must appeal to some kind of disliking to capture the sense of what it is to prefer the lesser of two evils.

Again, it is sometimes plausible to interpret "I prefer a rather than b" as meaning nothing more than "I want a rather than b". Such an interpretation is particularly useful for describing habitual behaviour. For example, if someone were to ask me why I eat spaghetti by wrapping it around the prongs of my fork without resting the whole mess on a spoon, I might say that I prefer to eat it my way rather than the other way. If asked why I prefer my way to the other way, I could (and have) replied "That's just how I eat spaghetti" I could say that I never use a spoon and a fork because I never need both, but that would not be a report of my reason or motive for not using a spoon. The fact is that it had never occurred to me to use both utensils to eat spaghetti and the first time someone asked why I did not use a spoon and a fork I was pretty surprised. I am sure that I wanted to eat spaghetti the way I had always eaten spaghetti rather than some other way, but the want was not based on any reasoned view. It was based on or generated by habit. People often like to do the things they do in the sense that they have reasoned pro-attitudes toward and find pleasure in doing some things. But we are capable of just doing things because we want to. "I want to do or have this rather than that because I have always done or had this rather than that" can be an appeal to tradition or habit or an expression of the total lack of any reason for the want. Although it may be the case, as some psychiatrists and psychoanalysts seem to assume, that no one does anything without a reason, people frequently seem to be immediately unaware of and even unable to discover reasons for their wants. "I don't know why I want this one (or to do it this way) rather than that" seems to be the sort of remark that most people would make at some time in their lives and the fact that some people (even those who have undergone analysis) sometimes cannot identify any reason for some of their wants might well be explained on the hypothesis that there is, after all, no reason at all for some wants. Wants, it might be said, are often only causally explicable. At any rate, that is precisely the view adopted here. Furthermore, as I have just indicated, there is some reason for believing that expressions and descriptions of preferences may often be nothing more than expressions and descriptions of wants.

Given these preliminary remarks about the meaning of 'prefers' and its cognates, there are at least two concepts that merit attention. The first is that of blunt preference, i.e.

(1)   x bluntly prefers a to b = x wants a, and does
                                    df
           not want or else is indifferent toward b; or else
           x likes a, and is indifferent toward or else
           dislikes b; or else x is indifferent toward a,
           and dislikes or else does not want b.

          I call this concept 'blunt preference' because
the concepts of wanting, liking and disliking employed in it
are unlike our ordinary concepts in that the former are not
supposed to admit of degrees of intensity whereas the latter
are. As the terms are used in (1), for example, it cannot
be said that the intensity of x's liking of a is greater
than the intensity of his liking b. That is, the concept of
liking used in (1) is merely qualitative in the usual sense
of this term, and similarly for disliking and wanting. In
other words, the comparative aspect of ordinary preference
has been eliminated in the definiens in favor of
conjunctions. Strictly speaking, nothing in the definiens
is compared to anything else.

          Blunt preference does manage to captaure some of
the sense of the ordinary concept insofar as it might well
be adequate to describe someone's preference for some a over
some b.   For example, one might say "I prefer Carter to
Trudeau" and mean nothing more than "I am indifferent toward
Carter and dislike Trudeau." What is even more interesting
about this concept is that it involves a relation which is
non-transitive, non-intransitive and non-asymmetric.   That
is, it is logically possible that for some x, a, b and c

(2)   x bluntly prefers a to b, b to c and does not
           prefer a to c. (non-transitive)

(3)   x bluntly prefers a to b, b to c and a to c.
           (non-intransitive)

and

(4)   x   bluntly   prefers   a   to b and b to a.
           (non-asymmetric)

          The importance of (2) may be seen by considering
the combat superiority of ships.   It so happens that
destroyers tend to be superior to submarines, submarines
tend to be superior to battleships and battleships tend to
be superior to destroyers. Thus, if one had to bet on the
outcome of certain battles, one would be wise to prefer a
destroyer over a submarine, a submarine over a battleship
and a battleship over a destroyer.   Moreover, given a
non-transitive concept of preference, it is logically
possible for one to have such preferences. That is the
virtue of (2). A transitive concept would be such that

anyone preferring destroyers to submarines and submarines to battleships would be committed logically to preferring destroyers to battleships. That is why I have avoided constructing a transitive concept of blunt preference. There are equally compelling arguments for preferring (3) and (4) to intransitive and asymmetric concepts of blunt preference, but these may be safely ignored. (See Michalos (1967).)

From a logico-mathematical point of view, what (2) and (4) tell us is that the relation involved in blunt preference does not guarantee an order, since the latter implies transitivity and asymmetry. From a descriptive or empirical point of view, what (2) to (4) tell us is that the relation involved in blunt preference is on the right track toward an explication of ordinary preference. Contrary to the wishes of most researchers in the field of decision-making, people often display or express preferences that are apparently unordered. Although such preferences may be regarded as irrational in some sense of this term from a formal point of view, it has been repeatedly demonstrated, using examples like those in the preceding paragraph, that as a matter of fact people do and should have such preferences. (See, for example, Fishburn (1970).) Usually an appeal is made either to the criteria of or the conditions in which evaluations occur in order to account for the lack of order in a set of preferences. For example, when a situation schematized by (2) arises, it might be claimed that x changed his criteria or standards of preference as he passed from appraising a and b and b and c on the one hand to a and c on the other. If 'a', 'b' and 'c' are interpreted respectively as apples, bananas and cherries, then x might prefer apples to bananas and the latter to cherries on the basis of their taste, but cherries to apples on the basis of their price. Alternatively, it might be the case that x prefers cherries to apples because he has suddenly discovered that apples give him heartburn, i.e., it is the presence of new evidence that creates his unexpected preference for cherries over apples. According to (1), however, situations schematized by (2) may also be the product of what could be called one's preferring attitude toward what is preferred. One might, for instance, want apples instead of bananas and bananas instead of cherries, but still like cherries and dislike apples. In such a case his unexpected preference for cherries over apples is not created by an alteration in his evaluating criteria or background evidence, but merely in his preferring attitude toward the fruit.

Whatever one wishes to make of the fact of non-transitive sets of preference, their existence must be admitted. Therefore, any adequate explication of the ordinary concept of preference must be such that it does not render such preferences logically impossible. However one idealizes the workings of the human spirit, one should not go so far as to make it logically impossible for a person to have or express preferences that are unordered or, perhaps, more seriously muddled or confused. As primitive as blunt preference may seem, it does provide us with an analyzable concept of preference which satisfies this condition.

To obtain an explication for our ordinary concept of preference from that of blunt preference, essentially comparative concepts of liking, disliking and wanting must be added to blunt preference. These will enable us to say things like "x likes a more than b" where the connective of comparison "more than" is not eliminable in favor of conjunctions. In other words, we are now going to allow different intensities of liking, disliking and wanting, and this additional sophistication of our primitive terms will allow us to define the common notion of preference. I propose then that

(5)   x prefers a to b = x bluntly prefers a to b;
                          df

         or else x likes or wants a more than b; or else
         x dislikes b more than a.

According to (5), this concept of preference has properties similar to those schematized in (2) to (4) (i.e., it is non-transitive, non-intransitive and non-asymmetric) and it is essentially comparative.

5   INDIFFERENCE BETWEEN

It has already been emphasized that the concept of indifference introduced here differs from that which is usually employed because this one is essentially qualitative while the other is comparative. To mark this difference I have used the phrases 'indifferent toward' and 'indifferent between', the latter clearly involving a comparison. If more than two things happen to be compared, 'between' would naturally be replaced by 'among' for grammatical reasons. I shall specify two concepts of indifference between, one blunt and the other ordinary.

To obtain a definition of blunt indifference between, it must be assumed (as in blunt preference) that the concepts of liking, disliking and wanting do not admit of gradations of intensity. That is, it must be assumed that these concepts are qualitative in the more usual sense of this term. So one may simply like or not like, want or not want and dislike or not dislike something. Then

(1)   x is bluntly indifferent between a and b =
                                                df

> x likes, is indifferent toward, dislikes, wants
> or does not want both a and b.

Like its analogue, blunt preference, this concept of blunt
indifference between lacks the essential characteristic of
our ordinary concept of indifference between, namely, it is
not essentially comparative. In fact, it is not comparative
at all. On the other hand, the relation involved in blunt
indifference between is non- transitive, non-intransitive
and symmetric.

Beginning perhaps with Armstrong (1930), several
writers have found the idea of a non-transitive and
non-intransitive relation of indifference eminently
reasonable. After all, it is urged, the interval between
two adjacent entities in the pairs a, b and b, c might well
be too small to perceive, while the interval between the
extremes of each pair a and c might be perfectly
perceivable. In fact, the more pairs one puts back-to-back
as it were, the more likely such a result tends to become.
For example, one might be indifferent between holding one's
breath for one second or two, two seconds or three, ...,
sixty seconds or sixty-one, but clearly perceive a
difference between the first alternative and the last. In
the presence of possibilities like this then, non-transitive
indifference seems to be an acceptable fact of life.
Similarly, this relation seems to be typically
non-intransitive since the fact that one is indifferent
between two adjacent entities in two pairs seldom excludes
the possibility that one is also indifferent between the
extremes. For example, many people would be indifferent
between any pair of the triple, a half a glass of water,
three-fourths or a full glass.

To obtain an explicatum for the ordinary concept
of indifference between from that of blunt indifference
between, essentially comparative concepts of liking,
disliking and wanting must be added to blunt indifference
between. These will enable us to say things like "x likes a
exactly as much as x likes b" where the connective of
comparison "exactly as much as" is not eliminable in favor
of conjunctions. Then,

(2)   x is indifferent between a and b = x is
                                            df
           bluntly indifferent between a and b; or else x
           likes, dislikes or wants both a and b.

This concept of indifference between admits of gradations,
is essentially comparative, non-transitive and
non-intransitive. Therefore, it seems to be an adequate
explicatum of our ordinary concept of indifference between.

CHAPTER IV

Needing, Choosing and Deciding

1   INTRODUCTION

In this Chapter the concepts appearing in its title are explicated in terms of several of those examined in Chapter Two. In the next Section, two kinds of needs are distinguished, namely, species and particularistic needs. This is followed by an analysis of covert and overt choosing. In Section Four, initial distinctions are drawn between choosing and deciding, and two concepts of deciding are explicated, namely deciding that and deciding to. The last Section reviews various relations between decision and choice behaviour on the one hand and mental acts of deciding and choosing on the other.

2   NEEDING

As Braybrooke (1967, 1968) has shown us in some detail and casual observation confirms, the differences between wanting and needing are frequently difficult to discern. Things that are needed tend to be and generally, perhaps, ought to be given some kind of priority over things that are wanted (Meyer (1974). I shall build up definitions of two kinds of needs which, following Braybrooke, I shall refer to as 'species' or 'course of life needs' on the one hand and 'adventitious' or 'particularistic needs' on the

other. Roughly speaking, the difference between the two
types is that the former are attached to individuals (in the
broadest sense) in virtue of their being members of a
particular species while the latter are attached to
individuals in virtue of their particular idiosyncrasies.
The whole analysis is guided primarily by these insights of
Braybrooke and by the assumption that each of the following
four schemata should be satisfiable by any adequate
explicatum of the concepts of needing and wanting.

x wants a and x needs a

x wants a and not (x needs a)

not (x wants a) and x needs a

not (x wants a) and not (x needs a)

As the terms are ordinarily used, I believe, for example,
that one may want a drink and need or not need it, and not
want a drink and need or not need it. Such examples could
easily be multiplied, but I shall not trouble either of us
with the multiplication. (See also Kuhn (1963).)

There are some problematic concepts that must be
employed in order to define by analysis the concept of a
need. The first is that of an entity being in some sort of
equilibrium with its environment. The etymology of the term
suggests an equal balance, and the image of a balance with
its pans loaded such that each is exactly the same distance
from its base quickly comes to mind. Assuming that the pans
are held in this position because of the symmetric
construction of the balance and the equal force of gravity
on each pan (to cite only the most obvious conditions), it
is easy to see how the concept of an equilibrium might be
appropriated by biologists, social scientists and
philosophers. All that is required is a plausible analysis
of the notion of an equal force in this or that area of
investigation. Unfortunately, such analyses are not
particularly easy to obtain, especially for social and
psychological systems. In order to identify those periods
in which, say, the "psychic force" or the "force of
personality" of one individual is equal to that of those
around him or, more precariously, to that of his physical,
social, moral, etc. environment, one must have at least
rough measures of such "forces" and plausible conversion
factors (i.e., to turn "psychic force" measures into some
other sort for comparison). Without such instruments one's
estimates of the equilibrium or disequilibrium of social and
psychological systems tend to be metaphorical guesswork.
One's conceptual scheme for such systems may be adequate in
many other respects, of course, but one will be unable to
determine as a matter of fact when this or that system is in
a state of equilibrium. That is a basic infelicity of the

discussion before you, an infelicity that I cannot
eliminate. Nevertheless, it is worthwhile to have a
coherent conceptual scheme even without a plausible
operationalization of it, because that provides us with a
logically adequate basis for our research programs.
Accordingly, I propose that

(1) $\underline{x}$ is in a state of equilibrium with $\underline{x}$'s
            environment = the present state and rate of
                        df
            development of $\underline{x}$ is normal and secure for a
            a member of $\underline{x}$'s species.

Needless to say, some of the key words in (1) are
as problematic as 'equilibrium' itself, but they are all
unavoidable. The normality or abnormality of a kind of
entity's present state and rate of development will
frequently be statistically definable. Provided that this
or that entity can be conceptualized as a member of a
fairly large homogeneous class of entities (perhaps by
"pooling" certain smaller classes that share significantly
similar characteristics), it will be possible to obtain
reliable measures of central tendencies and dispersions.
When such data are available, one may define normality and
abnormality precisely and analytically. In the absence of
such data, one is obliged to rely heavily on the intuition,
sensitivity or expertise of one's researchers - for better
or worse.

The term 'secure' has been added to (1) in order
to eliminate the possibility of more or less immediate
deterioration or outright extinction. The sorts of cases I
have especially in mind are those like species of animals
that are rapidly becoming extinct. If, for example, the
American bison and certain species of elk are in the process
of becoming extinct then it would seem to be misleading to
describe them as being in a state of equilibrium with their
environment. We can still identify normal and abnormal
development and existence for members of these species, but
if they are insecure to the point of being predictably
extinct in the not too distant future, evidently they are
not managing to balance the destructive "forces" of the
environment with their own defensive "forces". Hence, some
notion of security seems essential for a definition of
equilibrium. As in the case of the idea of normality,
however, it must be emphasized that as a matter of fact it
may be extremely difficult to determine when this or that
kind of entity's existence and rate of development are
secure. In the case of elk and bison, for example, the very
fact that their existence is now recognized as in jeopardy
may lead to extensive conservation programs which would
virtually reverse the present trend. Similarly, in the area
of social mores and customs, reformers often find that their
efforts to hasten the death of, say, Jim Crow often leads to
"his" resuscitation.

   Assuming that we have a more or less plausible and general concept of an equilibrium, we may say that

(2) $\underline{x}$ has a species or course of life need for $\underline{a} =$
                   df
    either $\underline{x}$ has too little or too much a
    to be in a state of equilibrium, or if $\underline{x}$ had too
    little or too much $\underline{a}$ then $\underline{x}$ would not be in a
    state of equilibrium.

According to (2), needs are inextricably bound to certain departures from an equilibrium. (Compare the "physiological theories of disease" in Engelhardt (1975).) But the force of the conditional disjunct of (2) is that one may have a need without ever having such a departure. For example, we all have a species need for sensory stimulation, but I would guess that the only people who have ever suffered from sensory deprivation are the victims of sensory deprivation studies. Unlike Braybrooke (1968), most philosophers and social scientists fail to capture this important aspect of needing in their explications. (For example, see Cameron (1947), Tolman (1951), Cole (1953), Sparshott (1958) and Handy 1969).)

   In order to obtain an explictum for adventitious or particularistic needs patterned after (2), slight modifications are required. First, we say that

(3) $\underline{x}$ is in a particularistic state of equilibrium
   with $\underline{x}$'s environment = the present state and
            df
   rate of development of $\underline{x}$ is normal and secure
   for $\underline{x}$.

The difference between (1) and (3) is that the equilibrium specified in (1) is defined in terms of features that are characteristic of a whole species, while the equilibrium specified in (3) is defined in terms of features that are peculiar to a certain member of some species. Using the ancient jargon of Aristotle, one might say that the equilibrium specified in (1) is essential to any member of a species in virtue of its being a member of that species, while the equilibrium specified in (3) is accidental to any member of a species in virtue of its particular circumstances. Following (2) then,

(4) $\underline{x}$ has a particularistic or adventitious need for
   $\underline{a}$ = either $\underline{x}$ has too little or too much $\underline{a}$ to be
    df
   in a particularistic state of equilibrium, or if
   $\underline{x}$ had too little or too much $\underline{a}$ then $\underline{x}$ would not
   be in a particularistic state of equilibrium.

Thus, a man who is pounding a nail into a wall may be said to have a species need for oxygen in accordance with (1) and (2), and a particularistic need for a hammer in accordance with (3) and (4). Similarly, a pianist has a species need for food and a particularistic need for a piano; and so on.

Clearly then, from the point of view of the continued existence of species, the sorts of departures referred to in (2) are considerably more serious than the sorts of departures referred to in (4). Indeed, the difference may be regarded as important enough for some people to reject (4) and any similar notion of an adventitious need. One might, for example, prefer to ignore such notions altogether, and try to get along with one strong concept of needing and a concept of wanting. I suspect, however, that it would be misleading to say that a pianist only wants a piano to carry on his or her practice. The piano is essential for the practice; it is not only wanted but needed. So, I would not opt for a single concept of needing.

To obtain a general explicatum for the ordinary concept of needing and its cognates from (1) to (4), I propose that

(5) $\underline{x}$ needs $\underline{a}$ $\underset{df}{=}$ either $\underline{x}$ has a species $\underline{or}$ a

particularistic need for $\underline{a}$.

This explicatum has the virtue of satisfying the basic adequacy criteria mentioned in the first paragraph of this Section concerning wanting and needing, and it captures the other features of our ordinary concept that have been cited, i.e., it allows for needs which one never happens to have unsatisfied and for adventitious as well as course of life needs.

One of the reasons that people engaged in arguments about wants have a tendency to try to pass off their wants as needs is that the latter are generally supposed to involve more serious and inescapable hardships when they are not met. Hence, their appeals are strengthened. But one of the reasons such maneuvers can typically be successfully repelled is that needs cannot be defined without making assumptions about what are to count as equilibria states and excessive departures from them. Thus, appeals to needs tend to generate the same sorts of haggles that are generated by appeals to wants. (For example, see Suchman (1967), Manzer (1974), Laframboise (1975), McCloskey (1976) and Michalos (1976b, 1976c).)

3   CHOOSING

Unlike wanting, liking, preferring and needing, choosing is an action. One can choose well or poorly, rapidly, carefully, deliberately, skillfully, but not intensely, strongly, mildly or severely. Furthermore, as is the case with other actions, it makes perfectly good sense to request, command or forbid someone to choose something. Although it is true that the first person singular "I am choosing ..." is seldom used, it is easy to think of cases in which it could be used quite sensibly. For example, imagine that I have left you outside a shop while I run in "for a minute" to buy a tie. Several minutes later you storm in to find out what is holding me up. You say, "Will you choose one so we can go!" and I reply, "I'm choosing one right now, this one" which I wave in your face.

It has been suggested by Daveney (1964) and Dower (1971) that an act of choice might be regarded as a "transition point between a state of uncertainty (cf. trying to solve a problem) and a state of certainty or knowledge (cf. knowing the answer to a problem)." (Dower (1971) p. 192) While this view has the advantage of parsimony, it has the disadvantages of implying that (a) acts of choice (which constitute some sort of change in the world) do not take time; (b) they are superfluous, since they do not have any consequences at all (Edwards (1967)); and (c) strictly speaking they are not acts at all, for people do not perform transition points. It seems to me that one would be straying much too far from common sense and ordinary usage to accept these consequences. (See also Lewis (1955), Chisholm (1968) and Chapter V.)

To say that choosing is an action is to make a claim that is at once vague and ambiguous. It is vague because the concept of a human action has yet to be explicated in a generally acceptable fashion, but I am prepared to live with the vagueness. Its ambiuity, however, is another matter. It is absolutely essential to distinguish choosing as a mental act from choosing as a bit of behaviour which is generally assumed to be correlated and somehow integrated with such acts. I refer to mental acts of choosing as 'covert choosing', and behaviour which is generally assumed to be correlated with such mental acts as 'overt choosing', 'choice behaviour' or 'behaving as one would expect someone to behave who had performed a covert act of choice.'

Although it might be thought that it is misleading to refer to a mere bit of behaviour as an "overt choice", such references seem to be quite commonplace. Just as we occasionally refer to our bodies as ourselves (e.g., with sentences like "I burnt myself"), we occasionally refer

to certain kinds of overt behaviour as making a choice.
This comes out most clearly when we say things like
"Although she preferred cake to fruit cocktail, she chose
the latter", or "Although he preferred to have Frank rather
than Tom on the team, he chose Tom". In such cases
"choosing" seems to be nothing more than acting as one would
be expected to act if one had performed a particular sort of
mental act or, perhaps, merely had a particular sort of
mental state. (See also Hancock (1968).)

Another reason for insisting upon a distinction
between covert and overt choosing is that it is possible to
choose covertly at one time and display the appropriate
choice behaviour at a later time. (Nowell-Smith (1958),
Daveney (1964) and Brand (1970a) have all expressed this
view.) For example, prior to election day I can choose the
candidate I am going to vote for and then "register" or make
my choice overtly on election day. Similarly, one might
covertly choose to buy a particular item before performing
an overt act of choice. Indeed, confronted by ambitious
salesmen determined to show me this, that and the other
thing, I have often said something like, "You're wasting our
time. I've already made my choice." But my remarks and the
salesman's zeal would both be misguided if a distinction
between covert and overt choosing were not made. On the
other hand, if "choosing an item to purchase" only meant
something like settling my own mind about what I wanted then
my overt behaviour would be superfluous to me and the
salesman. But in fact there is an important sense in which
I have not chosen anything until I display some sort of
behaviour, e.g., I say "I'll take that one please". Thus,
for example, Drucker (1969, p. 54) could write "A decision
[choice] without a definite action-plan and without adequate
control of its execution is not an effective or even a
finished decision." Similarly, Majone (1975, p. 57) claimed
that "... implementation is regarded as an essential part of
decision making, rather than a matter of administrative
routine, because new constraints are very often discovered
in the process of implementation." Furthermore, it may well
be the case that having said "I'll take that one please," I
am stuck with it. If I try to convince the salesman that my
utterance was a slip of the tongue, for instance, he might
insist that I made my choice when I asked for that one and
now I will just have to live with it. In other words, as
Dower (1971, p. 194) has recently observed, some verbal
choice behaviour has the force of what Austin called a
"performative utterance". The mere utterance of say, "I'll
take that one" or "I choose the one over there" may in
appropriate circumstances constitute an act of overt
choosing.

If choice behaviour only had the force of a
performative utterance, there would evidently be no need to
have a peculiar kind of mental act correlated with it and,

consequently, no point in trying to provide an analysis of such acts. Unfortunately, as I have already suggested, choice behaviour frequently seems to be a direct expression of some kind of mental act, namely, that of covert choice. Hence, it will be worthwhile to explicate the latter concept. So far as choice behaviour or overt choosing itself is concerned, there is very little to be said. Virtually any kind of behaviour could be properly regarded as making a choice in certain circumstances. I might, for example, overtly choose a particular tie by pointing to it, nodding my head at the appropriate instant, saying "I'll take that one", "I'd like this", by asking someone to buy it for me or even by stealing it.

As suggested in the last Chapter, the term 'choice' is often used interchangeably with 'option' and 'alternative'. Hence

(1)   I had no choice.

might have the same meaning as

(2)   I had no alternative.

or

(3)   I had no option.

Such equivalences seem to suggest that the existence of alternatives is a necessary condition of choosing. Indeed, according to Daveney (1964), not only must there be alternatives for one to be able (logically) to make a choice, but one must know that there are alternatives. On this view, choosing is analogous to perceiving in the ordinary sense of this term. Just as one might argue that if as a matter of fact there is no lion in my room then there is no lion there to be seen and, therefore, I cannot (logically) see a lion in my room, one might argue that if as a matter of fact I have no alternatives then I have no alternatives from which to make a choice and, therefore, I cannot (logically) make a choice. While there is some truth behind this line of reasoning, it is seriously misleading as a result of oversimplification.

Insofar as choosing is regarded as merely a mental act (i.e., insofar as covert choosing is concerned), it is only analogous to perceiving in the sense that both are acts. With respect to the question of alternatives, however, covert choosing is analogous to believing. A proposition does not have to be true to be believed and very often things are covertly chosen which do not exist in the normal sense of this term. If as a matter of fact I have no alternatives then I might still believe that I have alternatives from which to make a covert choice and, therefore, make such a choice. This happens all the time. For example, imagine that I am trying to choose an appropriate color combination for my livingroom walls. I consider several "possibilities" and finally choose red and white. When I call at the hardware store to buy the paint, I find that neither color has been available for months. Again, one might covertly choose to see a certain movie tonight on the assumption that it is still playing and then be disappointed to find that last night was its final night. Finally, one might covertly choose to buy a certain secondhand book rather than a new lamp, but on returning to the bookstore discover that the book has been sold. In all of these cases the entities chosen do not exist any longer, i.e., there is no red or white paint, and the picture and book are gone. Strictly speaking what exists are <u>beliefs</u> that the entities exist as live options, and it is these that are absolutely necessary for covert choice, not the entities themselves. If I did not believe that I could buy the book, or obtain red and white paint, or that I could see the picture (i.e., if I did not believe that these were live options, alternatives or that I had these choices) then I would find it impossible (psychologically) to <u>count</u> anything I could do as choosing. For example, again, I would find it impossible to choose to become pregnant, President of the United States or Prudence of Bobtail Haven (my dog) this afternoon, because I do not believe that any of these are live options for me. On the other hand, if perchance someone were to convince me that I could, say, become President this afternoon then I might very well make such a choice. Undoubtedly my believing that I could become President this afternoon would not logically imply that I would make such a choice, but it would remove a significant obstacle. In other words, my believing that I could become President this afternoon is a necessary but not sufficient condition of my choosing to become President.

So far as covert choosing is concerned then, it would be a mistake to posit the existence and knowledge of alternatives as necessary conditions. Belief in the existence of alternatives is all that is required. With respect to overt choosing or choice behaviour, however, the situation is somewhat complicated. Sometimes the non-existence of alternatives rules out the possibility of an overt choice and sometimes not. Consider first, a case in which the non-existence of alternatives does not eliminate the possibility of overt choice. I walk into a store in which brown and black socks are apparently being sold, and I covertly choose a particular brown pair to buy. Then I say to the salesman "I'd like to buy this pair", i.e., I display choice behaviour appropriate to my inner determination. If it should turn out that that particular pair of socks has already been sold then in an important sense it is not a live option for me. Nevertheless, I could display the very same kind of verbal behaviour that I would display if it were a live option, i.e., I could say "I'd like to buy this pair please" whether or not it is for sale. Here, as in the case of covert choosing, it appears that belief in the availability of alternatives is all that is required for overt choosing. If I did not believe that that particular pair of socks was a live option then it would be silly for me to behave as if it were.

Now consider the following case in which the non-existence of alternatives plainly destroys my opportunity to make at least a certain kind of overt choice. Suppose I am at a party in which a box of assorted chocolates is being passed around. The understanding is that each guest will choose whatever he or she likes. When the box finally reaches me, it is empty. Since my host does not realize that it is empty, he urges me to choose a chocolate and pass it on. So I reply "But I can't choose a chocolate because there are no chocolates!" Then my host apologizes, not only for running out of chocolates but for urging me to do the impossible.

It seems to me that those who insist upon the existence of alternatives as a necessary condition of choosing probably have cases like the empty box of chocolates in mind. What must be emphasized is that because such cases are not the only kind, generalizations from them alone are hazardous. A more adequate specification of the role of alternatives in choice would run something like this. Belief in the existence of alternatives is necessary for covert choice; while the very existence of alternatives is sometimes necessary for overt choice and sometimes not, depending on the particular kind of choice behaviour required.

I shall have much more to say about alternatives (objects of choice) in Chapter VI, but it will be worthwhile now to distinguish <u>real</u> alternatives or <u>live</u> options from those that are merely presumed to be. Thus,

(4) a is a presumptive option or alternative for x
    $=$ x believes that a is a live option or real
    df
    alternative.

and

(5) a is a live option or real alternative for x
    $=$ x could (in every sense) obtain, bring about
    df
    or perform a if x tried.

According to (5) then, real alternatives are those over which one has control. (I have more to say about controllability in VIII 6.)

The only remaining feature of our ordinary concept of choosing which has to be considered is that of preference. As Rescher (1969b) has admirably shown, the role of preference in choice has been a subject of philosophical dispute for over two thousand years. Hence, it does not seem likely that the position adopted here will satisfy everyone. At any rate, my view is roughly that covert choice always involves preference, but overt choice does not. More precisely, I propose that

(6) x covertly chooses (chose, will choose, etc.) a
         over b $\underset{df}{=}$ a and b are presumptive options for
         x and x initiates (originates, forms or generates)
         a preference for a over b.

and, as I have already suggested,

(7) x overtly chooses a over b $\underset{df}{=}$ x behaves as one
         would expect someone to behave who had covertly
         chosen a over b or as one would expect someone to
         behave who preferred a over b.

Insofar as we have an ordinary concept of choice, I should think it would be adequately explicated by

(8) x chooses a over b $\underset{df}{=}$ x covertly and overtly
         chooses a over b.

Several aspects of (6) to (8) require some clarification. First, the idea that I am trying to capture with the terms 'initiates', 'originates', 'forms' and 'generates' in (6) is that of human agency. To say that human beings can make covert choices is to say that they can make, bring about, cause or produce changes in the world insofar as their psyches or mental states are part of the world. All the terms designating human agency in the preceding two sentences have been drawn upon by contemporary writers. For example, Dower (1971, p. 192) claims that an "act of decision [or choice] is the initiation of a (prior) intention to act in a certain way." Hampshire (1959, p. 134) writes that "To decide to do something is necessarily to form the intention of doing it." According to Taylor (1966, p. 112) "... nothing can be represented as a simple act of mine unless I am the initiator or originator of it." Finally, Brand (1970a, p. 91) tells us that when a person has chosen something he has "...intentionally brought about a change in the world."

Second, the concept of preference employed in (6) is supposed to be the one explicated by II 4 (5). Hence, covert choosing is being analyzed in terms of the

origination or initiation of wants, likes, dislikes and
indifference. Choosing cannot be identified with wanting,
liking, disliking or being indifferent because choosing is
an action while wanting, liking, disliking and being
indifferent are not actions. However, the formation or
generation of a want, a liking, disliking or an attitude of
indifference toward something, in a word, of a preference
for something over something else does constitute an action,
which, in the presence of presumptive alternatives, is being
identified here with covert choosing.

Third, so far as I am able to discern, my view of
the nature of what is produced in an act of (covert) choice
is probably broader than that of any other writer. The
"intentions" that Dower and Hampshire cite are very similar
to the sort of dispositions referred to in my explication of
'wanting' (III 3 (3)) and having a pro-attitude toward
something (III 2). But the concept of preference designated
in (6) covers more than wanting and having a pro-attitude.
Similarly, Brand (1970a, p. 90) identifies one's choosing to
perform an action with one's "having committed himself" to
the performance of that action, and the idea of making a
commitment is analyzed such that it is very much like
forming an intention, want or pro-attitude. Brand's view is
especially interesting because he introduces the idea that
one prefers what is chosen as an additional feature of his
explicatum. Since he does not analyze the conept of
preference, we cannot be sure that his notion of making a
commitment with a preference does not contain a redundancy.
Obviously, on my view of preference, it would contain a
redundancy. Finally, it is interesting to notice that
Aristotle's view of choice as the 'deliberate desire of
things in our own power" (1112b) seems to be quite
compatible with all of those described here, though he
evidently shared Daveney's view of alternatives.

Fourth, the concept explicated by (7) is closely
related to one generally referred to in the literature as
'picking', 'taking' or 'selecting'. For example, Daveney
(1964, p. 518) claims that if there is no "aim which my
selection satisfies, it would be more natural to descibe an
action such as [taking a card from a desk] as picking a card
rather than choosing a card." This is perfectly compatible
with overt choice as explicated by (7), since according to
the latter there may well be no aim satisfied or no
underlying preference involved at all. Again, Brand (1970a,
p. 88) refers to choice behaviour in the absence of "beliefs
about alternatives" as "mere picking and taking". Dower
(1971, p. 196) tells us that if an agent considers
"alternatives as not relevantly different or gives up
determining a reason for taking one as opposed to any other,
he will simply select at random in an undetermined manner,
for he has no reason for taking the one that he does take.
It would then seem that in such cases no decision is made to

take [the alternative selected]." Finally, Rescher insists
that

> "... there is simply no reasonably
> defensible way of actually 'choosing'
> among alternatives in the face of symmetric
> knowledge .... It would be more
> rigorously correct to say that
> we have effected a selection."
> (1969b, p. 154)

The main difference between picking, taking or
selecting as explicated by these authors and what I am
calling 'overt choice' is that an underlying preference is
never required by the latter and it is never permitted by
the former. According to these authors, any instance of
choice behaviour which happens to have an underlying
preference correlated with it is by that very fact not an
instance of picking, taking or selecting, while the same
behaviour without an underlying preference is by that fact
an instance of picking, taking or selecting. On my view,
the mere presence of an underlying preference for a
presumptive alternative accompanying suitable choice
behaviour is not sufficient to explicate our ordinary
concept of choice. In order to capture the full sense of
'choice' some reference must be made to the initiation or
origination of preferences. Thus, I have proposed (8) as an
explicatum for our ordinary concept of choice rather than
(7) combined with the requirement of an underlying
preference.

It might be thought that there is another
important difference between picking, taking or selecting
and overt choice. One might want to distinguish random
choice behaviour from choice behaviour simpliciter but
insist that picking, taking or selecting is always random.
It is worthwhile to point out that this would be a mistake.
Some kinds of picking, taking or selecting are random and
some are not. If, for example, I take the only pencil on my
desk and begin to write with it, my selection can hardly be
described as random. If there is only one pencil available
then there is no set of objects available from which a
random selection can be made. This kind of case contrasts
sharply with, say, picking a card from a deck or flipping a
coin to effect a selection between one of two indifferent
alternatives. Thus, there is as much reason to distinguish
random picking, taking or selecting from mere picking,
taking or selecting as there is to distinguish random choice
behaviour from mere choice behaviour. (See also Shiner
(1973); and compare his view to that of Averroes in Rescher
(1969b).)

Finally, it is worthwhile to notice that my
proposed explication of covert choosing probably commits one

to the libertarian side of the libertarian - determinist controversy. According to Edwards,

> "The determinist argues that choices
> are always determined by the strongest
> desire which is itself the ultimate
> outcome of antecedents in the character
> and environment of the individual.
> In contrast to this, the libertarian
> should argue that the actual
> situation is just the reverse, that
> in those situations where choices
> occur it is the choice which
> determines what the 'strongest
> motive' is to be."
> (Edwards (1967, p. 72))

Insofar as initiating a preference might be regarded as equivalent to determining a "strongest motive", anyone who accepts the view proposed here is committed to the libertarian position as Edwards understands it. (See also Walter and Minton (1975).)

4   DECIDING

In ordinary discourse the terms 'choosing' and 'deciding' and their cognates are frequently used interchangeably. For example,

(1)   I decided to stay.

might be regarded as telling us no more or less than

(2)   I chose to stay.

Similarly, Edwards and Tversky (1967, p. 7) apparently felt no qualms when they wrote "Decision theory is an attempt to describe in an orderly way what variables influence choices." (Emphasis added.) And Gamson (1968, p. 21) also seems to have been satisfied when he wrote "To say that the choice is binding implies that it can be implemented without the necessity of any further group reviewing the content of the decision." (Emphasis added. See also Jungermann and de Zeeuw (1977, p. 3).)

This interchangeability is instructive in a couple of respects. First, it suggests that like choosing, deciding is an action. One can decide wisely or foolishly, but not intensely or mildly, etc. It makes perfectly good sense to urge one to decide, for example, with an imperative like, "Decide, will you!". But it would be as nonsensical to suggest that one might decide strongly as it would be to suggest that one might eat or bake a cake strongly.

Secondly, it suggests that like choosing, deciding is only possible in the presence of the belief that there are alternatives, although there may not be any as a matter of fact. From a linquistic point of view, it is easier to establish this point for deciding than it was for choosing. One can only be undecided or in a state of indecision if one believes that one has alternatives or options requiring a decision. Whether or not there are such alternatives, one might still believe that there are and be deeply disturbed about one's inability to come to some decision. For example, one might spend several days trying to decide whether or not a certain house should be bought, finally decide to buy it and then discover that the house was sold some time ago.

If one must believe that there are alternatives in order to make a decision, then sentences like (1) and (2) must be regarded as short for sentences like

(3)   I decided to stay rather than leave (or argue, run away, face Nancy, etc.).

and

(4)   I chose to stay rather than leave (or argue, run away, face Nancy, etc.)

There are, however, some interesting differences in the grammar and, I think, in the logic of the two concepts. These are revealed most clearly by examining objects of decision and choice, and I have therefore devoted a separate Chapter (VI) to such an examination. Here I shall only indicate briefly three fundamental distinctions.

In the first place, sentences beginning with "I decided that ... " seem to be quite natural when the dots are replaced by sentences, e.g., "I decided that John was drunk." But sentences beginning with "I chose that ..." turn out rather strange as, for example, "I chose that John was drunk". Moreover, if the dots are replaced by an ordinary noun, the peculiarity shifts, e.g., "I chose that hat" makes perfectly good sense, but "I decided that hat" is absurd. Thus, there is certainly some important grammatical difference between 'deciding that' and 'choosing that', although at this point one may yet be hesitant to say that this difference reveals any significant logical distinction.

Secondly, it seems to be the case that when very serious considerations or needs are at stake, talk about making choices tends to give way to talk about making decisions. This claim is extremely difficult to justify without appealing to examples. Therefore, consider the following pairs of sentences.

> I decided to let him die.
> I chose to let him die.
>
> I decided to amputate his leg.
> I chose to amputate his leg.
>
> I decided to bomb the village.
> I chose to bomb the village.
>
> I decided to punish him.
> I chose to punish him.

Each of these pairs tends to reveal a subtle difference between some kinds of 'deciding to' and 'choosing to'. I grant immediately that all of these sentences make perfectly good sense, i.e., not one is meaningless or absurd. Hence, from the point of view of logic and grammar, one is free to use both members of each pair. Nevertheless, all of the sentences with 'chose' rather than 'decided' seem peculiar, primarily, I think, because the former term suggests a kind of freedom, license or warrant that generally does not exist in the presence of the infinitives following it. For example, normally one would decide to punish or not to punish someone for some reason that would typically involve certain principles or rules. If punishment is warranted at all by these principles or rules then one has a <u>prima facie</u> good reason to punish. In other words, there is a moral or social <u>need</u> for punishment. In such cases then, one's preferences would seem to be beside the point. They would be overridden by the reasons, considerations or needs codified in the rules or principles one is citing. Similarly, under normal circumstances a doctor would not amputate a patient's leg for the sake of anyone's preferences. Normally, I suppose, there would be a diagnosis of the case leading to a decision (not a choice) to amputate or not. What would be essential for the decision would be some assessment of the need, necessity or reasons for amputation. It would be odd, I should think, to say that the doctor was trying to <u>choose</u> whether or not an amputation was needed, necessary or reasonable.

Assuming that one is willing to grant that preferences are usually and ought to be overridden by special considerations or needs of one sort or another, it does not <u>follow</u> that choices share the same fate unless one adopts the explicatum of the concept of choosing offered here or one similar to it. After all, someone might say, why should not some reference to overriding considerations or needs of one sort or another be built into this explicatum? I already have likes, dislikes and wants packed into it. Why not needs? The answer is in the previous paragraph, precarious as it may be. It is just this: The most distinctive feature of those cases in which one would typically use and recognize some incongruity if one failed to use "decided to" instead of "chose to" is the presence of an overriding consideration or need of some sort. Thus, some reference to such considerations or needs should be built into an explicatum of "decided to" but withheld from an explicatum of "chose to".

Third, explicata of ordinary concepts of choosing and deciding must be distinguished because there are two mutually irreducible concepts of deciding ('deciding to' and 'deciding that') but only one concept of choosing ('choosing to'). The detailed arguments for the mutual irreducibility of the two concepts of deciding are presented in Chapter VI, but the following paragraph may relieve some anxiety.

The most plausible "bridges" between the two concepts of deciding involve some notion of acceptance or of believing, for what one would like to do is analyze something like

(5)   I decided that p.

into

(6)   I decided to believe (or, to accept the proposition) that p.

Unfortunately, neither notion (accept or believe) will do the job, because "to believe' and 'to accept the proposition' can only occur redundantly in (6). Hence, in neither case does one obtain an analysis of 'deciding that' out of 'deciding to'. (Other writers who have indicated differences between 'deciding to' and 'deciding that' include Hampshire (1959), Tukey (1960), Blanchard (1961), Edgley (1969), Price (1969) and Dower (1971).)

Now we may proceed immediately to our explicata. We will need additional explications of presumptive and real options in order to accommodate the concept of deciding that something is or is not the case. If 'p' and 'q' are placeholders for propositions then I propose that

(7) p is a presumptive option or alternative for x
           $=$ x believes that p could (in every sense) be
           df
           believed by x.

and

(8) p is a live option or real alternative for x
           $=$ p could (in every sense) be believed by x.
           df

According to (7), a proposition is a presumptive alternative
for someone if and only if one believes that it is not
inherently unbelievable, i.e., one believes that it is not
logically incoherent, nonsensical or utterly absurd. Thus,
the famous remark (among theologians) attributed to
Tertullian about the incarnation of Christ, namely, "I
believe it because it is absurd." is here regarded as
logically devoid of sense, unless the absurdity referred to
is some sort of nonlogical peculiarity.

Since propositions cannot be obtained like
objects (e.g., chocolates, ties, etc.), brought about like
states of affairs (e.g., having a stain on one's jacket,
being to the left of the door, etc.) or performed like
actions (e.g., riding a bicycle, eating a banana, etc.),
they are significantly different sorts of alternatives from
those specified in 3(4) and 3(5). Armed with these new
kinds of options then, we can say that

(9)   x covertly decides (decided, will decide, etc.)
         that p rather than that q = p and q are
                                    df
         presumptive alternatives for x and x initiates
         (originates, forms or generates) a belief that
         p rather than that q.

and

(10)   x covertly decides to a rather than to b
         = x covertly chooses a rather than b or
         df
         else x assents to a need for a rather than b.

It should be noticed that I have taken some
liberty with the interpretation of the variables a and b in
(10). Heretofore, prepositions and articles have been
included in the interpretation of these variables. For
example, 'x chose a' might have been interpreted as 'x chose
to run' or 'x chose an apple', and so on. However, since I
am using 'to' and 'that' following 'decide' in order to
distinguish two kinds of decision without introducing
special nomenclature (e.g., subscripts or superscripts), the
interpretation of the variables must be slightly
abbreviated. I believe this is a mere technicality without
philosophical significance.

The idea of assenting to a need in (10) has
considerable philosophical importance. The notion of assent
employed in (10) is precisely that used by Falk (1945), Hare
(1952), Horsburgh (1954) and Frankena (1958) in their
discussions of assenting to an obligation. It is difficult
to capture the sense of the concept without using metaphors,
but the general idea is that assent involves more than mere
acknowledgment, recognition or intellectual apprehension.

Frankena (1958, p. 66-7) claims, for instance, that "It may be part of the ordinary 'grammar' of such words as 'assent', when used in connection with ethical judgments, that they are not to be employed except when 'mere intellectual apprehension' is accompanied by a responsive beating of the heart." I am suggesting that the use of 'assent' in connection with needs is analogous. Indeed, it seems likely that the idea of assenting to an obligation is a species of the generic notion of assenting to a need, for obligations are, or at least require for their specification, certain kinds of needs. Furthermore, according to Falk (1945, p. 140), "when we try to convince another that he ought to pay his bills, we expect our argument if accepted to effect some change of heart in him." Similarly, when we try to convince someone that something is not merely wanted but needed, we expect that our argument will "effect some change of heart in him, if he accepts it. As emphasized in Section Two, one of the primary reasons for using rhetoric appropriate to needs to talk about wants is that needs are more constraining than wants. Thus, when one assents to a need one is inclined to feel bound to a course of action that has some prospect of satisfying it. In this respect then, assent is certainly more than "mere intellectual apprehension" as Falk (1945) expresses it.

To explicate 'overt deciding that' and 'overt deciding to', I propose that

(11) $\underline{x}$ overtly decides $\underline{to}$ $\underline{a}$ rather than $\underline{to}$ $\underline{b}$ $=_{df}$

          $\underline{x}$ behaves as one would expect someone to behave who had covertly decided $\underline{to}$ $\underline{a}$ rather than $\underline{to}$ $\underline{b}$.

and

(12) $\underline{x}$ overtly decides $\underline{that}$ $\underline{p}$ rather than $\underline{that}$ $\underline{q}$ $=_{df}$

          $\underline{x}$ behaves as one would expect someone to behave who had covertly decided that $\underline{p}$ rather than that $\underline{q}$.

Insofar as it is appropriate to speak of "an ordinary" concept of deciding then, I would propose that

(13) $\underline{x}$ decided $\underline{that}$ $\underline{p}$ rather than $\underline{that}$ $\underline{q}$ or $\underline{to}$ $\underline{a}$ rather than $\underline{to}$ $\underline{b}$ $=_{df}$ $\underline{x}$ covertly and overtly decided that $\underline{p}$ rather than that $\underline{q}$ or $\underline{to}$ $\underline{a}$ rather than $\underline{to}$ $\underline{b}$.

In view of everything that has gone before, (11) to (13) do not seem to require any special explanation or clarification. It is perhaps worthwhile to mention, however, that notwithstanding the present analysis, there is at least one philosopher who believes that "decision is an irreducible, extra-logical connective .... it is non-conceptualizable" (Gallagher (1964, p. 493)). Moreover, most writers on the subject seem to be content to define a single concept of deciding in terms of a single unanalyzed concept of choosing. That is, most people do not try to distinguish 'deciding that' from 'deciding to' or even covert from overt deciding, although the latter distinction is typically presupposed by their remarks about the differences between making a decision and implementing it. (See, for example, the explicata of deciding offered by Gore and Silander (1959), Dahl (1960), Shackle (1961), Wilson and Alexis (1962) and Bachrach and Baratz (1970).)

5   RELATIONS BETWEEN COVERT AND OVERT CHOOSING AND DECIDING

If covert choices and decisions were somehow open to inspection, one would expect to find certain types of them more or less perfectly correlated and integrated with certain kinds of behaviour. For example, one would expect to be able to identify the covert choice of a particular apple with, say, a verbal request for it. While covert choices and decisions are not open to inspection, they are to some extent open to introspection. This is of fundamental importance. One is frequently able to recognize a certain unsettledness of mind which accompanies problem-solving. One typically knows how it feels to be in doubt about what to do and then to resolve one's doubts with a firm decision. One knows how it feels to decide to do this or that but to disguise one's decision or to pretend that one has made a different decision, e.g., I can decide to vote for Smith, be certain of that decison, convince you that I have decided to vote for Jones and then vote for Smith. I can identify the covert decision to vote for Smith in the sense that I can distinguish the state of mind I am in following that mental act from other states of mind, like say, those in which I have decided to vote for Jones or to abstain altogether.

Usually then, we think of behaviour and covert decisions and choices as coming in pairs. Of course, as has already been suggested and shall become clearer as we proceed, one may be present without the other. If one makes a covert choice or decision and behaves as one would ordinarily be expected to behave having performed such a mental act in given circumstances, then I shall describe one's covert and overt acts as <u>in agreement.</u> For example, if one decides to telephone a friend and then behaves as one usually behaves having made such a decision (e.g., picks up the receiver of the phone, dials the friend's number, waits for an answer, etc.) then one's behaviour is in agreement with one's covert decision. If one decides to telephone a friend and does not behave in appropriate fashion (e.g., picks up the receiver and uses it as a hammer to pound a nail into the wall) then one's behaviour and mental acts are _not_ in agreement.

Besides the relations of agreement and disagreement, overt and covert decisions and choices may be temporally related, i.e., a covert decision or choice may be prior to, simultaneous with or later than its correlated behaviour. Taking these five attributes together, we have six possible states of affairs which are briefly summarized below.

1.   mental act _before_ behaviour _and_ agrees

2.   "   "   "   "   " disagrees

3.   mental act _simultaneous_ with behaviour _and_ agrees

4.   "   "   "   "   "   "   " disagrees

5.   mental act _after_ behaviour _and_ agrees

6.   "   "   "   "   "   " disagrees

By interpreting the mental act referred to above as that of deciding or choosing to vote for a certain candidate and the behaviour as that of turning a lever on a voting machine, the logical possibility of each of these six cases becomes apparent. The first and third cases seem to be nearest to what one would be inclined to regard as "normal" in the sense of having the greatest frequency of occurrence or in the sense of being the states of affairs most people might imagine when they think about relating the variables in question. In case 1, one decides or chooses to vote in a certain way and then behaves appropriately in accordance with his covert decision or choice. In case 3, although he never makes up his mind until he turns the lever, at that instant he is totally committed to the act. Case 5 is evidently peculiar, but still not impossible. Suppose our voter is responsible for setting up the machines and unwittingly turns a lever that registers a vote for Smith. Later he decides or chooses to vote for Smith and turns the lever again. So far as the voter's lever-turning behaviour is concerned, it might have been practically the same before and after his decision or choice.

The even-numbered cases are slightly more complicated, but nevertheless evidently possible. Case 2 would schematize accidents, deceptions and dramatic performances. One could, for example, choose or decide to vote for a certain candidate and turn the wrong lever by accident, or turn a different lever merely to deceive an unwanted observer, or turn a different lever in a mock election or dramatic performance. Insofar as case 4 occurs as an accident, it is unproblematic. At the very moment when I choose or decide to vote for Smith, I reach out and turn the lever casting a vote for Jones. But can case 4 schematize deception? Can one choose or decide to and behave deceitfully in the same instant? One is inclined to say that deceptive acts require some sort of planning, even if it is rather slipshod. But a little reflection on our hypothetical voter reveals a different story. Suppose he is committed to deceiving an observer but does not know how he is going to vote. He can make his decision or choice and deceive the observer merely by considering joint acts as options. That is, he must either decide or choose to vote for, say, Smith and vote for Jones, or else decide or choose to vote for Jones and vote for Smith. Then he deliberates, goes into the booth and (assuming that he has trained himself well) performs his covert act of opting for Smith at the very instant that he is turning the lever for Jones and simultaneously deceiving the observer. All of this is obviously logically and psychologically possible, and that is all the example is supposed to demonstrate. Now what about 4 as a schematization of a dramatic performance? In view of the last example, the answer is readily available. If the observer knew that our voter was going to act as described then the latter's performance would be virtually that of any theatrical performer. He would be performing extemporaneously as it were and no one would be deceived.

That case 6 may be appropriately regarded as a schematization of an accident is apparent, e.g., a voter sets up the voting machine, accidently turns the lever registering a vote for Smith and later chooses or decides to vote for Jones. But could case 6 schematize deception? This is a difficult question to answer. A voter, for example, is supposed to register a vote for one candidate, then decide or choose to vote for another and, roughly at the same time, deceive an observer. What is tricky about this case is that the voter can apparently only deceive the observer by behaving in one way or another, but at the moment the behaviour is required, the voter is undecided. It seems to me that although there is a way for the voter to deceive the observer in this case, it is slightly different from any of the deceptive examples considered so far. Clearly, an undecided voter can deceive an observer by pretending to prefer the candidate whose lever he turns. He has made no decision, but his behaviour leads an observer to believe that he has (because the observer imagines he is working in a case 1 situation). While this is deception, it is not of the sort considered above. In the other cases our voter has a decision to disguise. Here he only disguises his indecision. Nevertheless, deception is evidently possible in a case 6 state of affairs.

CHAPTER V

Decision Processes

1 INTRODUCTION

In this Chapter I explicate the general concept of a process and then consider decision processes as an important species. In Section Two the generic properties of processes are reviewed. This is followed by an elucidation of two main species of processes referred to as 'active' and 'passive'. Decision processes are classified as primarily active but possibly passive or somewhere between these two main species in Section Four. In the following Section it is shown that decision processes are as heterogeneous a group of processes as they could possibly be with respect to the generic properties of processes cited in Section Two. In the Penultimate Section decision processes are examined very briefly from the point of view of their being reasons for and causes of decisions. The conclusion reached is that decision processes logically can be but need not be the causes of or reasons for decisions. Finally, the possibility of an infinite regress of processes and acts is considered in Section Seven.

To simplify the language of the exposition, in this and following Chapters I generally use the single term 'decision' instead of the occasionally more accurate disjunction 'decision or choice'. Moreover, I also tend to use 'decision' instead of 'choice' as much as possible for the sake of parsimony.

2   PROCESSES

Although I have insisted that decisions ordinarily are and for analytic purposes should be regarded as acts, the overwhelming majority of writers seem to hold the view that decisions are primarily if not only processes. For example, Barnard (1938, p. 206) refers to "the process of decision" as "one of successive approximations -- constant refinement of purpose, closer and closer discriminations of fact -- in which the march of time is essential". Taking a similar line, Stein (1952, p. xiii) claims that a "decision itself is fundamentally a process rather than an act, without temporal dimensions". Again, Lundberg (1962, p. 168) tells us that "an administrative decision would be the process involved whereby one person came to make a choice ...". Finally, Kuhn (1963, p. 253) asserts that a decision is "the process of selecting responses ...".

It is easy to see the plausibility of such a view. One frequently hears and perhaps says things like 'They are in the process of deciding right now', 'That's a very time-consuming decision process', 'What sort of decision process did they use?' 'There's nothing wrong with the decision makers; it's their decision processes that are fouled up'. All of these sentences suggest that what one is talking about when one talks about decisions or deciding is a kind of process.

If, like Stein, one believed that acts do not have temporal dimensions, then I suppose the temptation to think of decisions as processes would be overwhelming. But there is little to be said for the view that acts do not take time. On the other hand, there is no rule stipulating the length of time acts and processes must take. Some processes may take less time than some acts and vice-versa. For example, it could easily take more time for me to strangle someone than it would take to burn a small piece of paper, i.e., the combustion process might well take less time than the act of murder. But the coverse could also be true, depending on such things as the size of the paper and the person to be strangled, the amount of oxygen available, and so on. Thus, the question of the most plausible genus for decisions, namely, acts or processes, cannot be answered by appealing to the temporal dimensions of these two genera, because those dimensions are not rigorously specifiable.

Fortunately, however, it is not necessary to identify the most plausible genus for decisions. The vagueness of the two terms 'act' and 'process' permit one to use either without putting too much stress on one's philosophical conscience. I have used 'act' to designate the genus of decisions because I want to use 'process' to

designate the genus of decisions because I want to use
'process' to designate the genus of whatever it is that
leads to decisions (in senses of "leads to" that are
explained later), and it would be cumbersome and perhaps
confusing to have to talk about processes leading to
processes. (Some authors, e.g., Wilson and Alexis (1962) use
'choice' to designate that to which decision processes lead,
without raising the question as to whether
'choice'designates an act or a process.) Thus, hereafter I
shall continue to assume that decisions are acts as
explicated in Chapter IV and that decision processes lead to
such acts.

Now what is a process? Consider the following
paradigms.

active process   passive process

ironing a shirt   growing old

baking a cake   recovering from chicken pox

tuning a car   combustion

painting a picture   orbiting the sun

pasteurizing milk   becoming psychoanalyzed

To save space, I have already grouped them into two species.
But to keep the horse before the cart, let us first enquire
into the generic properties of the items listed. There seem
to be two, namely, a sequential nature and a unifying
principle.

a) Sequences. All of the items in the two
columns above may be described as having a sequential
nature. Those on the left may be characterized as sequences
of acts, actions or doings. Those on the right may be
characterized as sequences of transitional stages through
which someone or something passes, or as sequences of
changes that one or something undergoes or suffers. Using
'event' as a neutral word referring to acts and sufferings,
we may say that all of the processes listed here consist of
sequences of events. Moreover, this seems to be
characteristic of all processes.

The events involved in any process are not only
distinguishable genetically, i.e., on the basis of their
originating with human action or not. They may also be
distinguished with respect to divisibility. Some
processes, e.g., growing old, are apparently more or less
continuous. Others, e.g., baking a cake, are more or less
discrete. Of course, we can and it is useful to analyze the
continuous processes into discrete ones and vice-versa. We

instead of a body, two arms, two legs and a head. The ease
with which one   performs   such   analytic   operations   should
caution   one   against   identifying   either   continuity   or
discreteness with the "real essence" as it were of any
process. However, it is worthwhile to be aware that certain
processes seem to be conceptualized more or less "naturally"
as   continuous   while   others   seem   to lend themselves more
readily to a discrete analysis. (For an interesting case
study involving divisibility and death, see Morison (1971)
and Kass (1971).)

Again, the events of the sequences constituting
processes may be <u>regularly</u> or <u>irregularly</u> ordered. The
process of psychoanalysis may (although it need not) proceed
more or less irregularly, with neither analyst not patient
knowing exactly what is coming next. Similarly, March and
Simon   (1958,   p.   178)   have   noted   "considerable
arbitrariness about the sequence in which problem-solving
steps are taken and in the order in which they are
assembled."   The pasteurization process, on the other hand,
tends to be regularized, especially in large dairy plants,
and   automobile   mechanics   are taught to use regular routine
procedures in tuning an engine.

A fourth variable feature of the sequences of
events   constituting   processes   is   their <u>hierarchical</u> or
<u>nonhierarchical</u> order. The process of <u>education,</u> for
example, is hierarchical in the sense that certain tasks can
not   be   accomplished   until   others have been accomplished,
e.g., one learns to play single notes on a piano prior to
chords   and   arithmetic   prior   to   algebra.   Planning and
problem-solving have also been characterized as hierarchical
by Suchman (1967) and March and Simon (1958), respectively.
There   is,   however,   nothing   especially hierarchical about
ironing a shirt, i.e., once the ironing process itself
begins, no part of the shirt must be ironed before another
can be ironed. Similarly, once the hose is turned on, no
part of the lawn must be watered before another part can be
watered.

Insofar as a process is hierarchical it tends to
be regular, since the former usually has the effect of
imposing a certain order on a sequence of events indicating
the direction of dependencies. For example, if some concept
cannot be understood without first understanding another
then a regularity of the process of teaching someone both
concepts   is   entailed   by   the   hierarchical relationship
between them. An example of a hierarchical but irregular
process would be that of play-writing. Having created a
certain character one may be obliged to restrict his actions
in certain ways without being able to submit those actions
to any regular or routine sequence. Regular processes need
not be hierarchical, since the regularity or routine may be
merely the result of planned convenience or efficiency. For

example, one might routinize the process of ironing a shirt
without creating a hierarchical order.

b)   Unifying principles.   The second generic
property of processes   is what I have referred to as their
'unifying principles'.   Usually unifying principles indicate
nothing more than the   end   states, goals   or   products of
certain sequences of events, e.g., paintings, tuned cars and
ironed shirts. But they may also indicate other distinctive
features in   the   absence of end states or goals, e.g.,
orbiting the sun. (For a contrary view see Munsat (1969).)

If   's' is a placeholder for the names or
descriptions of sequences of events, then   what I wish to
propose is that

(1)   <u>s</u> is a process = <u>s</u> can (in some sense) be
                          df
          conceptualized from the point of view of some
          unifying principle <u>and</u>, as a matter of fact,
          <u>s</u> has a tendency to act in accordance with that
          principle.

Both conjuncts of this explicatum are important, and so far
epistemologists and philosophers of science have not reached
general agreement about the precise relations between them.
The first conjunct emphasizes the fact that processes are to
some extent <u>mental constructs</u>, i.e., this or   that   sequence
of events may be conceptualized as one which has a certain
unifying principle or theme. The second conjunct emphasizes
the fact that there   is   a   natural   correctness   or
incorrectness about such conceptualizations to the extent
that certain sequences of events are or are not unified by
the constructive principle. For example, consider the case
of a person dropping a certain amount of flour, shortening,
sugar, salt, water and a couple of eggs into a bowl.
Insofar as this sequence of acts is perceived   or
conceptualized as having the production of a cake as its
unifying principle (in this case its goal, final cause or
that for the sake of which the acts are performed), it is
regarded as a cake-making process.   The   idea   of   a
cake-making process is a mental construct superimposed on
the sequence of acts, and the unifying theme of the
construct is the particular goal of producing a cake. The
very same sequence of acts may be conceptualized as a
process of education, therapy, entertainment, propaganda,
retribution, or something else by assigning it different
goals, by viewing it as leading toward or as a means to
different ends.   But clearly conceptualization is   not
entirely free of unrestricted.   More precisely, as the
second part of my explicatum insists, one normally does not
and should not think of a sequence of events as leading
toward or as a means to some end unless the sequence <u>does</u> as
a matter of fact tend to reach the alleged end.   If, for

example, sequences of acts similar to those cited above displayed no tendency to result in cakes, it would be a mistake to regard them as cake-making processes. It would not be a linguistic error, any more than a person's reference to a particular dance as a rain-making process must involve a linguistic error. The error involved is factual. The sequence of acts does not as a matter of fact tend to culminate in rain. Most people would not call the sequence of acts performed in a rain dance a rain-making process because it is apparently independent of the production of rain.

Lest anyone suspect that I imagine "dumb" natural processes like combustion and aging have aims or goals, I should say definitely that I do not. The world is such that certain things tend to be more or less "constantly conjoined" to others. Some of the latter are called 'goals', 'ends' and 'aims', but that does not imply that the processes involved regard these things as their goals, ends or aims. Only people have the capacity to regard anything as anything, not processes.

3   ACTIVE AND PASSIVE PROCESSES

Assuming that processes may be adequately characterized (briefly) as sequences of events conceptualized with a unifying principle, one would like to know something about the number and kinds of species within this genus. Since any combination of the properties of processes cited thus far might be used as a differentia for a distinct species, at least thirty-two species might be suggested, e.g., processes that are regular, hierarchical, divisible, sequences of acts and goal directed; irregular , hierarchical, and so on. This would certainly be a large number of distinct kinds, although it is not clear that it would be at all useful to be mildly familiar with all or even most of them. Hence, instead of proceeding along this more comprehensive and exhausting route, I shall focus my attention on two species that are especially pertinent for our purposes and illustrated amply by our lists of paradigms in the previous Section.

If the sequences of events designated in 2(1) are acts, actions or doings then I call the process active. Active processes are such that all the properties ordinarily attributed to acts may be attributed derivatively to active processes. For example, like all skills, we may speak of teaching and learning active processes, where what is taught or learned is a set of acts, skills or techniques. Moreover, one can learn such processes rapidly or slowly, well or poorly, and so on. Insofar as 'methods' and 'procedures' are used as synonyms of 'processes', it must be active processes that are involved. This becomes clearer on consideration of passive processes. (See also Munsat (1969).)

If the sequences of events designated in 2(1) are transitional stages that something or someone suffers or undergoes then I call the process 'passive'. None of the distinguishing properties of acts are attributable to passive processes. For example, one cannot be taught or learn to grow old. Growing old is not a skill that one tries, with more or less success, to perfect. One is not held responsible or regarded as praiseworthy or blameworthy for growing old. Of course, there are many skills that one can learn whose effect is to allow one to grow old, i.e., there are survival techniques. But what one learns when one learns such techniques is not how to grow old, but how to avoid or escape this or that particular peril.

Some processes might be adequately characterized as mixtures of active and passive processes, i.e., of sets of acts and transitional stages. One might, for example, want to describe the process of becoming psychoanalyzed as a mixture of the two types rather than as a passive process. Perhaps it is more like the processes of education and socialization than like the process of maturation. I would not dispute the existence of such mixtures for an instant. All I want to insist upon is that one and the same term, 'process', can be used to refer to sequences of events that are in significant respects quite different, and that what one can properly predicate of this or that process depends in large measure upon where one locates the process in question with respect to the two species described.   I suspect, for example, that one of the reasons teachers seem to be divided between what I call the 'sponge theorists' and the 'horse theorists' is that they see the education process as nearer to one or the other of our two types of processes. The sponge theorists seem to think that students are like sponges, and that the longer they are "held under" (i.e., kept in class under close supervision - not to say surveillance) the more they "sop up". For these people then, the process of becoming educated leans heavily toward the passive species. The horse theorists, on the other hand, seem to think that students are more like horses than sponges, and that one can "lead them to the water" (the fountain of wisdom I suppose) but cannot force them to drink. For these people, the eduction process is more like drinking than basking, more active than passive. Hence, the pedagogical recommendations of "sponge" and "horse" theorists may be regarded as more or less direct consequences of their conceptualization of the process of education as more or less like one or the other of the two species described. (See also Fox (1969) and Steffen (1973).)

4   SPECIES OF DECISION PROCESSES

Having explicated the generic concept of a process and two important species, the question before us now is this: How should one classify decision processes? Should one conceptualize them as primarily active processes, as passive processes or as mixtures? Lest anyone be kept in suspense too long, I shall say immediately that I think some decision processes fall more or less naturally into each of these groups, but that most decision processes tend to be active.

Consider the following typical kinds of answers to the question "How did you reach that decision?" I:

- consulted someone (a friend, relative, expert, etc.)

-applied some decision rule, e.g., Bernoulli-Bayes, minimax, etc.

- left it to chance (flipped a coin, drew a card, etc.)

- followed an example (did what you did or would have done or did the opposite)

- prayed

- used dialectic (discussed it with someone)

- bargained with someone

- experimented (used systematic trial and error)

- derived it from some beliefs I hold (or from some theory, principle, rule, etc.)

- guessed (wildly or wisely ("educated guess"))

- diverted my attention (played golf, chess, drank, etc.)

- slept on it

- reached it very carefully (with "fear and trembling", cheerfully, etc.)

This is a fairly suggestive smorgasbord of replies to "How did you reach that decision?". With the exception of the last answer in the list, each one gives us some idea of the sort of process engaged in or passed through on the way to a decision. The last answer is quite different from the others in that it is concerned with the manner of the occurrence of a process. The last reply tells us in what way, fashion or manner a process occurred and the others tell us roughly and briefly what process occurred. Both kinds of replies are instructive because they strongly suggest that decision processes are primarily active. With the exception of "sleeping on it", all of the replies suggest that decision processes tend to be active rather than passive. Consulting, applying rules, bargaining, copying, deliberating, praying, discussing, experimenting, deriving, guessing and diverting one's attention are things that one does rather than suffers. One can be taught and learn to consult, apply rules, etc., and one can consult, apply rules, etc., wisely, cautiously, foolishly, rationally, responsibly, fairly, skillfully, irresponsibly, creatively and routinely without stretching the meanings of these terms beyond recognition. One cannot however, sleep wisely, cautiously, etc., although one can wisely, cautiously, etc. go to bed with the intention of sleeping or put oneself to sleep. The process of sleeping is not a sequence of acts, but whatever it is that initiates that process may be a sequence of acts.

Since a decision maker may use the processes of consultation, deliberation, experimentation, etc. to reach a decision in much the same way that a craftsman uses his tools to practice his craft, we may regard the processes as instruments or means of reaching decisions. This might have been expected because our original question "How did you reach that decision?" could be interpreted as "What instruments or means were employed to reach that decision?" Whether or not the processes could be regarded as instruments, of course, is irrelevant to their being largely active or passive. One may use passive processes like ageing, going blind, and recovering from illness (e.g. to gain sympathy) as well as active processes like writing a book, painting a picture and baking a cake.

5   DIFFERENTIA OF DECISION PROCESSES

Having identified the species of decision processes as primarily but not entirely active, we should consider their differentia more carefully. More precisely, we should determine which properties of the genus process are attributable to decision processes. Briefly, my view is that the latter are adequately characterized as goal directed processes which may be discrete or continuous, regular or irregular, and hierarchical or nonhierarchical. In other words, the species of active processes that we refer to as 'decision processes' is as heterogeneous as it could possibly be with regard to the generic properties cited.

With respect to the first two properties, discreteness and continuity, I believe it is fair to say that it is most natural to conceptualize decision processes as discrete. The processes of consulting, applying rules, flipping coins, etc. can readily be described by listing sequences of discrete acts. We might say, for example, that the process of consulting an expert consists of putting a set of fairly specific questions to him regarding certain problems in the light of certain restrictions. The questions, problems and restrictions then, would be more or less discrete components of the consultation process. Similarly, the process of applying, say, the Bernoulli-Bayes rule would involve the description of alternative courses of action, states of nature, probabilities, outcomes and utility values, and each of these components would be more or less clearly distinguishable from the others.

While it is most natural to analyze these and most other decision processes discretely, such an analysis is not necessary or necessarily more fruitful than a continuous one. It might, for instance, be more useful to think of the process of discussing a problem with someone as a more or less continuous exchange of signals, information, sensations, etc. From this point of view there would seem to be less chance of neglecting any of the "dynamics" of a dialogue and more chance of identifying transactions that might occur "between the lines" of ordinary descriptions of certain events. (See, for example, Key (1972) and Evans (1972).)

Decision processes can be more or less regularized and proceed according to a set routine, or irregular to the point of being randomized. The stock clerk who reorders certain goods as soon as a red mark is visible in a bin or the number of items on hand reaches a certain number is involved in the sort of process I am calling 'regular'. The processes of deliberation, consultation and discussion are irregular in the sense that one is typically unable to describe a priori the sequences of individual acts that will occur in them. Randomization processes like that of flipping a coin in order to decide what to do are extreme forms of irregular processes.

Following Simon (1960), Alexis and Wilson (1967) seem to use the terms "programmed" and "nonprogrammed" to designate regular and irregular decision processes, respectively. Unfortunately, however, their discussion is muddled by a failure to distinguish decision processes and their products, decisions. It will be instructive to quote the relevant passage completely.

> "Broadly speaking decision processes may
> be classified as either programmed
> or non-programmed. Most decisions lie

somewhere on the continuum between these
two poles. Decisions are said to be
programmed to the extent that they are
repetitive and routine and a definite
procedure has been worked out for
handling them. Decisions are characterized
as nonprogrammed to the extent to which
they are novel, unstructured, and
consequential."
(Alexis and Wilson (1967) p. 222)

They begin by telling us that there are two kinds
of decision processes, but the definitions they propose seem
to involve both processes and their products. In the fourth
quoted sentence, for example, "unstructured" would seem to
be a property of the process leading to a decision, while
"consequential" would seem most likely to be predicated of
the decision itself. Even if one assumes (contrary to the
view adopted here) that the products of decision processes,
decisions, should also be regarded as processes, the
proposed definition would still be objectionable since it
fails to distinguish producing-processes from
product-processes.

Applications of some decision rules, copying
certain examples and some experimental techniques are
illustrative of hierarchical decision processes. It is, for
example, impossible to apply the Bernoulli-Bayes rule of
maximizing expected utility to some set of alternatives
without first determining the probability and utility of the
outcomes possible with those alternatives. The "management
audit system" described by Greenwood (1969) is another
example of a hierarchical decision process. "Following
operations research analysis techniques", he writes, "the
strategic decisions within each departmental area have been
structured in a hierarchically descending order of
importance and scope. Evaluations have been made as to
which decisions of broader scope tend to affect subsequent
decisions and which, therefore, should be made in this
descending order. Contrariwise, no decision should be made
before another decision of broader scope, which could affect
and limit the prior decision and thereby require that it be
revised." (Greenwood (1969) pp. 213-214) Praying,
discussing and guessing are examples of nonhierarchical
processes. Finally, it's undoubtedly the case that decision
processes typically have goals as their unifying principles
and that these goals are decisions. That is, decision
processes are normally initiated in order to produce
decisions and one would be hard-pressed be justify one's
identification of a particular process as a decision process
if it did not in fact usually lead to such acts. Granting
this, however, there is still an extremely difficult problem
of the precise meaning of "lead to" in the last sentence.

In exactly what sense do decison processes "lead to" decision acts?

6   PROCESSES "LEAD TO" ACTS

Although we have arrived at our present position while elucidating some of the specific attributes of various paradigms of decision processes, the problem before us arises naturally as a result of interpreting the question "How did you reach that decision?" in two prima facie plausible ways, namely, as "What reasons did you have for making that decision?" and "What caused you to make that decision?" Answers to both of these questions are suggested by some of the replies in the list in Section Four.

Citing the fact that I consulted someone (an expert, friend, etc.)), followed someone's example, discussed it with someone or derived it from some other premises would seem to be suggesting answers to the question "What reasons did you have for making that decision?" They suggest, for example, that an expert, friend, etc. advised me to make that decision and I did; that because someone else made that decision (or its opposite) in similar circumstances, I did; that the conclusion of my discussion with someone was that I should make that decision, so I did; or that in order to behave in a manner consistent with my usual behaviour or principles, I made that decision. Citing the fact that I flipped a coin, drew a card or rolled dice to reach a decision suggests that I had exactly as much reason to make that decision as any other (which is perhaps none at all), and that I left it to chance to provide the decisive consideration. In certain cultures the occurrence or nonoccurrence of what we might call 'chance events' are sometimes taken as evidence of the will of supernatural beings and as such, good reasons for making certain decisions. (See, for example, Cohen (1960).)

If decisions can be caused by decision processes, some of the replies in our list might be taken as answers to the question "What caused you to make that decision?" For instance, if I tell you that I reached a certain decision by consulting Hazel and you know that my relationship with her is such that whenever I talk to her I end up doing exactly what she thinks I should do, then you might take my reply as a report of the cause of my decision. Similarly, if I were known to be a very religious person and I told you that I reached that decision by praying, then you might take my reply as a report of what I believe to be the cause of my decision, namely, an act of God. If I were known to be a psychologist who frequently experimented with drugs on myself and I told you that I reached that decision by experimenting, then you might take my reply as a report

about   the   cause of my decision, namely, the action of some
drug.

All of these examples seem fairly realistic   and
suggest   an   affirmative   answer   to   the   question: Can
decisions be caused by or   causally   connected   to   decision
processes   or   parts of these processes? Consider the three
examples cited above.   In each case I am   supposed   to   have
initiated   and   actively participated in a process whose aim
and outcome was the production of a certain decision,   i.e.,
I   initiated   the   decision processes of consulting, praying
and experimenting.   Each of   these   processes   involved   the
activity of other people or things, namely, Hazel, God and a
drug.   It   is   the activity of these other people or things
that I   am   especially   referring   to   as   "parts   of   those
processes"   in the question before us.   Thus, one might want
to say either or both of the following.   (i) The   processes
that I initiated caused or were merely causally connected to
the decision that was finally made.   (ii) The processes that
I   initiated caused or were merely causally connected to the
actions of other people and things and the latter caused   or
were   causally   connected   to   the decision that was finally
made.   By holding both (i) and (ii) one asserts a duality if
not a plurality of causes and causal connections.

Considering only (i), since the processes that   I
initiated   could   (logically)   be   necessary,   sufficient or
both, and prior to, simultaneous with   or   later   than   the
decision   that   was   finally made, there are 9 permutations.
These may be outlined as follows.

1.	decision	process	is	prior	and	necessary	for	decision
2.	"	"	"	"	"	sufficient	"	"
3.	"	"	"	"	"	both	"	"
4.	"	"	"	simultaneous	and	necessary	"	"
5.	"	"	"	"	"	sufficient	"	"
6.	"	"	"	"	"	both	"	"
7.	"	"	"	later	"	necessary	"	"
8.	"	"	"	"	"	sufficient	"	"
9.	"	"	"	"	"	both	"	"

Considering only (ii), we have a similar   set   of
relationships that might obtain between the processes that I
initiate   and   the   actions   of other people and things, and
another set of relationships that might obtain   between   the

latter and the decision finally made, i.e., there are 3X3X3X3=81 possibilities. Combining (i) and (ii), we have 9X81=729 possibilities. Following the pattern set out above for the simplest solution, the construction of a table including all 81 or 729 cases is a routine task - but not one that I am about to undertake. The fact is that all of the problems concerning the causal connections between decision processes and decisions can be examined by a careful consideration of the 9 possibilities indicated above.

Case 2 is one of the two of the 9 that outlines a situation in which a decision process logically could be appropriately described as the cause of a decision. Moreover, there is apparently no contradiction involved in the supposition that the processes of consulting, praying and experimenting which were cited in our examples could be prior to and sufficient for a particular decision, i.e., they could be appropriately described as causes of such an act. As is typical of the identification of the sufficient conditions of virtually any event, one can usually introduce special circumstances that have the effect of eliminating certain conditions or changing the significance of others. Granting such maneuvers, however, it seems quite plausible to suppose that the processes cited could (in every sense of this term) have the required relationship to certain decision acts. Certainly sentences patterned after the following are not self contradictory:

(1)   x consulted y before making that decision and it is not the case that x could have consulted y without making that decision.

And the laws of nature have always permitted enough fast-talking y's and gullible x's to exist to warrant the enactment of laws against inciting, provoking, instigating, forcing, tricking, inducing or coercing people into doing things or believing things that they ought not and normally would not do or believe. Just as the laws of nature allow people to force and trick people into doing this or that, they allow people to force and trick people into decidng that this or that ought to be done or into deciding to do this or that. Similarly, just as civil, criminal or ecclesiastical laws prohibit forcing and tricking people to do this or that, they prohibit forcing and tricking people to decide to do this or that or to decide that this or that is the case.

Case 5 is slightly more problematic than case 2 but nevertheless instantiable and outlines the other case in our list which indicates causation. Suppose, for example, that you enter into a discussion with someone with the aim of reaching a decision about a certain issue and in the course of that discussion you reach a decision. The temporal span of the discussion is, by hypothesis now and probably usually in fact, longer than that of the decision act, but insofar as the act occupies any duration at all, it is simultaneous with the process of discussion. The process and act occur <u>at</u> the same time but not <u>for</u> the same time. In this respect the processes and acts would be simultaneous or contemporaneous in the same way that a telephone call can come at dinner, a pain can arise during an operation, a sour note can be played in a symphony and a clap of thunder can occur in a storm. Furthermore, as suggested earlier, since the length of time required for both decision processes and acts is anybody's guess, it is logically possible that, say, a short decision process might last almost or perhaps exactly as long as some decision act. On the basis of these considerations, then, I conclude that case 5 is, as I have just illustrated, possible to instantiate. That is, sentences patterned after (2) describe states of affairs that are possible in every sense of the term.

(2)   <u>x</u> discussed the issue with <u>y</u> while making the decision <u>and</u> it is not the case that <u>x</u> could have consulted <u>y</u> without making that decision.

Thus, decision processes have again been shown to be plausible candidates for the causes of or merely causally connected to decisions. (Further discussion of the issues involved in this Section may be found in Brand (1970b) and Munsat (1969). My discussion has been extremely brief because I do not think I could improve upon Brand's discussion and I am in substantial agreement with his conclusions.)

7   ELIMINATING AN INFINITE REGRESS

Before closing this discussion of processes leading to acts, it will be worthwhile to consider and dispel some suspicions that one might have about the possibility of an infinite regress arising from the view of the causal relations between decision processes and decisions that I have just presented. A regress may be alleged to arise as follows. Suppose I initiate a decision process with the aim of reaching a decision about some issue represented by 'S'. Since the initiation of a decision process is something that I do, it is something that I decide to do. But in order to decide to do something (e.g., to initiate a decision process), I must initiate a decision process, in this case, one whose aim is a decision about whether or not I should initiate a decision process to initiate a decision process to reach a decision about S. Clearly we are well on our way up the garden path now, because there is no way to prevent the extension of this sequence of initiating acts. That is, the view of the possible   causal   relations   between   decision processes and acts that I have   presented   in Section   Six   leads   to   an infinite regress and must, therefore, be rejected.

There   are   at   least   two   errors   in   the above argument.   First, it is false that if I do something, I must decide to do it.   Examples of actions   that   people   perform without   decisions   include   habitual   or routine tasks like shaving, combing one's hair, drinking from a glass, steering an automobile,   putting   a   teaspoon   of   sugar   into   one's coffee,   cutting   a   steak, etc.   These are actions that one performs intentionally, but   does   not   normally   decide   to perform   or   think   of   as   having decided to perform.   (See above IV 3 and Katona (1953).)

The second infelicity in the regress argument   is its third premiss, namely, that in order to make a decision, one   must   initiate   a   decision process.   This is certainly false.   It is quite possible that someone who has   something to   gain   by talking me into making a certain decision would initiate   a   decision process leading to   the   required decision.   Again,   I   might   be   called   upon by someone to discuss a certain issue   and   end   up   making   a   particular decision   as   a result of that discussion.   Finally, I might make a decision and be unable to identify any process   as   a decision   process   leading to that decision.   That is, there may not be any sequence of events such that one   could   with propriety   describe it as occurring in order to produce that particular decision.   In such cases, answers to the question "What caused that decision?" would be "Nobody knows".

Although the view defended here does not lead   to an   infinite   regress   with   necessity,   it   is   possible to generate   such   a   regress   by   systematically   selecting appropriate   alternatives.   Consider,   for   example,   the sequence of odd-numbered sentences below.

1.   I decide to initiate a decision process to   reach a decision about S or I do not decide to initiate such a process.

2.   If not, no regress arises.

3.   If   I   decide   to   initiate a decision process to reach   a   decision   about   S   then   I   decide   to initiate   a   decision process to reach a decision about initiating a decision process   to   reach   a decision about   S or not.

4.   If not, no regress arises.

5.   If   I decide to reach a decision about whether or not   I   should   initiate   a   decision   process   to decide whether or not I should initiate a process to...

By   selecting   only   the   odd-numbered   sentences   in   this
sequence, an infinite regress   arises,   and   it   is   clearly
possible   to   fall   into   this   trap.   But, as I have argued
above, the even-numbered   sentences   indicate   live   options
too.   So a regress is not necessary.   (See also Fox (1973).)

Part II
Decision Fields

CHAPTER VI

Objects of
Decisions and Choices

1   INTRODUCTION

In this Chapter I examine the concepts of
choosing and deciding from the point of view of their
objects, i.e., from the point of view of what can logically
be chosen and decided. The results here constitute little
more than the "other side of the coin" with respect to those
obtained in Chapter IV. In that Chapter I examined the
internal structures of the concepts of choosing and deciding
with the aim of revealing their main similarities and
differences. Here I examine the external relations of the
concepts with the same aim. The two lines of investigation,
internal and external, tend to emphasize similarities and
differences, respectively, but the facts revealed by each
approach are basically in agreement.

In Section Two the necessity of positing the
existence of choice and decision objects and of
distinguishing overt and covert species is established.
This is followed by a Section showing that logical and
empirical truths and falsehoods may be the objects of
decisions. In Section Four, as anticipated in IV 4,
choosing is distinguished from deciding on the basis of the
fact that the former concept admits of no analogue for
deciding that something is the case. It is then argued
that the decision objects designated by adverbial and
adjectival clauses are no different from those assumed in IV

4, namely, propositions, persons, objects, states of affairs and actions. In Section Six a second detailed step is taken toward distinguishing choosing from deciding, and deciding that from deciding to. The former distinction is based on the facts that one can choose to believe or disbelieve that something is or is not the case, but one cannot decide to believe significantly although one can decide to disbelieve significantly that something is or is not the case. The latter distinction is based on the impossibility of transforming cognitive into practical decisions or vice-versa. A final step toward making both of the distinctions just cited is taken in the Seventh Section, this time on the basis of the fact that the phrase 'to accept the proposition' cannot serve as a "bridge" between choosing and deciding on the one hand and deciding that and deciding to on the other. In the last Section some descriptive and prescriptive features of negative decisions are cited.

2   EXISTENCE OF OVERT AND COVERT OBJECTS

One can distinguish the act of eating from what is eaten, that of reading from what is read, and that of painting from what is painted. What is eaten, read or painted may be called the 'object' of eating, reading or painting. Then, one may proceed to characterize both acts (eating, reading, painting) and objects (things eaten, read, painted). Similarly, one may distinguish acts of deciding and choosing from what is decided or chosen. The former (acts) have been referred to as 'decisions' and 'choices'. Decisions have been analyzed into a mental component alternatively called a 'mental act of deciding', 'covert decision', or 'decision act', and a physical component alternatively called 'decision behaviour', 'overt decision' or 'behaving as one would expect someone to behave who had made a covert decision'. Choices have been analyzed analogously into a mental component called 'covert choice', etc. and a physical component called 'choice behaviour', etc. I shall refer to what is chosen as an 'object of choice' or 'choice object' and to what is decided as an 'object of decision' or 'decision object'. This usage is at least as old as the Ethica Nicomachea . There Aristotle wrote: "...that which has been decided upon as a result of deliberation... is the object of choice" (1113a) and "choice is praised for being related to the right object...." More recently March and Simon (1958) and Gamson (1968) have used the term "content of decisions" to designate what is decided, and it is evidently this aspect of decision-making that Lasswell and Kaplan (1950, p. 74) were focusing upon when they defined a decision as "a policy involving severe sanctions". The question before us then, is what kind of entities can be the objects of choosing and deciding when these terms are used in their normal or standard senses?

It might be thought that the apparent reasonableness of sentences patterned after

(1)   x decided calmly.

and

(2)   x chose right after y chose.

indicates that choosing and deciding do not require objects of choice and decisions. "Calmly" and "right after y chose" are certainly not answers to the question: 'What was chosen or decided?'. Such a view, however, is mistaken, for sentences patterned after (1) and (2) must be regarded as incomplete in themselves. For example, (1) and (2) might be short for

(3)   x decided to remove y calmly.

and

(4)   x chose pudding right after y chose pie.

To see that sentences patterned after (1) and (2) are incomplete in themselves, consider the denial of this claim, namely, that such sentences are complete and not essentially abbreviations of sentences with objects. Suppose, for example, that (1) is complete and objectless. It would follow that one could just decide calmly without deciding anything in particular or general. If we asked someone who had allegedly made such a decision exactly what had been decided, an appropriate reply might be "Oh nothing. It was just a very calm decision." This reply is logically incoherent. If nothing is decided then nothing is decided calmly, quickly or any other way. 'Nothing' does not denote something that can be decided, but the absence of a decision. One cannot decide without deciding something any more than one can merely believe, perceive, know, doubt, etc. without believing, perceiving, knowing or doubting something.

The certainty with which we assert the existence of objects of decision and choice is matched by the certainty with which we assert the existence of two types, namely, objects of overt and covert deciding and choosing. We know that one's overt behaviour and mental acts may fail to be in agreement. (See IV 5.) The decision or choice that one would appear to have made on the basis of his behaviour may be quite different from that which one has covertly made, if indeed any covert choice has been made at

all.   In   such   cases, if we did not posit the existence of
two distinct decision or choice objects   then   we   might   be
obliged   to   regard   certain   decisions   or   choices   as
incoherent, merely because our analysis   is   oversimplified.
For   example,   consider the case of a person who has decided
to vote for Smith and to persuade you that he has decided to
vote for Jones.   If our analysis permitted him to have   only
a   single   decision   object   then   we would have to say that
either his behaviour or his mental act of   deciding   was   in
some   way   incoherent.   We would have to say that either the
object of his decision or   of   his   feigning   behaviour   was
inappropriate,   and   that   the result was nonsensical, i.e.,
the idea of a decision act of voting for Smith whose   object
was   that   of   voting   for   Jones, and of feigning behaviour
providing evidence of a decision for Jones whose objcct   was
that   of voting for Smith are both logically incoherent.   If
the concept of a decision object is going to make any   sense
at   all,   it   must   be   explicated   such that both overt and
covert decision objects must agree with   the   behaviour   and
decision acts of which they are objects. Hence, in the light
of   examples   like those just cited, it follows that we must
admit that whenever a decision is made at least two decision
objects may be involved,   namely,   an   overt   object   and   a
covert object.   The only difference between these objects is
that   the   former   is   the   object of a decision which one's
behaviour would   lead us to say has been made and the latter
is the object of a decision which has covertly been made.

From the point of view of determining what   kinds
of entities can be the objects of choices and decisions, the
distinction   between   overt   and   covert   objects   is
inconsequential.   Hence, in the remainder of this Chapter   I
shall   omit the qualifying terms 'covert' and 'overt' before
'choice objects' and 'decision objects'.

3   PROPOSITIONS AS OBJECTS OF DECISIONS

The   decision   objects   indicated   by   sentences
patterned after

(1) $\underline{x}$ decided that ...

are   propositions.   Letting a single demonstrative 'that' do
double duty to identify a   particular   species   of   deciding
(deciding   that   such   and   such is   the   case),   sentences
patterned after (1) would be completed by propositions   like

(2)   that Bob is wise

and

(3)   that Chicago is dirty.

Decisions whose objects are propositions are often called
'cognitive decisions'. The question before us in this
Section is: Can all kinds of propositions be the objects of
cognitive decisions? This question may be answered
exhaustively if it is granted that every proposition must be
either logically true (or analytic), logically false
(self-contradictory), empirically true (true synthetic) or
empirically false (false synthetic). Although these
concepts have generated many interesting and still
unresolved philosophical problems and although there are
plenty of sentences which can only be regarded as borderline
cases as members of one or another class of propositions,
the fourfold distinction does provide a useful heuristic
device for analysis and it is in this spirit that the
classification is adopted here. I shall consider each kind
of proposition in turn as a decision object.

          a) _Logical truths_. Could propositions with
self-contradictory denials be decision objects? For
example, could one decide that A=A, that a horse is a horse,
or that _p_ or not _p_ is the case? There are two good reasons
for answering these questions affirmatively and one _prima
facie_ plausible reason for answering them negatively. The
first reason for answering them affirmatively is that
sentences patterned after

(4)   _x_ decided that _p_ or not _p_.

do not appear to be self-contradictory, i.e., it is
apparently logically possible to make such decisions.

          Secondly, the so-called effective decision
procedures employed by logicians frequently lead to
conclusions like

(5)   that _p_ or not _p_.

One _could_ say, of course, that logicians are mixed up and
that what they call 'decision procedures' really have
nothing to do with decisions at all. Rather, one might say,
they are concerned with _conclusions_ or _solutions_ . As a
matter of fact, this line has been suggested by some
contemporary writers, e.g., Tukey (1960) and Myers (1969).
In Tukey's case it was motivated by a recognition of a need
to distinguish cognitive decisions from so-called practical
decisions, i.e., deciding _that_ from deciding _to_. I have
already emphasized the importance of this distinction, but
it seems to me that it would be a serious mistake to mark
the distinction by delimiting the denotation of 'conclusion'
and 'decisions'. Why should not the solution of a problem
or the conclusion of an argument also be the object of a
decision? After all, given say

(6)   that $\underline{p}$

I can perfectly well conclude and decide (5). I can say that on the basis of 'that $\underline{p}$' I have concluded 'that $\underline{p}$ or not $\underline{p}$' and I have decided 'that $\underline{p}$ or not $\underline{p}$'. One may want to say that 'concluding' suggests a more systematic means of reaching 'that $\underline{p}$ or not $\underline{p}$' than 'deciding', but I am not at all sure that it does and even if it did, it would not be sufficient to prove that concluding and deciding are or ought to be regarded as mutually exclusive acts. Similarly, 'solving a problem' may suggest more structure than 'deciding', but that does not make the two acts incompatible or exclusive. (See also Hampshire (1959).)

The only prima facie plausible reason I can think of for resisting the temptation to allow logically true decision objects is that one might have the suspicion that no one would be inclined or, perhaps, able to believe that the denials of such objects (propositions) would be live options. I shall consider this view under the rubric of

b) Logical falsehoods. If, as I have insisted in Chapter IV, (i) one must believe that, say, that $\underline{p}$ is a live option or alternative in order to decide that $\underline{\bar{p}}$, (ii) one would not be inclined or able to regard a logical falsehood as a live option, and (iii) the denials of logical truths are logical falsehoods; then logical truths could not be the objects of decisions. While this argument seems to have some plausibility, I think it is unsound because (ii) is false, i.e., people are inclined, able to and do regard logical falsehoods as live options. It is commonplace, for example, to find individuals unwittingly asserting and trying to defend contradictory (=logically false) views. Moreover, religious people frequently assert and try to defend such views wittingly, e.g., when they subscribe to the doctrine that Jesus Christ was "fully God and fully man" which implies among other things that he was eternal and temporal (=non-eternal), omniscient and non-omniscient, human and not human. Such activities are usually explained by postulating the existence of beliefs actually held which correspond to the claims uttered and defended. Alternatively, such activities have been (erroneously I think) identified with the beliefs themselves. In either case, however, it is granted that an individual can and frequently does hold contradictory beliefs. (See also Edgley (1969, p. 75).) Indeed, much of the whole enterprise of research (philosophical, scientific or whatever) consists of a quest for a totally consistent set of beliefs, which means that the more or less natural state that researchers (all too often correctly) imagine themselves to be in is one in which they are holding inconsistent beliefs. Accordingly, then, if one can believe a proposition of the form 'that p and   not p', then one can regard it as a live option. No doubt the contradiction would frequently have to be fairly well disguised in order for one to believe it and regard it as specifying a genuine alternative, but both of these conditions are unfortunately easily and often satisfied. I conclude therefore, that logical falsehoods can be the objects of decisions and, consequently, that the sole prima facie plausible reason for rejecting logical truths as decision objects is not plausible after all.

c) Empirical falsehoods. Much of what was said in the previous paragraph is again pertinent. There are, I suppose, no ghosts, gods or gremlins. But the fact that people believe that there are such beings is enough to demonstrate the "existence" and, therefore, the logical possibility of the propositions that there are ghosts, gods and gremlins as objects of decision and belief. Besides, if such falsehoods are eliminated as decision objects then it would follow that whatever one decided about the world must ipso facto be true. That of course, is quite ridiculous. Hence, such propositions must be admitted as decision objects.

d) Empirical truths. These are apparently unproblematic. If true synthetic propositions are eliminated as decision objects then whatever one decides about the world must be false. Moreover, without such decision objects, two different individuals could not decide that a different one of two empirical contradictory propositions is true. Both of these consequences, however, are patently absurd. Hence, empirical truths must be admitted as objects of decision.

In general then, the conclusion I have reached regarding the kinds of propositions that may be the objects of decisions is just this: Every kind of proposition can (logically) be a decision object. This is not to say, of course, that every kind of proposition and a fortiori every particular instance of every kind can be the object of a good, wise, rational, etc. decision. On these . questions I shall remain silent until I have considered the concept of rationality as it is related to decision-making.

4   PROPOSITIONS AS OBJECTS OF CHOICES

As suggested in Chapter IV, sentences patterned after

(1)   x chose that....

do not seem to have any normal sense when the 'that' introduces a proposition. For example,

(2)   x chose that Roger is thirteen years old

seems to be extremely odd to say the least. The proposition

(3)   that Roger is thirteen years old

just seems to be unsuitable as an object of a choice.   On
the other hand, when the 'that' introduces a noun or noun
phrase (1) yields a perfectly meaningful schema, e.g.,

(4)   x chose that proposition.

Similarly, one would apparently be making sense if "that..."
were eliminated from (1) as in

(5)   x chose the proposition that Roger is thirteen
             years old.

          Granting that appearances may be deceptive, I
would like to consider the possibility that (2) might be
regarded as short for something like (5), and that the
latter is equivalent to

(6)   x decided that Roger is thirteen years old.

If the equivalence of (5) and (6) can be established then
one might say that there are such things as cognitive
choices. If not, this fact should be counted as further
evidence for the view that propositions are not suitable
objects of choice and that there are no cognitive choices.
If the latter view can be sustained then a fairly secure
logical "wedge" will be driven between choosing   and
deciding.

          The   non-equivalence of (5) and (6) can be
demonstrated by adducing cases in which one is true while
the other is false. Such cases are not difficult to find.
For example, one might choose the proposition that Roger is
thirteen years old from a list of propositions in order to
please, surprise, deceive, anger or appease someone, to win
a bet, make money, attract attention, and so on. If any of
these motives are operative it is possible for (5) to be
true while, at the same time, (6) is false. For instance,
one might not be able or interested in deciding that Roger
is or is not thirteen years old, but one might still choose
the proposition that Roger is thirteen years old in order to
amuse or surprise a friend who has confronted him with the
alternatives.   Apparently   then, (5) and (6) are   not
equivalent.

          A plausible move to make following the argument
in the paragraph above might be this. One might grant that
(5) is not equivalent to (6), but insist that an equivalence
may be obtained by modifying (5) to

(7)   x chose the proposition that Roger is thirteen
             years old as an object of belief.

However, (7) will not do the job either, because one might
choose the proposition as an object of belief for someone
else, but not for oneself. One might choose the proposition
for someone who believed other propositions that entailed
(3), without deciding that Roger is thirteen years old.
Similarly, I might choose the proposition that Jesus Christ
is the son of God as an object of belief that is appropriate
for any Christian, although I have not decided that Jesus
Christ is the son of God.

             It is not much of a trick to cover ourselves
against this objection. Change (7) to

(8)   x choose the proposition that Roger is thirteen
             years old as an object of x's belief.

Is (8) equivalent to (6)? I still think not. Schema (8)
seems to be a confusing way to say no more or less than

(9)   x chose to believe that Roger is thirteen years
             old.

However, as I shall show in detail in Section Six, (9) is
demonstrably not equivalent to (6). But (9) is the end of
the line as far as I can see for modifying (5) to obtain
something equivalent to (6). I conclude therefore, that the
evidence adduced here (which is admittedly dependent upon a
"promisory note" to be redeemed in Section Six) supports the
conclusion that no variant of (5) can be produced that is
equivalent to (6). In other words, the evidence supports
the view that nothing can be done to sentences patterned
after

(10)   x chose ...

to make them equivalent to sentences patterned after

(11)   x decided that ...

Therefore, I believe that the view announced at the
beginning of this Section that propositions are to be
excluded as objects of choice has been provisionally
vindicated.

5   ADJECTIVAL AND ADVERBIAL CLAUSES INDICATING OBJECTS OF
     DECISIONS AND CHOICES

          The   decision   objects   required   for   sentences
patterned after

(1)   x decided that (which, whether, who, how, why,
             where and when)...

are no different from those considered so far.   They may be
propositions, states of affairs, objects, persons or
actions.   That is, for example, 'deciding what...' may be
analyzed in terms of 'deciding that...' or 'deciding to...'
So no new decision objects are required in order to
accommodate adverbial and adjectival clauses.   I shall
defend   this   claim   by   presenting   some   apparently
generalizable illustrations.

          Apart from any particular background information,

(2)   x decided what was to be done.

means nothing more or less than

(3)   x decided that a certain action was to be
             performed or to perform a certain action.

To see that this is so, consider the following analysis of
(2). Ignoring references to beliefs about alternatives to
simplify our task, (2) tells us that

     (i)   There is some individual x.

     (ii)   There is some action y.

     (iii) y has to be performed.

     (iv)   x decided that y was to be performed or to
            perform y.

Now analyze (3) and you will discover that (i)-(iv) contains
everything that is required and nothing further. Hence, (2)
and (3) are equivalent.

          Again, apart from any particular background
knowledge

(4)   x decided how to hang the mirror.

is equivalent to

(5)   x decided that the mirror could or should be hung
             in a certain way.

Schema (4) tells us that

        (i)   There is some individual x.

        (ii)   There is some mirror y.

        (iii)   There is some way z to hang y.

        (iv)   z is appropriate or possible (or both).

        (v)   x decided that z was the way to hang y.

But (i) - (v) consist of all and only the information that
is in (5). So, (4) and (5) are equivalent.

        Finally, apart from any particular background
information

(6)   x decided why the strawberries were missing.

is equivalent to

(7)   x decided that the strawberries were missing
             for a certain reason or due to a certain cause.

Schema (6) would be analyzed into

        (i)   There is some individual x.

        (ii)   There are some strawberries y.

        (iii)   There is some reason for or cause of y
                being missing, z.

        (iv)   x decided that z was the reason for or the
                cause of y being missing.

And (i) - (iv) constitute an analysis of (7) too.   So, (6)
and (7) are equivalent.

        On the basis of my analysis of (2) - (7), the
procedure that I have used to determine the equivalences
cited should be clear. I have made similar analyses for all
the adjectival and adverbial clauses indicated above, but
there does not seem to be any point in parading all of them
before you.   If any of the analyses reviewed here are
implausible, my claim in the first sentence of this Section

will be even more implausible. If all of these analyses seem plausible, you will probably be prepared to believe that claim and we can move on to choice.

The objects of choice suggested by sentences patterned after

(8)   x chose what (which, whether, who, how, why, where and when)...

are precisely those considered thus far, namely, objects, persons, actions or states of affairs. I shall defend this claim with examples.

Apart from any particular background information,

(9)   x chose what pleased him most.

is equivalent to

(10)   x chose the object or state of affairs that pleased him most or, to do that which pleased him most.

To see that this is so, consider the following analysis of (9).

(i)   There is some male individual x.

(ii)   There is some object y, state of affairs z or action w.

(iii) y,z or w is the thing that pleased x most.

(iv)   x chose y, z or w.

Now schemata (i) - (iv) may also be regarded as an analysis of (10), which means that (9) and (10) are equivalent.

Again,

(11)   x chose whether or not the painting was to be hung.

is equivalent to

(12)   x chose the hanging or the nonhanging of the painting.

since both may be analyzed into

(i)   There is some individual x.

(ii)   There is some painting y.

(iii) There is some action z.

(iv) z is the hanging of y.

(v) x chose z or non-z.

I have made similar analyses for all the adjectival and adverbial clauses indicated above and have, therefore, concluded that the replacements required by (8) are all possible. Further transformations are considered in the next section.

The upshot of this section then, is just this: No new kinds of objects of decision or choice need be postulated for adjectival or adverbial clauses.

6   OBJECTS OF PRACTICAL DECISIONS AND CHOICES

There is one large class of objects of decision and choice left to consider, namely, the class of all and only those things that can appropriately be regarded as objects of the decisions and choices indicated by sentences patterned after

(1) x decided to ...

and

(2) x chose to ...

Tradition has it that the dots should be replaced by verbs or verb phrases designating human action or "doings", e.g., "eat", "write a letter", "go fishing", etc. Acts of deciding to do something are often referred to as 'practical decisions'. Similarly, one might want to refer to acts of choosing to do something as 'practical choices'.

As indicated in Chapter IV, a necessary condition of deciding and choosing is that the decider or chooser must believe that whatever is decided or chosen is a live option or alternative whether or not it really is. Actions that are for one reason or another impossible to perform may be believed possible and, consequently, may turn out to be the objects of practical decisions or choices. Supposing that it is possible for one to decide or choose to perform acts that happen to be impossible, it does not follow that one can decide to do everything and anything. There are two acts in particular that are plainly possible to perform but, contrary to our assumptions so far, not so plainly possible to decide or choose significantly to perform, namely, those of believing and accepting. Obviously these are problematic and by no means independent notions, but they are of fundamental importance for our investigation and merit some attention. I shall consider the problems of deciding and choosing to believe in this Section, and those of deciding and choosing to accept in the next.

In some respects 'believing' is treated as a verb of action and in others it is a verb of passion. Sometimes it designates something that one does and at other times it designates something that one suffers. The title of William James's famous essay "The Will to Believe", is not metaphorical. People frequently talk as if they had more or less complete control over and ought to be held responsible for what they believe. They utter sentences like "I won't believe that" and "I refuse to believe that". They may believe or disbelieve wisely or foolishly, rightly or wrongly. They may give good or bad reasons for (as well as causal explanations of) their believing or disbelieving. Philosophers like Lewis (1955) who have insisted upon the possibility of an ethics of belief have based their views largely on considerations such as these. (See also Price (1966) and Chapter XIII.)

But there is something to be said for the other side, too. First, adverbs designating intensity of feeling may be appropriately applied to believing, e.g., one may believe strongly, very strongly, mildly, just barely, etc. Second, some adverbs that one would typically apply to actions do not appear to apply to believing, e.g., carefully, vigorously, slothfully, skillfully and rapidly. And finally, first person singular reports beginning

(3)   I am believing ...

do not seem to have any normal sense, although reports beginning

(4)   I believe ...

do.

Rather than attempt to eliminate one of the two views about believing that I have just reviewed, what I propose to do is to consider the verb 'to believe' as if it were only a verb of action and raise the question: Can one decide or choose to believe that something is the case? In other words, can one make a practical decision or a choice whose object is the act of believing something? If it should turn out that believing cannot be regarded as an act, action or doing, then ipso facto it could not (logically) be an act, action or doing that one chooses or decides to perform. If it is not an act at all then it is not an act that one could decide, choose, dream about or anything else.

On the other hand, if it should turn out that believing can
be appropriately regarded as an act then it would be
interesting and worthwhile to know whether or not it is the
sort of act that one can decide or chose to perform.

Consider the schema

(5)   x decided to believe that Emil is ill.

If the infinitive 'to believe' occurs essentially rather
than redundantly in (5), then its elimination should alter
the meaning of (5). But

(6)   x decided that Emil is ill.

tells us precisely what (5) tells us. After all, deciding
to believe that something is the case is nothing more than
initiating the belief that something is the case. If this
were not so,

(7)   x decided that Emil is ill and does not believe
           that Emil is ill.

would not be self-contradictory, which it patently is. If
one has not come to believe that something is the case
having decided that it is, then of what does such a decision
consist?   What, if anything, has one done when one has made
such a decision?

It will not do to say that (5) really means
something like

(8)   x decided to try to believe that Emil is ill

(which is weaker than (6)), for there is certainly a
difference between trying to do something and doing it.
Moreover, if one insists that the most one can hope to do
with respect to believing something is to try to believe it,
then it would seem that 'to believe' is not being treated as
a verb of action at all. In that case, as I mentioned
earlier, it is logically impossible for believing to be the
sort of action one might decide to perform, because it is
not any sort of action. I conclude, therefore, that insofar
as 'to believe' is regarded as designating an action, it
occurs redundantly in schemata like (5). Furthermore, by a
similar line of reasoning its occurrence in sentences
patterned after

(9)   x decided to believe that Emil is not ill.

may also be shown to be redundant. Therefore, it is not the
case that 'to believe' designates an act performed by x in
addition to x's deciding that Emil is or is not ill. 'To
believe' is redundant in (5) and (9) just as 'got' is

redundant in 'John has got a hat'. In other words, deciding
to believe that something is or is not the case is not, as
Ryle would say, doing two things, namely, deciding that
something is or is not the case and believing that something
is or is not the case. It is merely deciding that something
is the case or is not the case.

Now consider

(10)   x decided to disbelieve that Emil is ill.

In (10) the infinitive 'to disbelieve' is evidently not
redundant since the schema (6) that results from eliminating
the infinitive is not equivalent to (10).   Similarly, 'to
disbelieve' is not redundant in

(11)   x decided to disbelieve that Emil is not ill.

since (11) is not equivalent to

(12)   x decided that Emil is not ill.

Suprising as these conclusions may sound, there
does not seem to be any escape from them. One cannot decide
to believe significantly that something is or is not the
case, but one can decide to disbelieve significantly that
something is or is not the case.

The claim made in Chapter IV that it is
impossible to reduce deciding that to deciding to or
vice-versa has now been partially substantiated. One of the
prima facie possible "bridges" between these two concepts is
the alleged act of believing. As we have just seen,
however, insofar as believing is regarded as an action, it
is logically impossible for it to be an action performed in
addition to deciding that something is the case. Hence, it
is logically impossible to transform a cognitive decision
into a practical decision by means of an act of believing.

The situation with choosing is entirely
different, for reasons which are not novel. If the
infinitives 'to believe' and 'to disbelieve' are eliminated
from any of the following four schemata,

(13)   x chose to believe that Emil is ill.

(14)   x chose to believe that Emil is not ill.

(15)   x chose to disbelieve that Emil is ill.

(16)   x chose to disbelieve that Emil is not ill.

the resulting schemata re not merely not equivalent to the
originals, but they are extremely peculiar (unlike the

originals). Evidently then, one can say that one chooses to
believe or disbelieve significantly. This might have been
expected, since there is no such thing as cognitive
choosing, i.e., choosing that something is the case.
Furthermore, the fact that (13) turns into something strange
when 'to believe' is eliminated but that (5) is merely
equivalent to (6) proves that (13) cannot (logically) be
regarded as equivalent to (5) or (6). In other words,
"choosing to believe" cannot be regarded as equivalent to
"deciding to believe" . This is precisely the sort of point
that I promised at the end of Section Four to establish
here. In that Section, you recall, I claimed that

4(6)   x decided that Roger is thirteen years old

is demonstrably not equivalent to

4(9)   x chose to believe that Roger is thirteen years
            old.

The proof of this claim would be analogous to that regarding
(13), (5) and (6). More precisely, if 4(6) is equivalent to
4(9) then the latter must be equivalent to

(17)   x decided to believe that Roger is thirteen years
            old,

because (17) is equivalent to 4(6). But if (17) is
equivalent to 4(9) then 'to believe' must occur redundantly
in both schemata because they are identical in every other
respect. However, 'to believe' occurs redundantly in (17)
and significantly in 4(9). Hence, (17) is not equivalent to
4(9) and, therefore, 4(9) is not equivalent to 4(6).

7   DECIDING TO ACCEPT SOMETHING

        The verb 'to accept' and its cognates (accept,
accepts, accepting, etc.) is an extremely ambiguous verb and
its ambiguity is a bit difficult to characterize. Sometimes
it is synonymous with 'to believe' and

(1)   I accept that remark.

is meant to say no more nor less than

(2)   I believe that remark.

At other times such synonymity is ruled out, e.g.,

(3)   I believe that Ned is dead.

is not equivalent to

(4)   I accept that Ned is dead.

because (4) is so peculiar grammatically that it lacks a
normal or stock sense, though one might impute the sense of
(3) to it in certain circumstances. At still other times
accepting may be more or less implicitly contrasted with
believing.   Most of the laws and theories that are accepted
by scientists, for example, are not believed. (Scriven
(1961).)   Indeed, scientists and philosophers who happen to
be instrumentalists (e.g., Toulmin (1953)) would insist that
laws and theories are not the sorts of things that can be
believed or disbelieved, or be true or false. Those who are
not instrumentalists frequently accept laws and theories as
close approximations to the truth (and, therefore, known and
disbelieved falsehoods), as suggestive or fertile
hypotheses, as useful systematizers or organizers of large
amounts of data, as precise formulations of vague and
therefore untestable intuitions and as better than no
working hypotheses at all. (Bunge (1961)) The man on the
street also contrasts accepting and believing when he utters
sentences like

(5)   I believe that there is discrimination against
            minority groups in our society but I do not
            accept it as unchangeable, right or tolerable.

        What is required then, is some convenient means
of making the vrious senses of 'to accept' distinct and
explicit.   Some philosophers (e.g., Lakatos (1968)) have
suggested subscripting the term with numerals and providing
definitions for each resulting concept, e.g., 'accept$_1$'
means ..., 'accept$_2$' means ..., and so on.   I have also
employed this technique in Michalos (1971), but it is
clearly of limited value because the number of different
useful senses of 'accept' soon becomes unmanageable. The
best procedure seems to be the one used by the man on the
street and suggested in (5). That is, one merely has to
indicate the intended sense of 'accept' by qualifiying it
with an appropriate 'as ...' phrase, e.g., accept as a
working hypothesis, as better than nothing, etc. This, at
any rate, will be the procedure followed here.

        Now what can be said about deciding and choosing
to accept something. If 'to accept the proposition' is
regarded as synonymous with 'to believe the proposition' in
sentences patterned after

(6)   x decided to accept the proposition that p.

and if it occurs significantly in (6), then

(7) $\underline{x}$ decided that $\underline{p}$.

should not have the same meaning as (6). But (7) is
equivalent to (6). Hence, 'to accept the proposition' does
not occur significantly in (6), which is to say that it does
not designate an action performed in addition to deciding
that something is the case. Therefore, the phrase 'to
accept the proposition' cannot be used as a "bridge" between
practical and cognitive decisions when 'to accept' is
interpreted as 'to believe'.

       If 'to accept the proposition' is not regarded as
synonymous with 'to believe the proposition' then sentences
patterned after (6) might not contain any redundancy.
Suppose, for example, 'to accept' is qualified thus:

(8) $\underline{x}$ decided to accept <u>as a report believed by
$\overline{\underline{Francis}}$</u> the proposition that Ned is dead.

Clearly if the long phrase 'to accept as a report believed
by Francis the proposition' is deleted from (8), the
resulting schema is not equivalent to (8). Francis might be
the village idiot and one might very well accept the fact
that she believes the proposition that Ned is dead without
deciding that Ned is dead. But this remark is quite
generalizable. If 'to accept' is qualified in any way that
does not yield a phrase synonymous with 'to believe' then it
will always be possible to decide to accept a proposition
without at the same time deciding that whatever is asserted
by the proposition is actually the case. Hence, it is
logically impossible to "bridge the gap" between cognitive
and practical decisions by means of the phrase 'to accept
the proposition' when 'to accept' is not interpreted as 'to
believe'.

       Finally then, we must consider the possibility of
<u>choosing</u> to accept a proposition, e.g., as in

(9) $\underline{x}$ chose to accept the proposition that Ned is
             dead.

First, suppose 'to accept' is regarded as synonymous with
'to believe'. Then 'the proposition' is inessential for (9)
and the latter means nothing more nor less than

(10) $\underline{x}$ chose to believe that Ned is dead.

Schema (10) is analogous to

6(13) $\underline{x}$ chose to believe that Emil is ill.

So we know that 'to believe' in (10) and, consequently, 'to
accept' in (9) occur significantly. Hence, if 'to accept'

is regarded as synonymous with 'to believe' then one can
choose to accept significantly that something is or is not
the case.

We also know that under the present
interpretation of 'to accept'

(11) x chose to accept the proposition that p.

is not equivalent to (6), because if the phrase 'to accept
the proposition' is removed from (11) and (6) then the
schema resulting from the former is peculiar but the schema
resulting from the latter is just (7), which is perfectly
sensible. Moreover, since (7) is equivalent to (6), the
former is not equivalent to (11). Thus, if 'to accept' is
interpreted as 'to believe' the practical choice cited in
(11) cannot be transformed into the cognitive decision cited
in (7).

Suppose that 'to accept' is not regarded as
synonymous with 'to believe' in (9). It might, for example,
be qualified as in (8), giving us

(12) x chose to accept as a report believed by
         Francis the proposition that Ned is dead.

If the long phrase 'to accept as a report
believed by Francis the proposition' is removed from (12),
the result is strange. So (12) is not equivalent to (8).
If that phrase without 'the proposition' is removed from
(12), the result is sensible all right, but not equivalent
to the original (12) for reasons considered in Section Four.
It is easy to think of cases in which

(13) x chose the proposition that Ned is dead.

is true but (12) is false and vice versa, e.g., one might
choose that proposition to please a friend, although one is
aware that Francis does not believe it and, therefore, one
does not accept it as a report that she believes. The
qualified infinitive 'to accept' then, is undoubtedly
significant in sentences patterned after (12). Hence,
whether or not 'to accept' is interpreted as synonymous with
'to believe', it is logically possible to choose to accept
something. Again then, a difference between deciding to and
choosing to is revealed insofar as the former cannot be used
with a significant occurrence of 'believe' immediately
following it.

8   CHOOSING OR DECIDING NOT TO DO SOMETHING

Following March and Simon (1958), Lyons (1965) and Brand (1971), I hold that "choosing or deciding not to do something" should both be analyzed in terms of "choosing or deciding to do something else". For example, in order to analyze a sentence patterned after

(1)   x decided not to take the bus.

one should appeal to whatever x did decide. So, (1) might be analyzed as

(2)   x decided to walk.

or perhaps

(3)   x decided to take a taxi.

This view of the nature of what we might call 'negative decisions' or 'negative choices' has important consequences for the description and prescription of sets of alternatives. Since dichotomous classifications of alternatives of the sort 'do such and such or not' typically disguise a plethora of options under the rubric 'not', it is worthwhile to try to discover what factors determine the "cash value" of the latter and what factors rationally ought to determine that value. March and Simon (1958) hypothesize that at least nine factors affect the "character of an evoked set of alternatives" for a decison-maker in an organization. These include such things as the closeness of supervision, the complexity of the decision, the decision-maker's computational ability, the amount of perceived participation in decision-making, the incentive scheme and the behaviour of adjacent individuals. However, on the normative question of what factors rationally ought to affect the "character of an evoked set of alternatives" March and Simon are silent. But it is precisely this kind of question that must be answered by anyone interested in the evaluation of decision-making and, as I shall show in some detail in IX 7, it is by no means clear that any generally satisfactory and useful answer can be provided. It may well be the case that Kuhn (1963, p. 309) is right when he claims categorically that "there are no significant rules for the two most important steps of decision-making -- formulating the scope of the decision, and listing the alternatives to be considered within the set." If he is right then the practical value or actual usefulness of policy sciences for decision-makers would seem to be seriously limited. (See also Michalos (1971), Chapter VII.)

Possibilities, Restrictions and Resources

1   INTRODUCTION

In this Chapter we begin with an analysis of
alternative   concepts   of   possibility   and   impossibility.
Although   it   is   often   said   that   decision-makers   are
confronted   by   various   possible   states   of   the   world   or
nature, not quite enough has been said about the   nature   of
possibility   itself.   Following this discussion, in Section
Three the idea of a restriction   is   unpacked   in   terms   of
constraints,   restraints,   detours   and   limitations.   For
reasons which are given   in   the   third   Section,   it   seems
preferable   to   replace   the   term   usually   used   in   the
literature, namely, 'constraints', with   the   <u>prima   facie</u>
more   neutral 'restrictions'.   In Section Four I examine the
relations of implication that hold   among   the   concepts   of
constraints, restraints, detours and limitations as they are
explicated   here.   The   last   Section   is   devoted   to   an
explication of the concept of a resource.

2   STATES OF THE WORLD AND POSSIBILITIES

The element   of   decision   situations   which   has
traditionally   been   called the 'states of the world' or   the
'states of nature' consists of all the relevant   aspects   of
that   situation   that a decision-maker believes or knows <u>can</u>
arise at the time of the decision.   The word 'can'   must   <u>be</u>

emphasized because it is both essential to the definition of 'a state of the world' and highly ambiguous. Once its ambiguity has been noticed and systematically analyzed, it becomes clear that any adequate account of possible states of the world or nature must consist of a <u>set</u> <u>of</u> <u>sets</u> of alternatives rather than a single set of alternatives. In other words, the question: What can happen? gives way to: What can happen from an economic point of view? From a moral point of view? and so on. Thus, instead of imagining decision-makers pondering a single decision matrix summarizing possible courses of action or hypotheses, states of the world, outcomes and payoffs, I imagine them confronted by sets of matrices summarizing the relevant data emerging from conceptualizations of the world from different points of view. (Compare Zwicky (1967).)

A decision-maker is interested in determining what the world in which the decision must be made is going to be like, i.e., what relevant events, occurrences, or happenings will take place at the time of the decision. Clearly, the most reliable source of information about what will happen is what has and is happening, provided, of course, that some appropriate systematization of the past and present has been constructed. Hence, the ground, basis or warrant for a decision-maker's view of what can happen, lies in what is happening and has happened. That is to say, a decision-maker's information about present and past states of the world constitute a resource of fundamental importance. It is included among those items and aspects of a situation that can as a matter of fact be brought to bear on the problem at hand, although it may not all be equally controllable, manageable or clear. (Chapter VIII deals with these issues in detail.) On the other hand, the states of the world (themselves) that a decision-maker believes or knows on the basis of his informational resources <u>can</u> arise are not additional resources. Occurrences, <u>events</u> or happenings that are believed or known to be possible (in senses to be specified shortly) are not resources in the sense of items or aspects of a situation that can be brought to bear on a problem. They cannot be brought to bear on a problem because strictly speaking they are non-existent. They are mere possibilities. Undoubtedly knowledge and beliefs about such possibilities can be brought to bear or used in one way or another on a problem, but that is quite different from using the possibilities themselves, whatever that might mean.

Having distinguished possible future states of the world (what can happen) from present and past states of the world (what is happening and has happened), it is incumbent upon us to provide some explication of the senses of 'can' involved. I take it that this problem is tantamount to specifying various kinds of possibility, because of equivalences like

'<u>x</u> can ...' <u>if</u> <u>and</u> <u>only</u> <u>if</u> 'it is possible for <u>x</u> to ...'

Granting such equivalences, there are at least two significantly different ways to elucidate the concept of possibility, neither of which has been explained clearly in the literature so far. One way begins with the assumption that there are as many kinds of possibility as there are points of view from which a situation may be examined. Some years ago, for example, Arthur Pap (1949) suggested this approach by distinguishing logical, physical and technological possibility, roughly as they are distinguished below in 1-3. An occurrence is possible

1. <u>logically</u> if and only if the sentence(s) required for its description is (are) not logically false or contradictory. Hence, for example, it is logically impossible for an act of courage to fail to be courageous.

2. <u>physically</u> if and only if the sentence(s) required for its description does (do) not contradict any physical (including biological or chemical) laws of nature. Hence, it is physically impossible under normal circumstances for a lump of sugar not to be water-soluble.

3. <u>technologically</u> if and only if the sentence(s) describing the technological devices required for its production does (do) not contradict any of those required for a complete description of the sum total of available technological devices. Hence, it is technologically impossible for any available artificial heart to sustain the normal functions of an organism indefinitely.

Very little reflection is needed to recognize the arbitrariness of this triad. (See, for example, Austin (1956).) Why should not the list be extended thus? An occurrence is possible.

4. <u>economically</u> if and only if the sentence(s) describing the economic resources required for its production does (do) not contradict any of those required for a complete description of the sum total of currently available economic resources. Hence, it is economically impossible for me to have a one hundred thousand dollar house built for my family.

5. <u>legally</u> if and only if the sentence(s) required for its description does (do) not contradict any criminal, civil or common laws of the society to which it is referred. Hence, it is legally impossible for a murderer to receive the death penalty in England today. (Compare Majone (1975, pp. 58-59).)

6.   politically   if and only if the sentence(s) describing the political phenomena required for its production does (do) not contradict any of those required for a complete description of the sum total of relevant political phenomena.   Hence, it is politically impossible for a third party candidate for the office of President of the United States to win a national election.

7.   socially   if and only if the sentence(s) required for its description does (do) not contradict any of the codified customs, mores or accepted norms of the society to which it is referred.   Hence, it is socially impossible for a gentleman to completely disrobe himself in the midst of his guests for tea in England.

8.   psychologically   if and only if the sentence(s) required for its description does (do) not contradict any known psychological laws or any sentences required for a complete description of the psychological make-up of individuals whose action is required for its production. Hence, it is psychologically impossible for me to prefer death to life under normal circumstances or to find the idea of beating an old women to death with a chain appealing. (Compare Armstrong (1971).)

9.   esthetically   if and only if the sentence(s) required for its description does (do) not contradict any of the codified principles, rules or maxims, or any of the sentences required for a complete description of the esthetic attitudes of individuals required for its production.   Hence, it is esthetically imposssible for me to appreciate the sounds produced by many popular young musicians.

10.   religiously   if and only if the sentence(s) required for its description does (do) not contradict any of the doctrines, dogmas or sentences required for a complete desciption of the religious attitudes of individuals required for its production.   Hence, it is religiously impossible for a Theravada Buddhist to believe in the existence of or need for a Supreme Being or God in the Judaic-Christian sense.

11.   morally   if and only if the sentence(s) required for its description does (do) not contradict any of the principles, maxims, rules, laws or other sentences required for a complete description of the moral views of individuals required for its production.   Hence, it is morally impossible for me to beat an old woman to death with a chain.

      Assuming that the phrases 'required for its desciption' and 'complete description' can be satisfactorily explicated, there would seem to be as much merit in

specifying the last eight as there is in specifying the
first three kinds of possibility. The immensity of this
assumption has been amply demonstrated (e.g., in Kim (1969),
Davidson (1967a, 1967b, 1969) and Martin (1967), but for our
purposes it is enough to notice that without it even Pap's
triad collapses. The differences between, say, economic
and moral possibility as they are defined here seem to be as
significant as those between physical and technological
possibility. No doubt some people would be inclined to
reduce some of these kinds of possibility to others, e.g.,
everything but logical possibility might be regarded as a
species of physical possibility by a thoroughgoing
materialist; and some people would insist upon more
distinctions, e.g., those who believe that there are crucial
differences between biological and physical explanations
might want to define a 'biological possibility'. Whatever
one's attitude is toward these alternatives, it is important
to notice the underlying assumption from which they are
generated, namely, that there are as many kinds of
possibilities as there are points of view from which a
situation may be examined. Thus, examining a situation from
a moral point of view suggests moral possibilities and
impossibilities; a legal point of view suggests legal
possibilities; and so on. Tempting as this approach might
appear (at least until one draws out some of the multitude
of kinds of possibilities implied in it), it is not
inexorable. Indeed, I believe there is a plausible and
considerably more parsimonious alternative.

Instead of specifying many kinds of possibility
(corresponding to many points of view), one might specify
only two, logical and, for want of a more suitable term,
factual possibility. 'Logical possibility' would be
explicated as above, and

(1)   An occurrence is factually possible $=$ the
                                             df
      sentence(s) required for its description does (do) not
      contradict any true sentences.

Some of the true sentences that might be contradicted would
be physical, economic, civil or moral laws. Some would be
mere generalizations or, perhaps, simple statements of fact
about the psychology and behaviour patterns of certain
individuals, i.e., what Brand (1972) calls
"person-dependent" features. Still others would be
descriptions of customs, political institutions and so on.
In short, in order to exhaustively determine the factual
possibilities of a situation for any decision-maker, the
situation must be examined from as many different points of
view as that decision-maker recognizes.

The questions that must be raised repeatedly are
something like these: What is possible in this situation

from a _____ point of view? From a _____ point of view, is such and such possible in this situation? What can happen from a _____ point of view? In these questions 'possible' always has one of two meanings and the appropriate meaning is identified by the word inserted in the blank space. Rather than having many kinds of possibilities to consider, we have many points of view. Different points of view yield different reasons or different kinds of reasons for believing or knowing that something is impossible. What is imposible from a logical point of view (logically impossible) is excluded from all worlds because its description is self-contradictory. What is impossible from any other point of view (factually impossible) is excluded from some particular world(s) because its description contradicts some sentence(s) which is (are) not excluded.

Within the realm of factual possibilities and impossibilities one may distinguish those that are defeasible from those that are indefeasible. The difference between the two is that one may have control over the former but not over the latter. For example, one may alter one's own religious or political possibilities by changing one's religion or one's political affiliation. On the other hand, there is literally nothing anyone can do to, say, alter the course of time. That really is beyond our control. (Majone (1975) uses the terms 'conventional constraint' and 'empirical constraint' to draw roughly the same distinction.)

Of course, it may be extremely difficult to decide in any given situation whether one is confronted by defeasible or indefeasible possibilities or impossibilities. What appears to be beyond one's control may be merely beyond the price one is willing or able to pay. What one person is unwilling or unable to pay, another may find quite reasonable and within his means. So the latter person will have possibilities where the former has only impossibilities. (I have more to say about controllability and costs in Chapters VIII and XII, respectively.)

The advantage of the dualistic account of possibility (i.e., logical and factual possibility) that I have just explained over the multiplistic account explained previously is, as has already been suggested, parsimony. More precisely, it allows us to avoid the redundant positing of kinds of possibility corresponding to various kinds of viewpoints and reasons for believing or knowing that certain claims must be false. It might be thought, however, that the dualistic approach is heuristically less useful than the multiplistic approach because the latter provides a more perspicuous research program than the former. That is, a decision-maker using a multiplistic analysis of possibility might seem to have the advantage of having a check list of allegedly distinct fields to investigate for various kinds of possibility. He looks for physical possibilities and impossibilities, then moral, then legal, and so on until his list is exhausted. One using a dualistic analysis, on the other hand, would presumably look for reasons for believing or knowing that something is possible or not in one of the two senses. But, an objector might suppose, he would not have any systematic search procedure, any check list or extensive classificatory scheme to guide his investigation.

I think this objection has some force, because the multiplistic approach does have heuristic value. But it is possible to have both the heuristic benefits of the multiplistic approach and the simplistic benefits of the dualistic approach, although, as one would expect, these benefits are not obtained without some cost. Decision-makers might make a check list of points of view from which the world is to be examined, e.g., a moral point of view, a legal point of view, and so on. The points of view need not be exclusive nor exhaustive beyond a (devilishly difficult to identify) point of relevance. The emphasis is not to be put on kinds of possibility or even kinds of reasons for believing or knowing that something must or must not be the case. Instead, references to diverse points of view should be regarded as mere heuristic devices, as guides for research with no significant ontological import. We might even countenance the use of phrases like 'psychological possibility' so long as these are held to be equivalent to phrases like 'not excluded from a psychological point of view'. As long as one is clear about the abbreviative character of such phrases as 'psychological possibility', their use should be innocuous. Thus, by employing a check list of points of view, the heuristic benefits of the multiplistic approach may be secured. The costs incurred are just those required to provide some rough definitions of different points of view. I am confident, however, that these costs are negligible.

3   RESTRICTIONS

In the literature of operations research, cost-benefit analysis or programming-planning-budgeting research, a decision-maker's resources are generally contrasted with his "constraints". Roughly speaking, the idea is that in every decision situation a decision-maker will have certain things to bring to bear on a problem (resources) and certain others that must simply be lived with ("constraints"). The latter are "untouchable and/or unchangeable". (Hinrichs (1969)) Frequently the two terms are regarded as denoting the very same facts in different ways, since a record of everything that one can bring to bear on a problem is also a good indicator of what one cannot bring to bear on it. For example, if it is known that a decision maker can afford to spend $3,000 on a new car then this piece of information may be regarded as a measure of his economic resources as well as of his economic "constraints". He has all that money and that is all he has. Hinrichs has expressed this particular point of view about resources and "constraints" quite succinctly: "limited resources" he writes "are the prime constraints". (Hinrichs (1969, p. 14)) Another kind of "constraint" that is usually considered in this literature is formal or logico-mathemtical. To take a simple example, if probability values are to be assigned to the members of a set of events then the sum of the values for the total set must be one. This is just one of many rules or formal "constraints" to which a decision-maker would be committed in order to play the logico-mathematician's game.

Although the idea of a "constraint" is of fundamental importance for the foundations of decision-making, it is seriously in need of clarification. By explicating the concepts of constraining, restraining, limiting and detouring I shall justify the latter claim and, hopefully, eliminate some of the sources of confusion.

First, let us agree to use the word 'restricted' and its cognates (restrict, restriction, etc.) as a more or less neutral term explicated as follows:

(1)   x is restricted $\underset{df}{=}$ x is constrained
          restrained, restricted, limited or detoured.

Thus, hereafter when something or someone is described as restricting a decision-maker, it will be understood that this is merely an ambiguous way of describing that something or someone as constraining, restraining, limiting or detouring that decision-maker.

The terms providing the explicans in (1) may then be explicated as follows. If 'x' is a placeholder for the names or descriptions of individuals (including corporate persons and "dumb" animals), then

(2)   x is limited $\underset{df}{=}$ there is some activity or
          action such that if x were disposed to engage in
          or perform it, x could not.

x is restrained = there is some activity or
                 df
action such that x is disposed to engage in
or perform it and is prevented from doing so.

(4)   x is detoured = there is some activity or
                           df
            action such that x is disposed to engage in
            or perform it and is directed to engage in
            another.

(5)   x is constrained = there is some activity or
                              df
            action such that x is compelled to engage in or
            perform it.

After a few preliminary remarks about each of these explications, the four concepts will be elucidated and systematically related.

        First, notice that the conditional employed in (2) is not transpositional, since we have

        if x were disposed to engage in or perform it, x
        could not

but must deny

        if x could, then x would have been disposed to
        engage in or perform it.

The subjunctive conditional involved in (2) cannot be understood as truth-functional. In this respect it is like the non-truth-functional cookies-in-the-jar examples used in many introductory texts, i.e.,

        There are cookies in the jar, Junior, if you want
        them.

cannot be taken to imply

        If there are no cookies in the jar, Junior, then
        you do not want them.

The absence of cookies in the jar might be just the kind of thing that whets Junior's appetite. As a matter of fact, the conditional in (2) is even more like those involved in lawlike sentences than it is like those involved in the cookies-in-the-jar example, but the latter similarity will do for our illustrative purposes. (An excellent review of issues related to different kinds of conditionals may be found in Rescher (1964a) and Pears (1971, 1972).)

The consequent of (2), "x could not", is again ambiguous. In one sense of 'possible' or another, it is impossible for x to perform a certain action if x is so disposed or makes an attempt. The exact nature of that activity or action is difficult to specify without using metaphorical language. The "root model" or paradigm case that I have in mind consists of a physical barrier or boundary beyond which x cannot pass, e.g., like a horse in a corral, a chicken in a coop or a goldfish in a bowl. In each of these cases a barrier is set up; for the horse it is a fence, for the chicken a wire and for the fish, glass and a "sea of air". Although the physical barriers differ, each of these animals is in a similar situation insofar as each of them must operate within a distinctly limited environment. It might well be the case that none of them is ever inclined, tempted or moved to pass beyond the boundaries erected for them. Nevertheless, the boundaries exist and they place definite limitations on the movement of the animals. Similarly, by extending the concept of a barrier or boundary beyond the physical realm, we may speak of psychological, technical, political, etc. barriers or boundaries. Just as we speak of a decision-maker occupying some physical space, we may speak of his psychological, technical, economic, etc. space. That is, every point of view from which a decision-maker's situation may be examined generates a more or less hypothetical limited environment, space or sphere of operation. It is more or less hypothetical depending on who generates it when, where and why. Whether or not a decision-maker is ever inclined or disposed to pass beyond the diverse boundaries of his multifarious environments, those boundaries constitue limitations.

Like (2), (3) may be best understood by thinking about it first in purely physical terms, e.g., a pickpocket is engaged in stealing someone's wallet when suddenly the victim turns on the thief and bashes him over the head, knocking him completely unconscious. There is no alternative action that the pickpocket is obliged to perform, because he has just been knocked out. He has, however, been prevented, checked, stopped or restrained from doing what he set out to do. Broadening our conept then, we may speak of psychological, economic, moral, etc. restraint, on the grounds that it is plausible and often fruitful to think of a decision-maker being stunned or thwarted for psychological, economic, moral, etc. reasons. The only danger that one faces as a result of such an extension is that one may confuse some acts of detouring with acts of restraining. As (4) suggests, our pickpocket would have been detoured if, when he attempted to ply his trade, his victim redirected, rerouted or steered him toward some other goal, e.g., if he persuaded him to rob someone else, run away, see his priest, accept a loan or find a job.

(According to Bachrach and Baratz (1970), he would have been "influenced".) Insofar as the pickpocket's performance of any of these other actions prevented him from picking our particular victim's pocket, one might want to say that that performance had a restraining effect. Such a remark would surely not involve any extraordinary usage of the terms employed.   But   it   would   obliterate   the   important distinctions cited in (3) and (4), distinctions that already have been suppressed for too long in the literature.   For economic, moral, psychological, etc. reasons a person may simply be stunned, jolted, disoriented or have his intellectual and appetitive powers simply brought to a halt, and the temporary extinction of these powers should be distinguished from their redirection. Hence, I insist upon distinguishing   the   acts   of   restraining   and   detouring, marking the distinction by the use of two different terms. Because the terms are not ordinarily used in the unequivocal senses assigned to them here, there is some risk of confusion. Still, it seems preferable to risk confusion rather than to continue suppression.

Finally, (5) may be understood by analogy with the preceeding explicata, e.g., our pickpocket is physically constrained if the victim knocks him down and sits on him, ties him up, handcuffs him or locks him in a room. If he is forced to flee for moral, social, legal, etc. reasons then we may speak of him as morally, socially, legally, etc. constrained.   An excellent example of a decision-maker being constrained in the sense of (5) is given by Bachrach and Baratz (1970, p. 42).

> "There is reliable evidence" they write "that
> President Truman's 'decision' to order an
> atomic attack on Hiroshima in August 1945 was
> totally foreordained: although he and his
> top advisers were debating the pros and cons
> of the policy choice to the last moment, the
> technical arrangements for the attack were
> so complete that a decision to call it off
> was all but impossible."

On the basis of these preliminary observations,, it seems fair to say that there really are at least four different ideas that might be designated ambiguously by the term 'restrict' and its cognates. Furthermore, it seems that the kinds of things that are generally referred to in the literature as "constraints" are identical to those I have termed 'limits' or 'limitations'. (See, for example, Lasswell and Kaplan (1950), Gross (1966) and Gamson (1968).) By examining each of the four ideas in relation to the others, further light will be shed on all of them.

4   RELATIONS BETWEEN LIMITING, RESTRAINING, CONSTRAINING
AND DETOURING

First it is clear that

'x is limited' does not imply 'x is restrained.'

If a horse is locked in a corral then it is limited. But if
it never attempts to escape then it is never restrained.
When I am walking on the roof of my house cleaning leaves
out of the gutters, I am limited by each edge. But I am
hardly ever restrained from going beyond the edge by simply
leaping off the roof, because the prior condition for
restraint is hardly ever fulfilled, i.e., I seldom have the
inclination to jump off the roof of my house. On those rare
occasions when I would like to exit a la superman, I am
either simply stunned into a kind of stupor by the apparent
perversity of my inclinations, or I am prevented from
jumping by turning my attention to something else or
reflecting seriously about the likely consequences of
jumping. I am not, however, always restrained or detoured.
Usually the idea of passing over the side just never occurs
to me. It is typically as foreign to my ambitions as
walking to the top of the CN Tower or joining the RCMP. So,
usually I do not have to and, indeed, logically could not be
restrained or detoured from passing beyond the edge of the
roof of my house, although that edge constitutes   a
limitation of my physical environment. Thus, we also have

'x is limited' does not imply 'x is detoured'.

However,

'x is restrained' implies 'x is limited'.

and

'x is detoured' implies 'x is limited'.

In order to be restrained, one must first try to perform
some action, i.e., one must satisfy the antecedent condition
in the definition of being limited. But then one must be
prevented from performing the action, which satisfies the
consequent condition in the definition. Thus, if one is
restrained then one (logically) must be limited. Again, to
be detoured, one must be directed elsewhere from a path
already selected. Thus, when one is detoured, there is some
action such that one has tried to, been prevented from and,
therefore, is unable to (in some sense) perform, i.e., one
is necessarily limited.

For reasons similar to those invoked to show that
one could be limited without being restrained,

'x is limited' does not imply 'x is constrained'

A prisoner has his phsical environment limited by the size
of the cell he happens to live in, but he might not be
compelled to do anything within that cell. But the question
is: Do the walls of his cell compel him to remain inside
exactly insofar as they limit his access to the outside?
Or, to put the question more precisely: Is limiting a
person's activities to a certain physical space logically
equivalent to compelling him to perform at least one
particular action, namely, that of remaining within that
space?   I think not, because it seems to me that whenever a
prisoner is sleeping he is not performing any action and a
fortiori is not being compelled to perform any action.
Nevertheless, the prisoner is limited by the prison walls.
Thus, one can be limited without being constrained.

     As one may have expected

     'x is constrained' implies 'x is limited'.

Insofar as a decison-maker is forced to perform a certain
action, some kind of barrier has been erected between him
and alternative actions, e.g., insofar as he is compelled to
write a letter, a boundary has been put up as it were
between acts of his that would constitute refraining and
performing the task of writing the letter. The rather
cumbersome phrase "acts of his that would constitute
refraining" is necessary because, as I have already
suggested, in VI 8, one refrains not by doing nothing at all
but by doing this or that rather than something else.   For
example, one refrains from taking a third drink by smoking,
watching television, reading, working, talking to someone,
etc. There are any number of actions that one might perform
instead of taking the third drink which, in appropriate
circumstances, would be regarded as refraining from
drinking. Thus, since there are several candidates for
refraining actions that one is barred from performing when
one is constrained to perform some particular action, there
is (trivially) at least one.   Hence, when one is
constrained, one is limited.

Evidently,

     'x is restrained' does not imply 'x is
     constrained'.

and

     'x is restrained' does not imply 'x is detoured'.

for the very same reason. One might, as in the case of our
erstwhile pickpocket, be restrained by being rendered

totally unconscious and, consequently, unable to perform any action at all. (Compare Harre (1970).)

Again,

> 'x is constrained' does not imply 'x is
> restrained'.

because the antecedent requires the performance of some action while the consequent does not. Moreover,

> 'x is constrained' does not imply 'x is detoured'.

because one might be compelled to do something without ever considering an alternative.   To take a fairly obvious example, suppose Junior has been warned repeatedly about leaving his roller skates on the stairs, but he leaves them there anyhow. One night while Junior is asleep, father slips on one of the skates and nearly breaks his neck. In a fit of anger, he bursts into Junior's room, pulls him out of bed, drags him to the misplaced roller skate and makes him pick it up. All this time Junior is in the process of waking up.   In fact, the first fully conscious plan of action that occurs to him is precisely that which father is constraining him to perform, namely, to pick up the skate. Thus, Junior is forced to perform some action although there is no other action from which he is detoured.

> On the other hand,

> 'x is detoured' implies 'x is constrained.'

If a decision-maker is detoured from performing some action, then he must (logically) refrain from performing one that he set out to perform. Hence, he must perform some action that in the circumstances will count as refraining from performing the action originally intended. Thus, if he is detoured from performing some action then he is, for logical reasons, constrained to perform some action or other. Clearly, however,

> 'x is detoured' does not imply 'x is restrained.'

since the antecedent requires the performance of some action while the consequent does not.

The following matrix summarizes the relationships I have just elucidated.   The plus signs are short for 'implies', the minus signs for 'does not imply' and the single words 'constrained', etc. are short for the sentential functions 'x is constrained', etc. The zeros indicate the trivialities.

	constrained	restrained	limited	detoured
constrained	0	-	+	-
restrained	-	0	+	-
limited	-	-	0	-
detoured	+	-	+	0

To briefly illustrate the significance of the distinctions drawn in this Section, consider the following simple case. One frequently hears of and is personally confronted by economic "constraints" in the form of budget allowances. One allows oneself a certain proportion of one's income for food, clothing, entertainment, insurances etc. University departments have allowances for faculty and staff salaries, office supplies, travel assistance and guest speakers. Such allowances are evidently restrictions of some sort. But exactly what sort? If, for example, you are given a $400 guest speaker allowance, what kind of a restriction is that? It is most likely a limitation, because if you try to spend more, you will be prevented. It need not be restraining, because you might never be inclined to spend more. If you have always been determined to work within such an allowance, it would be misleading to say that it is constraining you. And finally, such an allowance probably does not include any directions regarding alternative amounts to be spent, although it clearly permits several alternatives. Now suppose you have a colleague named Smith who was given the same allowance in a different department. Smith is also limited. But he wants to hold a symposium with several invited speakers. So he has done all he can to obtain more funds, and he has failed. For Smith then, the $400 allowance is severely restraining. Moreover, it would be fair to say that it is constraining him to behave in ways that are not in accordance with his preferences. So, it is also detouring him.

Thus, although you and Smith are operating within the same allowance, it would be seriously misleading if not plainly false to suggest that you were both confronted with the same restrictions. You are each restricted in significantly different ways and any assessment of your decisions that was insensitive to these discrepancies would almost certainly miss its mark. Furthermore, any attempt to help or hinder you and Smith to make better decisions in your situations would also be guesswork if these distinctions were ignored.

5   RESOURCES

The idea of a decision-maker's resources   may   be explicated as follows:

(1) $\underline{x}$ is a decision-maker's <u>resource</u>   = $\underline{x}$ can
                                                              df
be brought to bear constructively on some feature of   a   decision situation by that decision-maker.

There are several parts of   this   proposal   that require   explanation and the remainder of this Section shall be devoted to just this task.

In the first place, by 'decision   situation'   I mean   the   circumstances,   context,   field,   environment   or setting in which a decision-maker operates.   It includes the decision-maker's beliefs   about   and   attitudes   toward   his circumstances   as   well   as the intersubjectively examinable features of   those   circumstances   about   which   he   may   be entirely   unaware   or   entirely   misguided.   The   so-called states of the world and points of view of   a   decision-maker that   were elucidated earlier would be important elements of his situation.   Others would be his objectives, preferences, alternatives, assessments of uncertainty,   restrictions   and resources.

Second,   according   to   (1),   resources   are   things that can be brought to   bear   constructively   on   something. The   phrase   "brought   to   bear   constructively"   suggests   the essence of the idea of a resource,   namely,   instrumentality. Resources are instruments or tools.   They   are   things (in the broadest   sense)   that may be used, employed, applied   or put to work in the service of a decision-maker.   They   are,   to use   a   much overworked term, the means to ends.   Of   course, one can collect   resources   as   our   dog   Penelope   collects pencils,   socks,   underwear,   combs,   etc. merely to have them rather than to use them, and in such cases it seems that the resources have become ends-in-themselves rather than   means. I   would prefer to say that the hoarding of resources is the end or   goal   in   these   cases   rather   than   the   resources themselves,   but the matter is not especially crucial in any case.   The important point is that resources are   the   sorts of entities that are usually needed or wanted as instruments or   means of obtaining things which are needed or wanted for themselves alone.   This   view   of   resources   seems   to   be completely   consonant   with   that expressed by most writers, e.g., Diesing (1958) and Gross   (1966).   According   to   the latter,

"Nonhuman resources [= man's biophysical environment] have no existence <u>as</u> <u>resources</u> apart from people.

Physical objects can become resources only when two conditions are met: (1) when there are people with certain interests to be satisfied, and (2) when there are people with the knowledge and technological know-how required to use such physical objects for the satisfaction of such interests." (Gross (1966, p. 192)

By classifying resources as instruments or things that can be brought to bear constructively on other things, the genus of 'resources' has been identified. Now a few remarks about species are in order. More precisely, what is the range of the variable 'x' in (1)? First, it includes the name or description of any item of a decision situation that might be identified as a result of examining such a situation from any point of view whatsoever. For example, 'x' might be a placeholder for the name or description of a certain sum of money, a moral rule, a physical event, a person, a procedure, a psychological quirk, and so on. Such items are typical of the sorts that might be turned up in the process of examining a situation from different points of view, and any of them might be brought to bear constructively on some feature of a decision situation.

Again, however, the very existence of alternative points of view or perspectives must be counted as a resource. For example, consider the case of an unwanted employee with a binding contract. From a legal point of view, it is impossible for his employer to get rid of him. Indeed, the only available relevant legal resources are entirely in the hands of the employee. He has a contract which remains binding even though his presence in the organization is a cause of some dissatisfaction to his employer. By reviewing the situation from other points of view, new resources may be elicited. Perhaps the employee has a psychological peculiarity that can be put to use somehow. If he dislikes writing memos, an extensive memo system might be intiated. If he is annoyed by the need for counter-signatures, more could be required. From a social point of view, more options arise. The employer and other employees can have parties and noticeably neglect to invite the unwanted employee. Considering the situation from a political point of view, the employer could begin to re-route important decisions or functions around the unwanted employee, i.e., the power structure of the organization may be altered so the employee gets fewer plums less often. Clearly then, the very existence of several points of view must be regarded as a resource.

The case of the unwanted employee illustrates the fact that resources must not be thought of merely as tools of implementation, i.e., they are not only the means of putting plans or decisions into action. In the case cited, they were used to create alternative courses of action.

But, as I have already suggested in (1) and the paragraph before this one, they might be related to any feature of a decision situation. Resources might be used to eliminate restrictions, to reassess uncertainties, re-order preferences, alter objectives, discover new possible states of the world, etc. Moreover, different resources can eliminate different restrictions, reassess different uncertainties, reorder different preferences, etc. For example, one might use moral persuasion to convince one's banker that a certain policy creates unnecessary and unjust hardships on some family, and thereby have the policy waived and an economic restriction eliminated. Similarly, one might use economic resources to alter political arrangements, e.g., by buying the votes of people who cannot be persuaded by any other means.

It might be the case that some things that are important resources for one time, place or situation fail to be of any service for another time, place or situation, e.g., as a motivating force, moral persuasion has been absolutely worthless on some but apparently effective on other people.

Shackle (1961) and others have referred to the "self-destructive" character of some resources, i.e., using them tends to be tantamount to using them up. While many resources are self-destructive in this way, others would be more appropriately described as self-constructive. For example, social customs, moral rules, legal processes and lines of communication are frequently strengthened by use. The more people draw upon, appeal to or generally make use of a principle like, say, "one man, one vote" the more strength the principle develops and the greater a resource it becomes. Similarly, as Wilensky (1970) and Foa (1971) have insisted, love and information are resources that "...can be given to others without reducing the amount possessed by the giver...". (Foa (1971, p. 345)) Gamson simply neglects these kinds of resources entirely when he hypothesizes that

> "With an appropriate means of control,
> [a] system not only contains influence but
> increases its total resources; with an
> inappropriate means of control, it may
> contain influence but so consume its resources
> in doing so that it diminishes its effectiveness
> in achieving collective goals."
> (Gamson (1968, p. 180))

Considering the number of points of view from which a situation may be analyzed and the number of features that might be uncovered as a result of an exhaustive analysis, it is apparent that a decision-maker is virtually always confronted with hundreds of (logically) possible sources of resources. There are, of course, important and difficult questions to be answered concerning the appropriateness, relevance or rationality of an exhaustive investigation of the features of a decision situation in search of resources. For now, however, I shall content myself with reviewing what logically can be done and ignoring the problem of the wisdom of doing it.

The phrase "can be" in (1) may be understood in either the multiplistic or dualistic sense explained in Chapter VII. The only point that must be insisted upon is that if, for any reason at all or in any sense of 'possible' at all, it is impossible to use something constructively, that thing is not a resource. This is a direct logical consequence of (1), and I take it that it is in accordance with common sense and ordinary ways of talking. Resources can be used constructively and whatever can be used constructively is a resource.

Finally, it should be mentioned that one might prefer to use (1) as an explication of 'potential resource' and refer to resources that are actually put to work as 'actual resources'. (See, for example, Gamson (1968).) I have no serious objections to this move. Clearly only some of the things that can be brought to bear on many situations actually will be, and one might just as well refer to the former as potential and to the latter as actual resources. On the other hand, no confusion will result if the additional qualifying terms are not introduced and we speak of used and unused resources instead of actual and potential resources. Hence, I will continue to use (1) as an explication of 'resource'.

CHAPTER VIII

Probability and Grids of Analysis

1   INTRODUCTION

Any feature   or any activity of any feature of a
decision situation may be predicated of that situation   with
(practically   speaking)   complete   certainty,   with   a
measurable probability of some   sort   or   with   uncertainty.
Features   or   their   activities   may   also   be completely or
partially   controllable   or   uncontrollable,   completely   or
partially   independent   or   dependent,   and   completely   or
partially clear or vague to a decison-maker.   The   task   of
this Chapter is to explicate all these concepts.

In   the   next Section a genetic classification of
interpretations of 'probability' and probability   statements
is introduced.   This is followed by three Sections reviewing
the   strengths   and   weaknesses   of   theories   of   obtaining
initial   probability   values   within   each   of   the   three
interpretations   explained   in   Section   Two.   (Most of this
material is examined in greater detail in Michalos (1969 and
1971.)   In Section Six the concepts of complete and partial
controllability, and complete and partial factual dependence
and independence are explicated.   Two important   species   of
dependence, namely, exclusiveness and complementariness, are
also   explicated   in this Section.   In the following Section
concepts of the complexity, perceived clarity and   vagueness
of   features   or   activities   of   features of situations are
explicated.   Finally, it is shown that and how all of   these
concepts   may   be systematically employed in the analysis of
any feature of a situation by means of a grid   of   analysis.

2   INTERPRETATIONS OF PROBABILITY STATEMENTS

Any feature of a decision situation may be predicated of that situation with (practically speaking) complete certainty, with a measurable probability of one kind or another, or with complete uncertainty. If a feature is predicated of a situation with a probability of one or zero, then its presence or absence in the situation is certain, i.e., it is certainly present or certainly absent. It is only uncertain if it cannot be predicated of the situation with any probability at all, even a probability of zero. For example, consider a certain physical resource, say time. A decision-maker may be practically certain that he has this or that amount of time to reach a decision, or he may have a measurable probability less than one but greater than zero that he has this or that amount of time, or he may be completely uncertain about his available time.

Extending traditional usage of the concepts of decision-makers operating under conditions of certainty, risk and uncertainty which are usually applied only to so-called states of the world, I shall speak of any feature of a situation as certain, risky or uncertain. Thus, preferences, alternative courses of action, objectives, resources, restrictions, etc. and even the existence of a particular decision-maker (which may be oneself) in a given situation may be certainly, with some risk or uncertainly predicated of a situation.

A question that naturally arises from the remarks in the preceding paragraphs is this: What is the meaning of 'probability'? Alternatively, one could ask: How should probability statements (i.e., statements that predicate probability of something) be interpreted? Examining the possible sources, grounds or origins of such statements, a threefold genetic classification of possible answers to these questions may be obtained. Probability statements may arise out of and be based upon physical, psychological or logical considerations. If the statements are generated from an analysis of certain physical properties of the world, I shall say that they and, more specifically, 'probability' and its cognates have a physical interpretation . If the statements are generated from an analysis of certain psychological properties of someone (e.g., a decision-maker), I shall say that they and, more specifically, 'probability' and its cognates have a psychological interpretation. If the statements are generated from an analysis of certain logical properties of a set of statements in some language, I shall say that they and, more specifically, 'probability' and its cognates have a logical interpretation.

Several other classifications of interpretations of 'probability' and probability statements have been used in the literature, usually with no criterion of demarcation being systematically employed. The most popular division is the dyadic one consisting of so-called <u>objective</u> and <u>subjective</u> probability. The interpretation I refer to as "physical" is generally classified as objective and the psychological interpretation is generally classified as subjective. What I refer to as the "logical interpretation" is sometimes regarded as objective and sometimes as subjective.

Once the question of the meaning or interpretation of 'probability' and probability statements has been settled, one's interest turns to a second problem, namely, that of measuring initial probability values. There is general agreement that any probability value should be a real number on the interval from 0 to 1, inclusive, but there is considerable disagreement about the methods that should be used to obtain such values in the first place. I shall briefly review some of the theories that have been suggested, and then present some of the advantages and disadvantages of these theories and/or the intepretations of 'probability' that they presuppose. As long as one is reasonably clear about the strengths and weaknesses of the various alternatives, it seems to me that each of them represents a live option in certain situations for certain individuals.

3   MEASUREMENT THEORIES FOR THE LOGICAL INTERPRETATION

For those who believe that probability statements are about logical relations holding among statements in some language, two measurement theories merit attention. According to the <u>classical theory</u> of Laplace (1812), one measures the initial probability of an event regarded as favorable by determining the ratio of the number of such cases to the total number of equally possible events of a certain kind. Since the entire analysis is carried out a <u>priori,</u> it is clear that the sort of possibility referred to in the phrase "equally possible" must be logical and that strictly speaking what the classical theorist is basing his initial probability appraisals on is not the relations among certain events but the relations among statements describing those events. Hence, on this view if it is asserted that the probability that God exists is 1/2, it should be understood that one who makes the assertion is assuming that neither 'God exists' nor 'God does not exist' are logically false (self-contradictory) and that only one of them is "favorable".

According to the <u>logical</u> <u>range</u> <u>theory</u> of Carnap (1950), one measures the initial probability of a statement by determining its logical range and adding the initial probabilities of all the state descriptions in that range. The terms 'logical range' and 'state description' are part of an enormous stock of technical devices employed by Carnap which do not lend themselves readily to partial interpretation. I hope, however, that the following remarks shall be adequate.

Suppose we have an imaginary world consisting of a single primitive property, redness, and two objects designated by '<u>a</u>' and '<u>b</u>' that might have or lack that property. Then there are four logically possible states of affairs in this world, namely

S1   <u>a</u> is red and <u>b</u> is red

S2   <u>a</u> is red and <u>b</u> is not red

S3   <u>a</u> is not red and <u>b</u> is red

S4   <u>a</u> is not red and <u>b</u> is not red

The four statements used to describe these possible states of affairs are called 'state descriptions'. Thus, a state description is a statement which indicates for <u>every</u> object in the world and for <u>every</u> primitive property, whether or not the object has that property. The logical range of a statement then, is the class of all those state descriptions in which it is true. For example, the logical range of the statement that <u>a</u> is red consists of the first two state descriptions, S1 and S2.

If every state description is assigned an intial probability then the initial probability values of every statement expressible in the language used to describe our imaginary world could be given an initial probability simply by adding the values of all the state descriptions in its range. For example, if all state descriptions were regarded as equally possible then each one might be assigned an initial probability of 1/4. So the probability that <u>a</u> is red would be 1/2.

There are at least five advantages to interpreting probability statements as logically true or false assertions about logical relations holding among certain other statements and to using either the classical or the logical range theories of measurement. First, one can usually obtain probability values that agree with one's intuition. For example, people who have never had any training in probability theory or statistics are quite often willing to flip a coin to decide certain issues because they believe this procedure tends to make everyone's "chances" equal. In accordance with such statements, the classical and logical range theories yield probability values of 1/2 for each of the alternatives involved in the toss of a coin. Second, one frequently obtains values that agree with observations. For example, when coins are flipped repeatedly, each side does tend to turn up about fifty per cent of the time. Third, in view of the second advantage, one can use statements about logical probabilities to appraise predictions and actual frequencies prior to observation. One might, for example, use the logical probability assessment that the probability of turning up a head on a flip of a certain coin is 1/2 as a good reason for doubting the truth of the prediction that the coin will never turn up heads. Fourth, the logical interpretation is always applicable. Any coherent statement can be assigned some logical probability value. And finally, one typically has easy access to such values, if not with the logical range theory, certainly with the classical theory.

There are two main disadvantages to the logical interpretation. First, given any theory of measurement for this interpretation, one is confronted by the problem of the proper application of Laplace's famous Principle of Non-sufficient Reason (Keynes's Principle of Indifference (1921)). According to this principle, in the absence of any reason for considering any events to be not equally possible, they may be considered equally possible. Thus, examining the imaginary little world constructed above, one might say (as I did) that every state description should be assigned an initial value of 1/4, because we have no reason to believe that they are not equally possible. Carnap, on the other hand, opted for the assignment of 1/3 each to S1 and S4, and 1/6 each to S2 and S3. As he saw it, there were three exclusive possibilities, namely, no object is red, one object is red or two objects are red. Someone else might reason that there are really only two possibilities, namely, both objects are red or not. Hence, Laplace's rule seems to countenance at least three different initial probability assignments to the state descriptions of our imaginary world. That, of course, is two too many. The problem of the proper application of this rule is just that of determining which assignment is "correct" when a number of alternatives are available. (See also Lenz (1956).)

The second disadvantage of using the logical interpretation given any theory for obtaining initial values is Ayer's (1957) objection that every probability statement involving this interpretation is as good as every other provided that it is not self-contradictory. On this interpretation probability statements are either logically true or logically false, and the former are supposed to be as equally unobjectionable as the latter are equally objectionable. What one would like to say, however, is that probability statements based on more evidence are more reliable than probability statements based on less evidence. But if all one's statements are necessarily true (if not self-contradictory) then the fact that some are based on more or less evidence would seem to be irrelevant to their reliability.

As argued in Michalos (1970b, 1971), I believe it is demonstrably false that all logically true statements are equally unobjectionable for all purposes. Anyone who has worked with axiomatic systems of logical truths (e.g., the propositional calculus) realizes that many tautologous formulae are more valuable than others in the derivation of certain other tautologous formulae. Thus, I am inclined to see this second disadvantage as less serious than Ayer and some others see it.

4   MEASUREMENT THEORIES FOR THE PHYSICAL INTERPRETATION

For those who believe that probability statements are about the physical attributes of certain features of the world, three measurement theories merit attention. According to the finite frequency theory advocated by Russell (1948), one measures the initial probability of an event regarded as favorable by determining the ratio of the number of such cases to the total number of events in an observed sequence of repetitive events of a certain kind. There are three fundamental differences between this theory and those considered so far. In the first place, the analysis is carried out a posteriori on the basis of observations. Second, the kinds of events involved are necessarily repetitive. An event is repetitive if it is repeatable an unlimited number of times, e.g., drawing a card from a deck with replacement, rolling a six with a fair die and kicking a football. In such cases strictly speaking it is the kind, sort or type that is repeated, not any particular event, e.g., one might enjoy as many kicks as one pleases, but cannot repeat, say, the first kick (or second, etc.). In contrast to kicking a football as a kind of repetitive event, the first kick (or second, etc.) is unique. Unique events, by definition, are not repeatable. Your own birth and death, the American Civil War, and the New York Jets's victory over the Baltimore Colts in the Superbowl are all unique events. Finally, this theory differs from the others considered because it requires sequences of repetitive events. By a "sequence" of repetitive events I mean an occurrence of at least two events of the same type. Thus, a two-membered sequence of coin tosses requires two coin tosses, a three-membered sequence requires three tosses, and so on.

According to the propensity theory developed by Popper (1959) one measures the initial probability of an event regarded as favorable by determining on the basis of one's experimental set-up and scientific theories the relative frequency of such cases in a sequence of events of a certain kind. The basic difference between this theory and the frequency theory just cited is that here probability statements are not reports about observed sequences, but reports about the tendencies of experimental set-ups to generate certain kinds of sequences. While the frequentist focuses merely on the outputs of experimental set-ups, the propensity theorist focuses on the set-ups themselves and on whatever scientific theories are available to account for their outputs.

Finally, a physical analogue of the logical range theory has been constructed by Kneale (1949). Although Kneale's physical range theory is much more primitive and has never received the attention of its logical counter-part, regarding it as an analogue of the latter is an accurate and easy way to suggest its basic nature. Instead of talking about logical possibilities and ranges, a physical range theorist talks about physical possibilities and ranges. Instead of carrying out his analysis a priori, he proceeds a posteriori. Instead of Laplace's Principle of Non-sufficient Reason, he employs a Physical Principle of Sufficient Reason which enjoins one to investigate phenomena and to consider events equally possible if there is some good reason to consider them so. While Laplace's rule is based on ignorance, the physical range theorist's is based on knowledge.

There are at least three advantages to interpreting probability statements as empirically true or false assertions about the physical attributes of certain features of the world, given any of the measurement theories just outlined. First, many people have the suspicion that probability statements ought to be as much about the physical world in which we live as statements like

The temperature in this room is $79\,^{\circ}$ F.

and this suspicion is vindicated by the physical interpretation. Second, the probability statements obtained with this interpretation tend to be stable because they are based on features of physical reality. And finally, they tend to be objectively, intersubjectively or publicly obtainable for the same reason.

The single disadvantage of interpreting probability statements as claims about physical attributes is that such statements are not available prior to observation. Without observation one has no information about the relative frequency of the occurrence of attributes

in sequences, about physical possibilities or about the
tendencies of experimental set-ups to generate certain kinds
of sequences. If, for example, one were committed to this
interpretation, confronted with an urn containing 9,999
black balls and one white one, and asked which color was
most likely to turn up when a single ball was drawn from the
urn, one would have to say that he did not have the foggiest
idea. On this interpretation the information provided about
the composition of the balls in the urn is absolutely
worthless, although most people would be inclined (rightly I
think) to bet against drawing a white ball.

There are two disadvantages to employing a
frequency theory. The first is the problem of selecting
appropriate reference sequences containing events regarded
as favorable. Suppose, for example, that Junior usually has
high marks on mathematics tests and that his overall
academic average is C. Using his past performance on math
tests as a reference sequence, one would say that the
probability of his obtaining a high score on such a test is
high. But using his past performances on all previous tests
as a reference sequence, one would say that the probability
of his obtaining a high score on a math test is low. The
problem then, is to make the "right" selection of one or the
other of these two possible reference sequences.
Interestingly enough, in the present case the probability
statement based on less information (i.e., Junior's past
performance on math tests) would be a more reliable measure
of his future performance on math tests than the statement
based on more information. Unfortunately, however, one
frequently lacks the information required to judge
confidently that this or that reference sequence is the
"right" one.

The second disadvantage of employing frequency
theories is the so-called problem of unique events. Since
by definition unique events are not repetitive and frequency
theories require repetitive events to begin with, it is at
least questionable and at most impossible to assign such
events probability values. Four more or less plausible
solutions to this problem have been suggested. Some
frequentists (e.g., von Mises (1939)) have insisted that
unique events simply cannot logically be assigned
probabilities. Others (e.g., LeBlanc (1962)) claim that
such events have a probability of one or zero, i.e., they
are regarded as constituting what may be referred to as
'degenerate sequences'. Still others (e.g., Reichenbach
(1949)) tell us that one may assign such events "weights"
which are nothing more than probabilities of repetitive
events related to the unique events as consequences. For
example, to measure the probability that George Washington
died in the year 1799 one might examine a sequence of
reports by different historians or historical documents.
Using such reference sequences, one could determine the

relative frequency of reports favorable to the hypothesis in question and regard that as the "weight" of the hypothesis. Finally, one might just deny that there are any "really" unique events, i.e., everything is like something somehow.

5   MEASUREMENT   THEORIES   FOR   THE   PSYCHOLOGICAL INTERPRETATION

For those who believe that probability statements are about the psychological properties (attitudes, beliefs, etc.) of someone, two measurement theories merit attention. According to what I shall call a simple judgment theory, one measures the initial probability of an event by simply assigning it a numerical value on the interval between zero and one inclusive in accordance with one's intuitive judgment concerning its occurrence or non-occurrence. For example, one might judge that a third world war is highly improbable and assign its occurrence a numerical value of .03.

Alternatively one might employ a personal odds theory introduced by Ramsey (1931) according to which if one is willing to give odds of m to n in favor of some event then the probability of that event is m/m+n. Thus, if one is willing to give odds of 3 to 1 that a certain senator will be elected then one has assigned it a personal probability of 3/4.

There are at least three advantages to interpreting probability statements as assertions about psychological attributes. First, with this interpretation probability statments may be available prior to observation to appraise predictions. Second, one acquires a means of quantifying talk about degrees or intensities of belief. Instead of merely judging that certain events are very doubtful, somewhat likely, very probable, almost certain, etc., one may assign them numerical values reflecting one's intensity of belief. And finally, one must admit that the ease with which one obtains probability statements on this interpretation given either of the measurment theories suggested is quite remarkable.

Two disadvantages are also apparent. First, one has the suspicion that probability values indicating nothing but one's own predilections can be extremely misleading guides. Morlock (1967) and others have shown that people tend to judge events that they regard as favorable as more probable than events that they regard as unfavorable. Second, probability statements obtained from either of the measurement theories considered with this interpretation may be unstable. One person at different times or two people at the same time may judge a certain event to have different

probability values although no new evidence is ever
introduced. (See also Shackle (1961) and Levi (1966).)

6   CONTROLLABILITY AND DEPENDENCE

Virtually every writer on decision-making has
paid some attention to probabilistic aspects of decision
situations. However, very few authors have considered the
controllability of features of such situations. Similarly,
the dependence and independence of features of a situation,
and the perceived vagueness and clarity of the setting all
have significance for a decision-maker. Thus, in the next
two Sections I shall explicate all of these relatively
neglected concepts, and then put the complete set of ideas
to work on grids of analysis.

Features or the activities of $\underline{any}$ features of
decision situations may be (practically speaking)
completely controllable, partially controllable or
completely uncontrollable. If $\underline{z}$ is a placeholder for the
names or descriptions of any activities or any features and
$\underline{x}$ and $\underline{y}$ are placeholders for the names or descriptions of
decision-makers then:

(1) $\underline{z}$ is completely controllable by $\underline{x}$ $=_{df}$ $\underline{x}$ can (in

            every sense) intentionally cause $\underline{z}$ to occur and
            fail to occur

(2) $\underline{z}$ is partially controllable by $\underline{x}$ $=_{df}$

            (i)   part of $\underline{z}$ is completely controllable by $\underline{x}$, or

            (ii) there is a $\underline{y}$ such that $\underline{z}$ is completely
                  controllable by $\underline{x}$ and $\underline{y}$ together, or

            (iii) part of $\underline{z}$ is completely controllable by
                  $\underline{x}$ and $\underline{y}$ together

(3) $\underline{z}$ is completely uncontrollable by $\underline{x}$ $=_{df}$ $\underline{z}$ is

            neither completely nor partially controllable
            by $\underline{x}$.

Several aspects of these proposals should be
emphasized. In the first place it should be remembered that
just as soluble substances may as a matter of fact never be
dissolved, controllable activities or features may as a
matter of fact never be controlled. (1) to (3) are concerned
with possibilities of control, not with control itself or
the exercise of control.   Second, as suggested by the

parenthetical "in every sense" in (1), if there is any sense
in which it is impossible for one to bring about some
activity or feature or to end it once it has begun, then it
is not completely controllable by that person. Third, the
concept of causality occurs essentially in (1) and,
therefore, in (2) and (3). (Dahl (1965)) Fourth, an
activity is not completely controllable by one who might
inadvertently or accidently cause it to occur and fail to
occur, but who cannot intentionally or wittingly produce
such results. Fifth, three kinds of partial controllability
are distinguished in (2). The first kind occurs when for
example, ten dollars are partially controlled by two people
who each have complete control over five. Instances of the
second kind occur when groups elect compromise candidates.
When nominating committees choose compromise candidates to
run in general elections, the nominee's final election is
partially controllable in the third sense specified.
Finally, it is perhaps worthwhile to note that (3) does not
commit us to a triad of mutually exclusive terms. Such a
result would be counter- intuitive, because if an activity
as a whole is completely controllable (uncontrollable) then
some part of it must be completely controllable
(uncontrollable). (Compare Rescher (1969a) and Walton
(1974).)
        If two propositions are related such that neither
implies the other or the negation of the other, logicians
say that the propositions are logically independent. If
either implies the other or the negation of the other then
they are logically dependent. The concepts of dependence
and independence that I shall explicate below are different
from these insofar as they involve factual rather than
merely logical relations. The difference between what I
shall call factual dependence and controllability is roughly
a difference between what causes what as a matter of fact
and what can intentionally cause what. Thus, if 'x' is a
placeholder for the names or descriptions of decision-makers
or events and 'z' is a placeholder for the names or
descriptions of the activities of or any feature of a
decision situation, then

(4)   z is completely factually dependent upon x $=$
                                                     df
         x is the sole cause of z.

(5)   z is partially factually dependent upon x $=$
                                                   df
         (i)   part of z is completely dependent upon x, or

         (ii)   there is a y such that z is completely
                dependent upon x and y together, or

         (iii) part of z is completely dependent upon x and
                y together, or

(iv) $\underline{x}$ is causally connected to $\underline{z}$, or

(v) $\underline{x}$ and $\underline{y}$ together are causally connected to $\underline{z}$

(6) $\underline{z}$ is completely factually independent of $\underline{x}$ $\underset{df}{=}$

$\underline{z}$ is neither completely nor partially dependent upon $\underline{x}$.

Obviously the identification of the "sole cause" of anything is largely a matter of ignoring aspects of a situation that are or ought to be for one reason or another irrelevant to one's analysis. I mean to suggest nothing more sophisticated or problematic with (4) than what is usually suggested when one asserts that this or that event or person is wholly responsible in a causal sense for the occurrence of some activity. For example, in a perfectly straightforward sense of 'cause', I am the sole cause of the movement of the pencil in my hand. I alone am moving it. If I throw a pencil at the painting on the wall, its takeoff would be partially factually dependent in the first sense on my action. By introducing various aspects of the situation as more or less important, we could obtain illustrations of the second, third and fourth senses of partial factual dependence.

There are 36 possible relations of implication among the six terms explicated in (1) to (6) which might be conveniently summarized in a 6 x 6 matrix. Using the plus and minus signs as in the matrix of restrictions in VII 4, only two plus signs would appear in the diagram, one indicating that complete implies partial controllability and the other indicating that complete implies partial factual dependence. Most of the implications that fail to hold are unproblematic, but a few may give one serious doubts about the suitability of (1) to (6) as explicata of ordinary concepts. The fact of the matter is that I have been extremely unsuccessful at discovering secure and significant guidelines regarding the ordinary or stock meanings of the terms in question. Thus, it might be more accurate to think of (1) to (6) as stipulations plain and simple, rather than as explications. Nevertheless, a few remarks about a couple of the relations among the defined terms and their "counterparts" in ordinary English may be instructive.

According to the proposals offered here,

(7)   '$\underline{z}$ is completely factually independent of $\underline{x}$' does not imply '$\underline{z}$ is completely uncontrollable by $\underline{x}$'

and it might be thought that this is unsatisfactory. However, the plausibility of (7) may be established by drawing out some of the consequences of its denial, namely,

(8)   '$\underline{z}$ is completely factually independent of $\underline{x}$
             implies '$\underline{z}$ is completely uncontrollable by $\underline{x}$'

Suppose (8) is asserted and only (3) and (6) are retained in
order to maintain the weak formal relations specified by (3)
and (6). From (3), (6) and (8) it follows that

(9)   '$\underline{z}$ is completely (and partially) controllable by
             $\underline{x}^\top$ implies '$\underline{z}$ is completely (and partially)
             factually dependent upon $\underline{x}$'.

But there are plenty of counter-instances of (9). Whenever
the activity of some person or thing is completely
controllable by more than one person or thing at different
times, complete factual dependence ordinarily would not be
regarded as a consequence of complete controllability. For
example, under normal circumstances one would say that the
water running from a faucet in my kitchen sink is completely
controllable by anyone in my family. But it is not
completely factually dependent upon anyone in my family.
If, for instance, I fail to exercise my control over it,
someone else might still exercise his or her control over
it. Again, suppose certain on-the-job activities of a
workman are completely controllable by a supervisor who
usually does not exercise his control. The result is that
the workman learns to get along on his own, i.e., he becomes
relatively factually independent. In view of examples like
these then, I have concluded that (9) is not ordinarily true
and that, therefore, (7) is acceptable.

       The converse of (7), namely,

(10)   '$\underline{z}$ is completely uncontrollable by $\underline{x}$' does not
             imply '$\underline{z}$ is completely factually independent of
             $\underline{x}$.'

might also be viewed with some suspicion. On the contrary,
however, one could say that the rotation of the earth is
completely uncontrollable by most of us, but none of us is
completely factually independent of that rotation. Hence,
(10) is more plausible than its negation.

       An important type of partial factual dependence
is exclusiveness. If $\underline{z}$ and $\underline{w}$ are two activities then

(11) $\underline{z}$ and $\underline{w}$ are completely mutually exclusive $=$
                                                                          df
             the occurrence of either causes the nonoccurrence
             of the other.

(12) $\underline{z}$ and $\underline{w}$ are partially mutually exclusive $=$
                                                                          df
             (i)   part of either and the other are completely
             mutually exclusive or

(ii)   there is another activity $\underline{u}$ such that $\underline{z}$ and $\underline{u}$ (together) and $\underline{w}$ are   completely   mutually exclusive, or

(iii)   part   of $\underline{z}$ and $\underline{u}$ (together)   and $\underline{w}$ are completely mutually exclusive   or part of $\underline{w}$ and $\underline{u}$ (together)   and $\underline{z}$ are completely mutually exclusive.

Examples of (11) include such things as investing resources in one area excluding their investment in another, adopting one course of action excluding another, and so on. If, as would typically be the case, one invests just enough of his resources in some activity to   preclude   undertaking another,   we   would   have a case of partial exclusion of the first kind.   If two people are playing a game that cannot be played with a third person then exclusion of the second kind occurs.   If two people   are   engaged   in   an   activity   that permits   more   than   two   to   participate   provided that all players agree but the players do not agree,   then   exclusion of the third kind occurs.

Another   important   type   of   partial   factual dependence   is   complementariness.   If $\underline{z}$ and $\underline{w}$ are   two activities then

(13) $\underline{z}$ and $\underline{w}$ are completely complementary   =   there
                                                                                                          df
is   another activity $\underline{u}$ such that $\underline{z}$ and $\underline{w}$ together cause $\underline{u}$.

(14) $\underline{z}$ and $\underline{w}$ are partially complementary   =
                                                                                                  df
(i)   there is another activity $\underline{u}$ such that   part part of $\underline{z}$ and $\underline{w}$ together cause $\underline{u}$, or

(ii)   there   is   a fourth activity $\underline{y}$ such that $\underline{z}$, $\underline{w}$ and $\underline{y}$ together cause $\underline{u}$, or

(iii) part   of   the   activity   of $\underline{z}$, $\underline{w}$ and $\underline{y}$ together cause u.

Examples   of (13)   include   such   things   as two people pulling at their oars to propel a   boat   through   the water,   several   people   performing   organizational tasks to create   a   productive   unit,   and   so   on.   The   foaming   of intersecting   waves produced by the joint action of two oars illustrates partial complementariness   of   the   first   kind. Similar   foaming   produced   by two oars and a child slapping the water with a stick could illustrate the second and third kinds.

7   CLARITY AND COMPLEXITY

          With the help of my explications of 'complete'
and 'partial factual dependence' and 'independence', it is
possible to explicate analytically useful concepts of
clarity and vagueness.   There is general agreement among
philosophers that the clarification of a concept has
something to do with the disclosure of all its implications.
(Carnap (1934), Rorty (1967), Niiniluoto and Tuomela (1973))
This insight may be generalized for the clarification of any
feature of a decision situation. To simplify matters, I
begin with a definition of 'complexity'.   If 'x' is a
placeholder for the name or description of any feature or
any activity of any feature of a decision situation and 'n'
is a placeholder for the name or description of a certain
spatio-temporal region to be analyzed, then

(1)   The complexity of x in n $\underset{df}{=}$ the total number
             of distinct factual dependencies of x in n.

          Three aspects of (1) require explanation. In the
first place, since it may be the case that everything in the
world is causally connected to everything else and since it
is certainly the case that one could (factually) never know
everything about everything, the only complexity defined in
(1) is that which is relative to certain features in
certain regions of space-time. By the phrase "region of
space-time" I do not mean a mere spatio-temporal manifold,
a mere physical "lump" of the world.   Rather I mean
everything that might be identified in such a region as a
result of examining it from any point of view. For example,
a complete examination of a political candidate's actions in
the week before an election would include reviews of his
physical presence in this or that place at such and such a
time as well as his social, moral, economic, etc.
behaviour.   Generally a decision-maker's interests,
purposes, resources and restrictions will largely determine
the size of the region to be examined and its scope or
intensity.   Second, as one might have suspected, the
qualifying term 'distinct' has been added to avoid
misleading duplication, e.g., by having a single dependency
counted twice under different descriptions.   Third, the
unsolved problem cited in VII 2 concerning the selection of
appropriate languages to describe the world is still with
us. The operationalization of the ideas suggested in this
Section presupposes a satisfactory solution to this problem.
Finally, since (1) involves a notion of causality
essentially, it might be useful to think of the complexity
specified in this explication as primarily causal.
Ontologically weaker notions might be preferred for some
purposes, e.g., structural complexity or a mere measure of
the total number of parts of a system.   (See also Bunge
(1961)).

Now,

(2) x is completely clear for n $\underset{df}{=}$ the ratio of
the   number   of   disclosed   distinct   factual
dependencies of x to its complexity in n is   one.

(3) x is completely vague for n $\underset{df}{=}$ the ratio of the
number of disclosed distinct factual dependencies
of x to its complexity in n is zero.

(4) x is partially clear for n $\underset{df}{=}$ x is neither

completely clear nor vague.

If the ranges of x and n are limited to concepts
and conceptual schemes, respectively, and if 'logical' is
substituted for 'factual' in (1) to (3), then (2) to (4)
yield prima facie plausible explicata for ordinary notions
about the clarity and vagueness of concepts.

8   GRIDS OF ANALYSIS

Considering any feature or the activity of any
feature of a decision situation, one may estimate its
location (usually in a very rough fashion to be sure)
somewhere along the continua between measurably certain or
probable and uncertain, completely controllable and
uncontrollable, completely independent and dependent, and
completely clear and vague. The term 'between' here must be
understood as neutral with respect to the inclusion or
exclusion of the end points of each continuum. As I shall
show shortly, it is occasionally necessary and illuminating
to think of some features or their activities as existing
within closed intervals (end points included) and others
within half-open intervals (one end point excluded).

One way to represent these continua and to
illustrate their heuristic value is with the help of graphs
that I refer to as 'grids of analysis'. If one is analyzing
the various features of a decision situation and all other
things are equal, one would prefer measurable certainty or
probability to uncertainty, complete controllability to
uncontrollability, complete independence to dependence and
complete clarity to vagueness. That is, provided that no
other information is available, these would seem to be the
usual preferences. Several writers have alluded to one or
more of these preferences.   For example, considering the
development of "technical assistance programs", Opler tells
us that

> "The ideal situation, it was thought, would
> be one in which the technically appropriate
> task has been accomplished without accompanying
> complicating problems [i.e., excessive
> dependencies] or with only such difficulties
> as have been anticipated [i.e., at least
> probabilistically], are controllable, and
> can be handled together."
> (Opler (1954, p. 67))

Charnes and Stedry argue against the idea of constructing
"organizational utility functions" on the grounds that

> "The complexity of such (hypothetical) functions,
> including interdependencies introduced by the
> dependence of one person's satisfaction with
> his lot on another's rewards and the not-soon-
> to-be-understood relationship between individual
> satisfaction and other aspects of organizational
> performance, is awesome."
> (Charnes and Stedry (1966, p. 153))

Finally, March and Simon (1958) emphasize the "demand for
control" by managers in the models of organizational
behaviour introduced by Merton (1940) and Selznik (1949).
Moreover, they claim that problem-solving processes for
human action are simplified when "each action program is
capable of being executed in semi-independence of the others
- they are only loosely coupled together". (March and Simon
(1958, p. 169); see also Horngren (1962), Gross (1964),
Thorsrud and Emery (1966), Suchman (1967) and Hinrichs
(1969).) There are, of course, situations in which each of
such preferences might be reversed e.g., one might prefer an
uncertain death to a certain one and a life of dependent
leisure to one of independent labor. But in the absence of
any special information about the various features of a
situation, most people would prefer knowledge to ignorance,
which is roughly what the cited preferences amount to. A
priori one would even be inclined to say that usually one
ought to prefer knowledge to ignorance, but this extra
normative claim is not necessary for my purposes here. (I
return to this issue in Chapter XIII.) The alternatives
listed might be diagrammed on a grid of analysis as in
Figure I.

FIGURE I: GRID OF ANALYSIS

Favorable   Unfavorable

estimated certainty/probability -------   uncertainty

estimated complete controllability ---   uncontrollability

estimated complete independence   ---   dependence

estimated complete clarity   -------   vagueness

　

If one is fortunate enough to have reliable and valid measurements of measurability, controllability, independence and clarity then these would be used instead of estimates in the grid of analysis. Usually, however, situations are much too complicated to expect to have more than estimates of these characteristics.

Before illustrating the use of grids of analysis, three possible points of confusion must be clarified. First, it must not be thought that probability values are represented on the top line of the grid. It is the estimated measurability of the occurrence or nonoccurrence of the activities or features that is indicated on the top line. If, for example, one is concerned about the chance of a riot occurring in some ghetto at some particular time, one might say that the chance involved is at best very roughly measurable and one might indicate the doubtfulness of any probability value obtained by marking the top line somewhere near the uncertainty side. Generally speaking, the more plausible measurement becomes, the farther to the left one's mark moves on the top line.

Second, since nothing can be used if it is completely uncontrollable, resources must always be to some degree controllable. Hence, when one thinks of locating a resource within the controllable- uncontrollable continuum, one must think of that continuum as existing withing a half-open interval. By definition, the end point designated by 'completely uncontrollable' is excluded from the points on the controllable-uncontrollable continuum that can (logically) be predicated of a resource. In other words, if one could measure degrees of controllability by a real number in the interval between zero and one, then resources would necessarily be assigned a value r such that

$$\text{completely} \quad 1 \geq r > 0 \quad \text{completely}$$
$$\text{controllable} \qquad\qquad\qquad \text{uncontrollable.}$$

Finally, similar remarks apply to restrictions. Insofar as anything is controllable, it is not restrictive. So, the idea of a completely controllable restriction is self-contradictory. Hence, when one thinks of locating a restriction within the controllable-uncontrollable continuum, one must think of that continuum as existing within a half-open interval. By definition, the end point designated by 'completely controllable' is excluded from the points on the controllable- uncontrollable continuum that can (logically) be predicated of a restriction. In other words, if one could measure degrees of controllability by a real number in the interval between zero and one, then restrictions would necessarily be assigned a value r such that

completely	$1 > \underline{r} \geq 0$	completely
controllable		uncontrollable

To illustrate the use of analysis grids, let us begin by abbreviating them as in Figure II.

FIGURE II: ABBREVIATED GRID OF ANALYSIS

F   U

_____

_____

_____

_____

Now suppose a decision-maker is considering from an economic point of view the possible states of the world in which his decision must be made. In other words, suppose he is considering the economic states of affairs that might lie before him. He imagines that there are only two possibilities that may be represented by 'S 1' and 'S 2'. For example, S 1 might be a placeholder for 'inheriting $10,000' and S 2 for 'inheriting $5,000'. In accordance with our assumptions about most people's preferences, he would prefer to have the information indicated on Grid I to that indicated on Grid II.

Grid 1   Grid II

F   U   F   U

S1S2   S1S2

Grid I tells us that the decision-maker's estimated information about S1 and S2 is virtually as good as it could be. The single line below F in Grid I represents the superposition of a line representing the decision-maker's information about S1 on top of another line representing his information about S2. He is certain or has a measurable probability about the occurrence of S1 and S2, and he figures these states are completely controllable, independent and clear. If he has complete certainty rather than mere probability, that is even better. Grid II illustrates the very opposite of Grid I, i.e., things could not be worse. The decision-maker does not have a clue as to how he might measure the probability of the occurrence of S1 and S2. Moreover, he believes that these features are uncontrollable, tied to several other aspects through various relations of dependency, and extremely vague.

Again, a decision-maker would prefer to have the estimated information summarized on Grid III to that on Grid IV, because the former is identical

GRID III

GRID IV

F   U

F   U

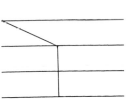

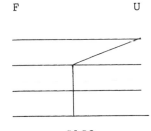

S1S2

S1S2

to the latter except for the fact that III indicates certainty or at least a measurable probability of the occurrence or nonoccurrence of the economic aspects involved.

Grids V, VI and VII are also in an order of preference from left to right.

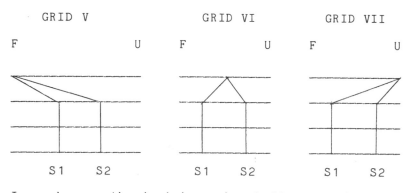

GRID V   GRID VI   GRID VII

F   U   F   U   F   U

S1   S2   S1   S2   S1   S2

In each case the decision-maker believes or knows that S1 is clearer, more controllable and has fewer dependencies than S2. But V indicates certainty or measurable probability, VI indicates that there is merely a possibility of measurement and VII indicates complete uncertainty about the presence or absence of the economic aspects involved.

　　　　　Finally, the following two grids seem to be equally complicated, less attractive than VII but still more attractive than II. (The path of S2 is crossed for ease of reference.)

GRID VIII   GRID IX

F   U   F   U

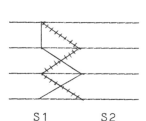

S1   S2   S1   S2

　　　　　Faced with the prospect of cases like VIII and IX, one has a strong inclination to search for some means of quantifying all the information geometrically represented on our grids. I shall not indulge this inclination any further than I have already. Instead, I want to present an example, in order to put more flesh on the skeletons I have been constructing. In particular, I shall characterize one of the alternative "strategies of administrative reform" suggested by Dror (1970a) with the help of an analysis grid. Similar grids may be constructed for all the other strategy options he has analyzed.

　　　　　An administrative system is centralized insofar as the decision-making processes of the system are hierarchical in the sense explained in Chapter V. More precisely, the hierarchy is such that lower echelon decisions tend to be routinized or significantly limited by higher echelon decisions, rather than vice versa. An administrative system is decentralized insofar as these processes are nonhierarchical, i.e., such that decisions made at lower echelons do not tend to be routinized or limited by higher echelon decisions. Alternatively the terms 'non-participative' and 'participative' decision-making processes might be used instead of 'centralized' and 'decentralized', respectively. (Rome and Rome (1971))

Anyone considering the possibilities of reforming an administrative system by altering its decision-making processes toward greater centralization or decentralization might begin by examining these alternatives in the light of an analysis grid. The result would probably look something like Grid VI above. In view of the fact that decision processes are frequently covert and that limitations are frequently reciprocal, one may be reluctant to regard an alteration toward greater centralization or decentralization as more than opaquely measurable. No doubt one can be reasonably certain and even have a plausibly measured probability of introducing certain formal procedures into a system, but one might still balk at the suggestion that the chances of significant alterations in the informal interpersonal decision-making processes might be measured. Hence, interpreting line S1 as centralization and S2 as decentralization, the two lines come together roughly midway between the extremes on the estimated certainty/probability-uncertainty continuum.

It is generally and correctly, I think, assumed that centralization provides greater controllability than decentralization. Thus, S1 is to the left of S2 on the estimated completely controllable-uncontrollable continuum. Since it seems likely that the more participation in and the fewer limitations placed upon decision-making at lower echelons the greater the variety of decisions and, consequently, the more distinct factual dependencies will be generated, S2 is to the right of S1 on the estimated completely independent-dependent continuum. And finally, if all other thigs are equal, S2 will be to the right of S1 on the estimated completely clear-vague continuum, because the disclosed proportion of the complexity entailed by centralization will probably be greater than the disclosed proportion of the complexity entailed by decentralization.

Part III
Rational Decision-Making

CHAPTER IX

Efficiency and Maximization Policies

1 INTRODUCTION

Supposing that we have a fairly good idea about the concepts of decision, choice, decision process, etc., what is required now is an explication of the concept of rationality as it applies to actions generally and decision processes and acts in particular. To prevent misunderstanding I want to reiterate the fact that the analysis to be provided in this and the following chapters is intended as a proposal regarding the <u>meaning</u> of 'rationality', not regarding the <u>criterion</u> by means of which one determines whether or not something is rational. As Rescher (1973a) explains, sometimes a proposal can provide both a meaning-analysis and a criterion of application, but the present proposal does not have this advantage.

The discussion opens with a very rough and provisional definition of 'rationality' in terms of efficiency. In Sections Three and Four several fairly well-known objections to this approach are met, e.g., that it is inapplicable in a world of complete abundance, that it disregards the importance of total benefits and that it does not permit the rationalization of ends. Section Five is devoted to a critical analysis of the Popperian notion that rationality may be explicated in terms of criticizability in order to avoid certain objections. In Section Six and Seven I try to show, contrary to the views of most writers on the subject, that all attempts to explicate rationality in terms of the maximization of something must be unsatisfactory. Finally, March and Simon's proposal concerning the replacement of maximizing with satisficing is criticized. (Roughly speaking, something satisfies if it is perceived as good enough.)

The view of rational decision-making that I shall recommend in the following chapters is based on efficiency and the rejection of maximizing and satisficing policies. Since many people seem to reject these premises, I have attempted to show immediately that the approach to rationality through efficiency is not as bad and that the ideas of maximizing or satisficing are not as good as might be thought. If I manage to put you in a more receptive frame of mind for the remaining chapters, I shall have come close to hitting my mark.

2 RATIONALITY AS EFFICIENCY

Rationality may be predicated of persons, acts, processes, beliefs, preferences, policies, organizations and goals as well as other things of less significance for this investigation. Although I am convinced that in every case it is not only plausible but analytically profitable to identify rationality with efficiency everywhere the term is used, here I shall only be concerned with actions generally and with decision processes and decisions in particular. Speaking very roughly and provisionally (for expository purposes), if 'x' is a placeholder for the names or descriptions of a person, act, process, etc. then

(1) $\underline{x}$ is efficient $=_{df}$ $\underline{x}$ produces a ratio of
benefits to costs (hereafter, a B/C
ratio) that is greater than or equal to one.

(2) $\underline{x}$ is rational $=_{df}$ $\underline{x}$ is efficient.

and

(3) $\underline{x}$ is irrational $=_{df}$ $\underline{x}$ is inefficient
(i.e., $\underline{x}$ produces a B/C ratio that
is less than 1. (Compare (1) to
(3) with Downs (1957) and Mises
(1960).)

Trained eyes of various sorts will notice immediately that (1) to (3) lack any reference to maximizing anything or even to satisficing activity. Broadly speaking again, as I shall explain more fully in the next few chapters, rationality lies between these more or less classical alternatives. It might be thought that there is some logical incoherence involved in the acceptance of efficiency without maximization. According to Diesing (1962, p.11), for example , efficiency" ... includes within itself the values of maximization and achievement". The reasoning behind this view seems to be that if efficiency is good or required, then more efficiency must be better and a fortiori required. This is certainly a non-sequitur. One could as well argue that if exercise is good or required, then more exercise must be better and a fortiori required. Similarly, fresh air, sirloin steaks and horseback riding are good, but more of any of them is not necessarily better. It depends on what one has, wants, needs and can tolerate.

(1) to (3) contain no explicit reference to the recipients of the benefits or the bearers of the costs involved in the determination of efficiency, but I suppose it will be granted by most people that there are no benefits or costs in the abstract. If something is beneficial or costly at all then it must be so for someone or something, in some circumstances and in some way or other. (Baier (1958)) The details of these and several other aspects of benefits and costs are elucidated in Chapter XII. For now it is enough to note that because these relational features of costs and benefits are logically unavoidable concomitants of efficiency, they are also logically unavoidable constituents of rationality. Consequently, when one uses the terms 'costs', 'benefits', 'efficiency' and 'rationality' without any explicit reference to who is receiving or paying for what, when and how, they must be understood as shorthand expressions or abbreviations. As a cursory inspection of the literature reveals, it is possible to use these terms as if they were not essentially relational without running into serious difficulties. Wherever possible I shall myself use the terms without qualifications. But some very fundamental questions about rationality cannot even be raised and others cannot be answered without a thoroughgoing investigation of its relational aspects. When the latter issues arise then, we shall be obliged to spell out all of the niceties involved.

3   A WORLD OF COMPLETE ABUNDANCE

One of the first objections that comes to mind when one considers the identification of rationality with efficiency is that while the latter is only important in the presence of scarcity, the former is always important. (Diesing (1962)) In the presence of complete abundance, it might be argued, there is no point in or reason for being efficient. Hence, there is nothing meritorious or virtuous in being efficient in such circumstances. On the contrary, however, one always ought to be rational. Again, it is at the very least not the case that mere abundance should be a sufficient condition for the elimination of rationality as a significant and good characteristic of human beings.   But mere abundance is sufficient to eradicate the importance and virtue of efficiency.   Hence,   the   objection runs, rationality cannot be identified with efficiency.

In response to this objection I would say that if a world of complete abundance is one in which one has everything that one needs and wants, then in such a world no activity can (logically) be warranted or reasonable in any ordinary sense of these terms. Ignoring the sort of account of rationality recommended   here   (to   avoid   blatant question-begging), try to justify the performance of any action in such a world. It could not be rational to wash, eat, sleep, exercise regularly, communicate with others or even read a good book. It could not be rational to wash because one would already be clean if one wanted or needed to be clean. Similarly, it would be irrational to eat because the need or want would already be satisfied; and so on. Clearly if 'complete abundance' means having everything one needs and wants, then rational action is excluded from such a world as much as efficiency.

But, it will be objected, obviously 'complete abundance' does not mean having everything one needs and wants. It "normally" means having everything that one needs and wants more or less readily available or available at virtually no cost (in any sense) at all. In a world with this sort of abundance, the objection continues, efficiency is certainly irrelevant. Indeed, in such a world B/C ratios are virtually nonexistent, exactly as nonexistent as costs. But it would still be rational to do or take what one needs and wants.   Thus, it would be a mistake to identify efficiency with rationality.

On the face of it this alternative sense of 'complete abundance' is more plausible than the former, but it is actually logically incoherent. In the first place, one who introduces this second sense of 'complete abundance' cannot be allowed the luxury of "virtual" costlessness.   If there are any costs at all in his world then it is logically possible to have definable efficiency ratios and rationality in the sense proposed here. Thus, an objector must posit a world without any costs at all in order to put teeth into his objection. In fact then, the hypothetical world we are imagining is very much like Paradise itself, since the costliness of an action is a necessary condition of its being harmful, evil or wrong.   To see that this is so, consider the absurdity of claiming that a certain action is harmful, evil or wrong although no one, including the actor, pays any price (in any sense) at all for its performance. If no price at all is paid then no moral, economic, esthetic or any other kind of price is paid. So, the action must be merely beneficial or neutral, or perhaps a mixture of both, i.e., beneficial for some and neutral for others. If the action is entirely neutral in the sense that it creates neither costs nor benefits then there is a serious question as to the rationality of anyone performing it. What, after all, is rational about doing something that has no value at all, positive or negative? The fact that it is also free is hardly a good reason for doing it, since its neutrality is a guarantee that one is paying absolutely nothing for absolutely nothing of any benefit to anyone. Evidently then, one must suppose that only beneficial actions will be performed in a completely abundant world, because only these could be reasonably warranted.

Unfortunately, even beneficial actions turn out to be unreasonable in a world of complete abundance. Our imaginary objector would like to say that in such a world one is simply able to satisfy one's needs and wants at no cost. As explicated in Chapter IV, however, one has a need for something if and only if, eithe one has too little or too much of it and is in a state of disequilibrium or if one had too little or too much of it one would be in a state of disequilibrium. But since the suffering of some state of disequilibrium must be regarded as costly for the sufferer, it is prohibited in an abundant world. It follows that in such a world either there are no needs to be satisfied or everyone has everything needed. The infelicitous consequences of the latter alternative were reviewed above. So, it must be maintained that in an abundant world there are no needs to be satisfied. Hence, the idea of a world of complete abundance in which needs and wants are satisfied at no cost is incoherent. It is an idea of a world in which there are no needs at all to be satisfied and in which there are needs that are satisfied at no cost.

Confronted by the conclusion just reached, our imaginary critic has but one move to make. Again he shall insist that I have erroneously defined the world of complete abundance. It must be defined hypothetically. That is, it is a world such that if anyone has any needs or wants then they are satisfiable at no cost. Given this specification of an abundant world, he might correctly claim, the contradition cited above cannot be derived. Yet in such a world one could be rational without being efficient; so my suggested definition fails.

Plausible as this may sound, our critic is still talking nonsense. In the presence of this third specification of a completely abundant world, one certainly cannot derive the contradiction cited above. But it is still undoubtedly the case that the world in question is one in which needs are a priori excluded. And this implies that it contains no people at all or that it contains people without needs. The former alternative is plainly irrelevant to the question of whether or not people could act rationally in a completely abundant world. If the world has no people at all then it has no rational, irrational or any other kind of people. Hence, our critic must be committed to the view that the world in question is populated by people without needs, and this is logically impossible. To be a human being is to have a species need for oxygen, food and water, to name only the most obvious needs. Thus, the supposition of a world populated by human beings without such needs is logically incoherent, because such beings would necessarily have and lack these needs. Hence, the third proposed definition of a world of complete abundance is also unacceptable. In the absence of alternative specifications then, I conclude that the suggestion that my proposed identification of rationality with efficiency breaks down in a world of complete abundance can only be regarded as a red herring. (See also Downs (1957), Grauhan and Strubelt (1971) and Majone (1975).)

4   TOTAL BENEFITS AND THE RATIONALIZATION OF ENDS

A second objection that might be raised against the suggested definition is that very often the total benefits obtainable from some action are high enough to outweigh considerations of benefits per unit of cost. To take a trivial example, if one were in need of a lump sum of $90 then, given a choice, it would be more rational to sell 30 items at $3 each than 10 items at $5 each. The marginal benefit (profit) or efficiency of the 10 item sale, it might be argued, is <u>greater</u> than that of the 30 item sale, but it is still more rational to make the latter sale if one has a choice. Hence, efficiency cannot be identified with rationality. (Compare Dror (1968, p. 45).)

This argument need not detain us long because the supposition that the choice in question would be rational "if one were in need of a lump sum of $90" reveals that the wisdom of the choice lies in its being an appropriate means to the end of obtaining $90. I shall have more to say about networks of means and ends with special reference to processes, products and what I call 'regions of analysis' as the discussion progresses, but for now it is enough to note that in cases like those just considered, it is more plausible to posit a slightly disguised or implicit goal for which the apparently rational action is an efficient means than it is to abandon the proposal of identifying rationality with efficiency.

A third objection that might be raised against the proposed definition of rationality is that it is too narrow because it is inapplicable to ends or goals. (Diesing (1962)) One wants to say that certain ends are more rational than others. According to Grauhan and Strubelt, for example,

> "...unless the instrumental rational (or optimal) models of policymaking are combined with a conception of rational goals, they can be neither rational nor optimal because their optimal quality will remain a formal facade behind which the real policymaking process can be empoisoned by the irrationality of the goals pursued." (Grauhan and Strubelt (1971, p. 254); see also Harsanyi (1969).)

Again, to take a somewhat homely example, if I set my sights on becoming the next heavyweight boxing champion of the world, that would be a highly irrational goal. If I decided to become the heavyweight champion of Guelph that would still be irrational but, I suppose, somewhat less so. If I merely aimed at improving my physical condition by regular exercise, that would be a completely rational goal. But all of these commonplace judgments, an objector might claim, are impossible given the identification of rationality with efficiency, because the latter is only applicable to means.

I agree that any adequate explicatum for the concept of rationality as it is normally used must permit us to predicate rationality of ends as well as means. I think, however, that the present proposal is safe on that score. Roughly speaking still, a goal may be regarded as rational in itself if and only if its realization produces a B/C ratio greater than or equal to one. The emphasized words in the preceding sentence are crucial, for ends are typically embedded in networks of means and ends of various kinds, and are frequently only accurately assessed with the network as a whole. Nevertheless, it is possible and illuminating to appraise goals as more or less independent producers of B/C ratios (i.e., as means to such ratios) in order to determine their rationality.

In response to the reply just offered, a critic might insist that it simply fails to apply to ultimate ends, to the rockbottom of all appraisals. According to my suggestion, he will say, an end is appraised by examining it as a means to a certain B/C ratio. But a B/C ratio is nothing more than a ratio of one set of realized ends called 'benefits' to another called 'costs'. Hence, it is only worth as much as the prior appraisal of what is to count as a benefit or a cost, i.e., it is worth as much as the appraisal of another set of ends. Hence, the latter must themselves be appraised. But that just leads to another set of ends, which leads to another ad infinitum. Alternatively, of course, one could refuse to be driven up this path by cutting one's analysis off at some point, but then our critic will claim that this point must be

arbitrarily   chosen.   Thus,   the   present   proposal   for
determining   the   rationality   of   ends   will   be   judged
worthless,   since both of these options, namely, an infinite
regress   of   evaluations   and   an   arbitrarily-selected
rockbottom of appraisals are worthless.

The   line   of   argument   taken   in   the   preceding
paragraph is   well-known   among   philosophers.   (See,   for
example, Bartley (1962, 1964) and Martin (1970).)   Moreover,
it   contains a fundamental and highly significant element of
truth.   As I see it, an ultimate end or   goal   is   one   such
that   there   is   no end "beyond" it in terms of which it can
(in any sense) be appraised.   Any end that admits of another
end in terms of which the former may   be   assessed   is   ipso
facto not an ultimate end.   Hence, anyone who claims to have
some   means   of   assessing   such   ends   is   uttering   a
contradition.   One might, of course, challenge   the   alleged
ultimacy   of   some end, and philosophers spend much of their
time doing just that.   But the very   fact   that   an   end   is
challenged,   questioned   or   criticized is evidence that its
ultimacy is not granted.   If it were granted by the   critic,
then the latter would be committed to the contradictory view
that   the end in question both has and does not have another
end in terms of which it may be assessed.   This then is   the
kernel   of   truth   in   the   skeptical   argument   under
consideration,   namely,   that   unappraisable   ends   are
unappraisable;   and   it   is   patently a logical truism. (The
view in this paragraph roughly follows that of Ayer   (1956).
However,   Will   (1974)   has   delivered   the most devastating
blows to skepticism.)

5   RATIONALITY AND CRITICISM

Before ending this discussion of   the   skeptical
argument   presented   in   the   previous   section,   it will be
instructive   to   consider   an   alternative but,   I   think,
unsatisfactory   reply   that   has   been   made to it by Popper
(1945) and   his   disciples   (e.g.,   Bartley   (1962,   1964)).
According to Popperians, the skeptical argument cannot begin
if   one   abandons   the   idea that something (e.g. a belief,
theory, position, etc.) is rational if and   only   if   it   is
justified or supported by some rational criterion.   In place
of this idea Popperians substitute the notion that something
is   rational   if   and   only   if   it is open to criticism and
survives severe testing.   It is easy to show, however,   that
insofar   as   the   skeptical argument has any bite at all, it
captures this definition of   rationality   as   much   as   any
other.   Because the results of any critical test can only be
as   valuable   as   the   test   itself,   critical tests must be
critically tested.   But the results of the latter   can   only
be   as   valuable   as the test itself; and so on ad infinitum.
Again then, we have the skeptical argument arising.

At least one Popperian has recognized this possibility. But he claims that while "this process of testing is, of course, in principle infinite, ... there is no infinite regress, because the aim of justifying or establishing has been abandoned". (Bartley (1964, pp. 28-29)). On the contrary, however, there is a regress insofar as no matter what one sets out to test, one is always driven to test one's test first. This is so because on the Popperian definition of rationality, a test cannot be regarded as rational unless it is criticizable and has in fact survived some test.

One way to avoid this regress is to abandon the second conjunct of the definiens of the Popperian definition. This would seem to be a plausible move to make, because according to this conjunct, any view that is too costly to test is irrational to hold. Thus, only the rich (in the broadest sense of the term) can afford to be completely rational!

Since I have already tried to show that the skeptical argument is not as troublesome as many people (especially Popperians) seem to think, the fact that the Popperian definition is open to it does not seem to be a serious difficulty. On this score, the Popperians are no worse off than anyone else. The serious problem facing the Popperian proposal is its vicious circularity, i.e., the explicatum must employ its own explicandum. Ordinarily, one would want to be able to assert that a given criticism may be mistaken, illfounded, silly, misleading, misguided, foolish, unwise, or, finally, irrational. To take a fairly important example suggested by the Popperians themselves, the criticism of straw men is unwise. (Popper (1968)) Similarly, it would be irrational to criticize a man for holding a view that the critic knows or firmly believes he does not hold. Thus, the only kind of criticism that it could be rational to make is rational criticism. Again, there does not seem to be anything especially rational about being open to irrational criticism. Indeed, if being open to such criticism implies the possibility of being overthrown by such criticism, then it would seem to be a mark of irrationality rather than rationality. What else can it mean to say that it is possible that some stupid criticism might overthrow a particular view? A rational view should exclude the possibility of being overthrown by irrational criticism Hence, the first conjunct of the Popperians' definiens must be the requirement of openness to rational criticism. Clearly, however, one who does not know what 'rational' means cannot know what 'rational criticism' means either. So, the definition is viciously circular.

To prevent such circularity from arising, one might claim that all criticism is rational. In view of the counter-instances cited in the previous paragraph, I would

find this impossible to believe. But a more general and
fatal criticism may be leveled against it, namely, that it
implies that criticism at any cost is rational. Thus, if it
cost one's own life and that of one's family to criticize an
evil regime, it would still be rational to level the
criticism! Granted that it might be rational to pay such a
price in some circumstances, it is difficult to imagine
anyone holding that any old criticism of anything at all is
always worth whatever it costs. But this outrageous
position would be required by the maneuver under
consideration.

6   THE REGRESS OF MAXIMIZATION

Having dispelled or at least allayed some doubts
about the general feasibility of explicating rationality in
terms of efficiency, I turn now to an attempt to defend the
view that all explications of rationality in terms of the
maximization of something must fail. Any proposed
explication of rationality that requires the maximization of
something must be unsatisfactory because the prescription to
maximize this or that cannot (in fact) be satisfactorily
specified. For example, consider the identification of
rational action with maximally efficient action, i.e., an
action is supposed to be rational if and only if (very
roughly speaking) it seems and/or is likely to produce a
ratio of benefits to costs that is at least as great as any
available alternative. According to this rough definition
then, what one is supposed to do to act rationally is to
choose those courses of action that are or, at least, seem
to be maximally efficient for one's ends. (This view is
supported by the overwhelming majority of writers; e.g.,
Savage (1954), Miller and Starr (1960), Churchman (1961),
Good (1962), Harsanyi (1972), Kuhn (1974) and Moor (1976).)
Ignoring the problem of choosing ends and the fact that
several actions ordinarily regarded as rational do not seem
to involve any choice or decision, the question is: From
what set of alternative courses of action should a maximally
efficient one be chosen? The answer offered by classical
economics, statistical decision theory and most management
science textbooks is the given set. (See, for example,
Luce and Raiffa (1957) and Wagner (1969).) But whether this
set is supposed to be socially (MacRae (1968)),
organizationally or environmentally "given" (March and Simon
(1958)), such a response to the normative question raised is
practically worthless. The question is a request for a
rational policy with respect to the selection of a set of
alternatives from which a rational course of action can be
selected. Looked at in another way, it is a request for a
general normative criterion of relevance for the selection
of sets of alternatives which would be analogous to a
general normative criterion of rational action given an

appropriate set of alternatives. It cannot, therefore, be answered by a mere report or description of the way such sets are usually determined. (No one has done a better descriptive job than March and Simon (1958).) Nor can it be answered by strategies that are question-begging in the sense that they assume one can always or often enough find "experts" or "rational managers" who, by suitably exposing their ideas to each other, will finally make appropriate selections. (Helmer (1966), Mason (1969)) Unfortunately, the more seriously one takes the normative aspect of the question, the more dubious one becomes about the possibility of providing an answer that is satisfactory from the point of view of a policy of maximization.

Suppose, for example, that one is reflecting upon the enormous mortgage payments that one is saddled with every month and wondering whether or not it is rational to continue paying them or to sell out and buy a new house. How should he specify his alternatives? For the sake of completeness, one might suggest that he should consider all logically possible alternatives. This would certainly be a fatuous piece of advice to give anyone, because there are an infinite number of such alternatives and no one could examine all of them. Moreover, a similar condemnation is applicable to the suggestion that all factually possible alternatives should be examined. To see that this is so, consider his options with respect to consulting a single realtor. He might call the realtor at any time, on any day, from any place and standing or sitting in any position, so long as no contradiction is involved in the description of the time, day, place and position. If the set of alternatives that is factually possible to construct on the basis of this handful of variables is not infinite, it is still ridiculously too large to be recommended as a desideratum. (See also Diesing (1955), Duncan-Jones (1957) and Kuhn (1963) on "the complexity of a 'simple' decision".)

At this point one is tempted to say that in any real decision situation a multitude of restrictions come into play to eliminate prima facie factually possible alternatives. (Dror (1968)) Thus, what one ought to do is let such restrictions generate a preferred set of alternatives. But this will not do. Even if, for example, it is assumed that realtors work a 5 day and 40 hour week, and that our prospective buyer is not going to leave town to make a phone call, we are still left with thousands of factual possibilities. There are, for example, 144,000 mutually exclusive seconds in the given work-week, any one of which might be chosen as the time to place the call. Clearly then, the appeal to de facto restrictions to solve our problem is hopeless.

What one hankers to say now is that only relevant alternatives should be considered. But this too is abortive. When one is thinking about buying a new house, one of the most relevant questions that can be raised concerns the price one can afford to pay for it. Normally one thinks of very round figures and intervals, e.g., anything in the $77,000 to $80,000 range would be possible. Hence, it is usually the case that as a matter of fact many more relevant alternative possible prices could be afforded than are ever examined individually. The $3,000 range mentioned in the previous sentence, for instance, implies 300,000 live options, namely $77,000.01, $77,000.02, etc.

One might insist now that because it is highly unlikely that anyone is going to ask or offer a sum like $77,000.02 for a house, such sums are not "really" relevant. "Really" relevant sums, it might be claimed, are those that have a fairly high probability of being asked or offered, e.g., $77,000, $77,500, etc. This strips our alleged 300,000 live options down to about 7.

The suggestion that "really" relevant alternatives are those with fairly high probabilities of being adopted seems to be rather promising and reminiscent of Schelling's (1960) analysis of tacit bargaining and Braybrooke and Lindblom's (1963) analysis of disjointed incrementalism. As a rule, however, it is seriously deficient. In the first place, normally one must already have a set of alternatives (a reference class or universe of discourse) before any probability values can be determined. (See VIII 2-5.) Needless to say then, the selection of the latter set raises precisely the kind of problem the present recommendation was supposed to solve. Second, when unique events are involved, there may be no probability values worth measuring, e.g., one may feel (as I and apparently Merton (1936) usually do) that one's psychological or logical probability assessments of what price he might offer or be asked to pay are not useful pieces of information to have. Third, insofar as these interpretations of 'probability' are applied, the more candidates for relevant alternatives one discloses, the less likely it becomes that any of them will have fairly high initial probability values. Thus, in order to obtain alternatives with high psychological or logical probabilities, one ought to generate as few as possible. Hence, an infelicitous corollary of the present recommendation would be: The fewer alternatives one uncovers, the better! Finally, insofar as the proposal might be construed as identifying the relative frequency of occurrence of something with its relevance, it would seem to be a recipe for stagnation and misjudgment. It would be a recipe for stagnation because it brands all highly novel alternatives as irrelevant, and it would be a recipe for misjudgment because frequently the very uniqueness or scarcity of many events (e.g., one's own death) makes them extremely important rather than simply irrelevant. (See also Bauer (1966).)

In response to the barrage of objections presented in the preceding paragraph, it might be insisted that the criterion of relevance employed there is perverse. One should, it might be claimed, attempt to consider only those alternatives that are "really" relevant, but nobody in his right mind would use the criterion of relevance that I have just used. Instead of appealing to the probability (in some sense) of an item's being selected, one ought to appeal to its value (in some sense) or, perhaps, to its probabilistically-weighted value. One might say then, that "really" relevant alternatives are those that have a certain kind of value or expected value. (See, for example, Harrison   (1952), Singer (1961), Gewirth (1964), Lyons (1965), Dror (1968) and Sobel (1970).) The so-called "cost of search" approach to alternative-set selection is a sophisticated species of this strategy. (Raiffa (1968))

This idea sounds promising, but it is useless for an efficiency maximizer.   For the latter it must lead directly to the prescription to search through all logically or factually possible alternatives to discover those with the appropriate sort of value. To demand less than this is to   admit   that any selected set of "really" relevant alternatives might fail to include plenty of other "really" relevant alternatives, some of which could well be much more valuable than any of those in the finally selected set. In other words, to demand less than this is, as Simon (1945, 1957) has insisted, to abandon the policy of maximization in favor of a weaker policy. Hence, a maximizer cannot escape from his herculean prescriptions. For reasons which have already been cited, however, he cannot hope to fulfill such prescriptions either.

Having gone up all these hopeless garden paths, one begins to realize that what a maximizer is seeking is a set of alternatives that is itself maximally efficient in the   sense   that   it contains the maximally efficient alternative from the set of all logically possible alternatives and as little extra as possible. That is to say then, that according to the maximizers what one is supposed to do to act rationally is (roughly speaking still) to choose maximally efficient courses of action from sets of alternatives which are themselves maximally efficient. But this is the beginning of an infinite regress.   Once again one cannot examine an infinite number of logically possible or an unmanageably large finite number of factually possible sets of alternatives to find the maximally efficient set. So one must find some smaller, more manageable set of sets of alternatives. But which set of sets in particular should one choose? Again it is the set that contains the maximally efficient set of alternatives and as few others as possible, i.e., again one finds oneself chasing an ever-elusive maximally efficient set of alternatives. Thus, since there can be no end to the search for a maximally efficient set of

alternatives, there can be no choice of a maximally
efficient course of action from such a set of alternatives.
Hence, there can be no rational action according to the
maximizer's proposal. But this, I should think, is patently
absurd and certainly not intended by most defenders of the
proposal.

This rather long regress argument against
maximization with respect to sets of alternative courses of
action is applicable mutatis mutandis to any sets of
alternatives that one might be required to have, e.g., sets
of alternative decision processes, allocations of resources,
possible states of the world and goals. Insofar as one must
be in possession of a maximally efficient set of
alternatives in order to act rationally, one cannot act
rationally because one cannot possess such a set.

Bales (1971) has attacked shorter but roughly
similar regress arguments on the ground that they fail to
distinguish what I earlier referred to as criteria of
application from meaning. Addressing his remarks to the
problem of what makes an act morally right, he claims
correctly that "...a proposed ethical theory ... could
provide a correct account of right-making characteristics
without spelling out a procedure which, if followed, would
crank out in practice a correct and immediately helpful
answer to questions like: "Ought I in this case to use
enough gas and electricity to keep my home warm?" (Bales
(1971, p. 261-262)) Therefore, he believes, it would be a
mistake to reject an account of "right-making
characteristics" if, as a matter of fact, it failed to
provide a satisfactory decision procedure as well.

The argument I have just advanced is free of that
error. My argument rests on the assumption that it would be
a mistake to accept an account of the meaning of any term
if, as a matter of fact, no satisfactory criterion of
application could be specified for it. I am not claiming
that an account of the meaning of a term should provide a
criterion of application as well. What I am claiming is
that an account of the meaning of a term should permit a
criterion of application. In other words, I am claiming
that it is self-defeating to propose explications of
concepts which by their very nature preclude their
application. To take a well-worked example, it would be a
mistake to explicate 'complete verification' such that a
priori one knows that no proposition could ever be
completely verified. (Malcolm (1950)) Similarly, it would
be self-defeating to explicate the concepts of a morally
right act or a rational act such that a priori one knows
that no acts could ever be morally right or rational.

7   BLUNT RATIONALITY, SELF-SUFFICIENCY AND EXCESSIVE COSTS

Supposing that the regress argument against maximization could be demolished, there are still three serious problems to be faced. In the first place, rationality is ordinarily thought to admit of gradations, i.e., there are supposed to be "degrees of rationality". (Diesing (1950), Friedrich (1964)) One's actions can be more or less, very, hardly, somewhat, slightly or highly rational or irrational. In this respect rationality is analogous to preference. However, when rationality is defined in terms of maximal efficiency, the result is a concept with a logical structure that is analogous to something between blunt preference and ordinary preference. More precisely, if 'x' and 'y' are placeholders for the names or descriptions of any actions, then

x is more rational than y

can only be analyzed as

x is rational and y is irrational,

never as

x is rational and y is rational and x is more rational than y.

For example, if all other things are equal and one is confronted by a set of four alternative courses of action with efficiency ratios of 1,2,3, and 4, then according to the maximizer's proposal, one is acting rationally if and only if one chooses that course of action with the ratio of 4. Any other choice in the given circumstances would be irrational. One who chose the action with a ratio of 4 would be more rational than one who chose the action with a ratio of 3 only in the sense that the former was rational and the latter was not. Moreover, one who chose the action with a ratio of 4 could only be described as choosing the most rational action in the set in the sense that he chose the one and only rational action in the set. Furthermore, it could not be said that one who chose the action with a ratio of 3 was more rational than one who chose the action with 2, because anyone choosing either action would be irrational. Of course, it could be said that one who chose the action with 3 was less irrational than one who chose the action with 2, but this does not eliminate the infelicity that I am citing. Ordinarily both rationality and irrationality admit of gradations, but on the maximizer's proposal there are no gradations of rationality. In this respect then, the maximizer's explication of rationality does not capture an important nuance of the ordinary concept. Instead, it merely provides us with a concept that is somewhere between what we might call 'blunt rationality' and ordinary rationality.

Another problem raised by the maximizer's proposal is that if all other things are equal, the choice of self-sustaining over self-developing action is always irrational. Roughly speaking, an action is self-sustaining if its B/C ratio is one and self-developing if its B/C ratio is greater than one. I have used the term 'self-developing' rather than 'self-aggrandizing' because the latter has a slightly pejorative connotation that the former lacks and I do not want to suggest that growth itself is necessarily undesirable. (Grauhan and Strubelt (1971) use 'self-enhancement'.) The point that must be insisted upon is that contrary to the maximizer's proposal, it does not seem to be a logical truism that if all other things are equal, it is irrational to choose to maintain the status quo rather than to develop it. Just as one might want to say that something is good enough in some sense although something else would be better, one might want to say that some action is rational enough although some other action would be more rational. On the present proposal, however, in the presence of an alternative with a higher efficiency ratio than that of the action chosen, the latter cannot (logically) be rational enough. Indeed, it cannot be rational at all!

It might be objected, following Diesing (1962, p. 44), that "it is reasonable to achieve the larger end as far as possible...because that is what it means to have an end." If this were true then it would be self-contradictory to assert that one has an end or goal which is not as large as it could (logically and factually) be but is large enough. The very idea of ends or goals that are just large enough would be logically incoherent. However, it seems to me that this idea not only makes perfectly good sense but it is absolutely essential for an adequate explication of the concept of rationality.

Finally, it is an unacceptable consequence of explications of rationality in terms of the maximization of something that, if all other things are equal, then no matter what the cost of an action, it is rational so long as it is not more costly than its "available" alternatives. For example, confronted by the alternatives of waging a war leading to 40 million casualties or one leading to 30 million casualties, a maximizer can act rationally by waging the latter rather than the former. Although I would agree that it is peculiarly less evil to destroy 30 million rather than 40 million people, the destruction of 30 million people still strikes me as the kind of action that ought to be regarded as irrational if not downright insane. The reason I think it should be regarded this way is that I have grave doubts that the benefits of such a war could (as a matter of fact) outweigh the enormous cost of 30 million lives. Again, consider the plight of Creon in Sophocles's Antigone. Creon must either uphold his own edict and destroy his niece or else spare his niece and undermine the law. What makes his situation tragic is the fact that the costs of any action he can perform are almost certainly going to outweigh the benefits. And this is typical of many tragedies. Man, the rational animal, finds himself in situations such that whatever he does is, as it were, contrary to his own nature. Whatever he does is "less" than it ought to be. In short, I am suggesting that explications of rationality ought to require more than making the best of any situation. In this world, it seems that the "best" actions in some situations can be so horrible that they cannot be described as rational without making a travesty of the concept. (See also Schwartz (1970), Wolff (1970), Conklin (1974), Majone (1975), Kerr (1976) and Fischhoff (1977).)

8   SATISFICING RATIONALITY

While the arguments presented in the last two sections against explications of rationality in terms of the maximization of something may be new, their conclusions are not. Maximization models of rationality have been under attack for some time, most notably by Simon (1945, 1957) and March and Simon (1958). According to Simon (1957, p. 202), "the approach taken in the theory of games and in statistical decision theory to the problem of rational choice is fundamentally wrongheaded ... It is wrong ... in seeking to erect a theory of human choice on the unrealistic assumptions of virtual omniscience and unlimited computational power." Furthermore, he claims that "the key to the simplification of the choice process in both cases is the replacement of the goal of maximizing with the goal of satisficing, of finding a course of action that is 'good enough'." (Simon (1957, pp. 204-205)) It will be instructive then, to provide at least a rough outline of the alternative these writers are suggesting in order to be able to evaluate and compare it with the proposal to be elucidated in the following chapters.

To begin with, it should be noted that although March and Simon claim to be primarily concerned with the "adequate" description of rational decision-making rather than with prescriptions about how people ought rationally to make decisions, it is doubtful that they or anyone else can keep these two tasks separate. The fact is that 'rationality' is an evaluatively-loaded word in the English language. Whatever they mean by the words, people like to think of themselves as and believe that they ought to be rational. While few of us would go so far as to assert that

rationality in a human being is everything, it is almost
certainly a necessary condition of many of the attributes
that we regard as important and distinctively human (e.g.,
moral virtue), and practically everyone regards it as a very
good thing -- whatever it is. As Berry (1973, p. 13) says,
" ... no one wishes to be labelled as nonrational".   Thus,
for example, to say that a man is rational or irrational is
not at all like saying that he is hairy or bald. Take away
a man's hair and you have a bald man, but take away his
rationality and you are on the verge of taking away his
humanity. Again, to say that someone is acting irrationally
is to say that he is not acting as he should act, that his
action departs from some norm. Moreover, since the farther
and longer he departs from that norm the more he tends to
become less human, it must not be imagined that   in
specifying the norm or classifying his behaviour in one way
or another with respect to it, one is merely engaged in
description.   To say that a man has the wits of a mule, or
conversely, that a mule has the wits of a man, is to make an
unfavorable appraisal of the man and a favorable appraisal
of the mule.   In short, with respect to the properties of
rationality and irrationality, there is no such thing as a
non-evaluative description. (See also Moor (1976, p. 7).
Davie (1973) makes a similar point with respect   to
prudence.)

        The main difficulties with the so-called
classical model of rational man, according to March and
Simon (1958, pp. 138-139), are as follows. (1) The model
postulates as given a set of "all" available alternative
courses of action, a set of "all" possible consequences
attached to each alternative and a   utility function
completely ranking each consequence according to its value
to the actor. But in fact these features are typically not
given or even obtainable. (2) It grants that one may have
certain, risky or uncertain information concerning possible
consequences, but does not recognize that one's information
concerning available alternatives and the value of
consequences may be similarly complicated. (3) By admitting
that one's information concerning a situation may be less
than perfect, the model implies a distinction between
subjective and objective rationality. But so-called
subjective rationality then seems to be a poor substitute
for "real" rationality and hardly worthy of the name
'rationality' at all. (4) The model fails to agree with
"common-sense notions of rationality". (See also Michalos
(1970d).)

        In the light of these objections to the classical
model of rationality, March and Simon propose an alternative
with the following simplifying features.

        (1) Optimizing is replaced by satisficing ---
        the requirement that satisfactory levels of the
        criterion variables be attained.

(2) Alternatives of action and consequences of action are discovered sequentially through search processes.

(3) Repertories of action programs are developed by organizations and individuals, and these serve as alternatives of choice in recurrent situations.

(4) Each specific action program deals with a restricted range of situations and a restricted range of consequences.

(5) Each action program is capable of being executed in semi-independence of the others -- they are only loosely coupled together.

(March and Simon (1958, p. 169))

Again, the "key" to the model of rationality proposed by March and Simon is satisficing instead of maximizing. Moreover, as this idea is unpacked by these writers and Simon independently, the "criterion of satisfaction is closely related to the psychological notion of 'aspiration levels'". (March and Simon (1958, p. 182)) Hence, the decisive factors in the determination of satisfactory solutions to problems or satisfactory levels of performance or achievement tend to be somewhat vague and, for want of a better word, subjective. What one regards as good enough depends upon what one is typically able to obtain. There is, in Simon's (1957, p. 260) words, a "rational adjustment that humans find 'good enough'", and there is apparently no means of deciding in an intersubjectively confirmable fashion just what sort of an adjustment this or that human ought to find rational or 'good enough'.

It seems to me that although March and Simon's proposal represents a distinct improvement over the classical model of rationality, it is still not an adequate view. Its inadequacy lies in the fact that according to it virtually any kind of action or behaviour is rational provided that the actor thinks it is good enough. This is a direct consequence of their explication of rationality in terms of individual satisfaction or aspiration levels, and it logically cannot be avoided unless some additional criterion of preferable levels is introduced, a criterion by means of which one can decide (probably roughly and precariously) that a certain individually selected level is too high or too low. Clearly, "too high or too low" is merely an abbreviation for something like "higher or lower than it rationally or reasonably ought to be". In that case then, rather than having rationality defined purely in terms of satisfaction or aspiration levels, it would be defined circularly in terms of rational or reasonable satisfaction or aspiration levels. Hence, no appeal to an additional criterion of preferable levels can be introduced and, therefore, any old satisfaction or aspiration level must be regarded as acceptable. Thus, for example, if Charles Lamb's fool burns down his house to roast pork, then we should regard his action as perfectly rational provided that he is satisfied with the exchange. Similarly, if he makes love to his pig and keeps his wife in a pen, then that behaviour too must be sanctioned as long as he regards it as good enough. In sum, no matter what action science or common sense tells us is strange, stupid or horrendous, we shall be obliged to regard it as rational provided that the actor regards it as satisfactory or satisfactorily suited to his levels of aspiration. If this fact is not sufficient to demolish the March and Simon proposal, I do not know what is. (See also Dror (1968) and Grauhan and Strubelt (1971).)

It might be thought that the way to dispose of the preceding objection is to distinguish subjective from objective rationality. That is, one might say, for example, that while Lamb's fool is not objectively rational (because almost everyone believes that the price he pays to roast pork is outrageously high), he is still subjectively rational (because as far as he is concerned the price is fair). Although I quite agree that such a division can be usefully made, it is a mistake to think that it eliminates the force of my objection. My objection is, briefly, that to identify rational action with satisficing action is to allow every individual to be the final judge of his own rationality. Even if it is granted that every individual is the final judge of his subjective rationality, it cannot be granted that every person is the final judge of his objective rationality. The question is then: Which kind of rationality is it that people like to think they have and believe that they ought to have? The answer to this question is undoubtedly both kinds. Since everyone knows that damn fools and psychopaths are capable of subjectively rational action, to be rational in that sense is hardly enough. One ought and would like to be objectively rational, i.e., not merely sensible in one's own eyes but in the eyes of the rest of the human race as well. Nevertheless, if one's objectively rational behaviour were never subjectively rational, never satisficing or suited to one's aspirational levels, then one would probably have a serious psychological problem. Such a person would be at best a very disturbed martinet, always doing what ought rationally to be done but never finding it personally satisfying or rational in his own eyes. Clearly then, granted that it is useful to distinguish subjective from objective rationality in some sense, no one should be inclined to abandon one in favor of the other. Hence, no one should be inclined to believe that anyone can be the final judge of his own rationality in every significant

sense of the term. Having cut the pie of rationality for
analytic purposes, one must still have both pieces in order
to remain a "normal" member of the human race.

CHAPTER X

Rational Decisions and Processes

1 INTRODUCTION

In this Chapter I assess the strengths and weaknesses of two kinds of evaluation strategies for decision processes and decisions, and present first approximations of explications of 'rationality' as applied to such processes and their products. In the next Section definitions of a priori and a posteriori evaluation procedures are stipulated. Five *prima facie* plausible objections to a posteriori appraisals are met in Section Three and three objections to a priori appraisals are met in Section Four. Following this salvaging effort, Section Five is devoted to disclosing several advantages of both kinds of appraisals. The upshot of these four Sections is that a priori and a posteriori strategies are shown to be neither as bad nor as good as their critics and advocates, respectively, would have us believe, but both plausible and complementary. (Many of the issues considered in these Sections have analogues in the controversy between deontological and teleological ethical theories. A review of some of the issues may be found in Broad (1930).) In the last two Sections, explications of 'rational' and 'irrational' as applied to processes and decisions are presented to serve as working formulae for the remainder of our investigation.

2   A PRIORI AND A POSTERIORI EVALUATION

When a decision process is evaluated by means of
an appraisal of the decisions produced by it or of the
decision situations in which it is used (including the
decision-makers involved), I call the evaluation of the
process 'a posteriori' or 'pragmatic'. When a decision
process is assessed independently of the decisions produced
by it and of the decision situations in which it is used
(including the decision-makers involved), I   call   the
evaluation of the process ' a priori '. Somewhat
analogously, I call the evaluation of a decision   'a
posteriori' or 'pragmatic' if it is based on the
consequences of the decision, and 'a priori' if it is based
on the decision itself, i.e.., the act and its object.

Since all evaluations require some standards or
evaluative criteria, one must not read more into the notion
of a posteriori or pragmatic evaluation than has been
stipulated above. There is no such thing as a posteriori
evaluation in the sense of an appraisal that is made without
prior selection (in some way) of criteria of appraisal.
Nothing can be better or worse, beneficial or costly in the
abstract.   It must be beneficial or costly in some more or
less specific respect, whether or not appraisers   are
consciously aware of that respect.

Because it is usually easier (in fact) to
distinguish decision processes from decisions than it is to
distinguish decisions from their consequences, my discussion
in the next three sections focuses on processes and their
products, decisions. The entire discussion is applicable
mutatis mutandis to the a posteriori and a priori evaluation
of decisions.

3   THE CASE AGAINST A POSTERIORI EVALUATION

A number of writers have taken the view that the
a posteriori appraisal of processes and decisions is not
merely possible but eminently reasonable. For example,
Aristotle (1142b) claims that "... to have deliberated well
is thought to be a good thing; for it is this kind of
correctness of deliberation that is excellence   in
deliberation, viz. that which tends to attain what is good."
Similarly, Diesing (1962, p. 178) tells us that "a
functionally rational decision structure is one which yields
adequate decisions for complex situations with   some
regularity." According to Buchanan and Tullock (1962, p.
338)

> "The 'theory of constitutions' concerns itself
> with a discussion of the effects of various
> possible democratic constitutions. These
> constitutions, in the book to which this essay is
> an appendix, are evaluated entirely in terms of
> their effects on individual citizens."

And Suchman (1967, pp. 31-32) stipulates quite generally
that an evaluation is

> "... the determination (whether based on
> opionions, records, subjective or objective data)
> of the results (whether desirable or undesirable;
> transient or permanent; immediate or delayed)
> attained by some activity (whether a program, or
> part of a program, a drug or a therapy, an
> ongoing or one-shot approach) designed to
> accomplish some valued goal or objective (whether
> ultimate intermediate, or immediate, effort or
> performance, long or short range)."

Finally, Grauhan and Strubelt (1971, p. 257) insist (roughly
following Dror (1968)) that "a full evaluation of policy is
possible only when its real output can be ascertained."

In spite of the fact that the idea of pragmatic
evaluation has had considerable support, some apparently
serious criticisms have been raised against it. I shall now
examine these in some detail.

In his thought-provoking _Non-Violence_ and
Aggression (1968), H.J.N. Horsburgh summarizes Gandhi's
"critique of the ultilitarian view of ends and means".
Although both Gandhi and Horsburgh were concerned primarily
with the moral and socio-political justification of human
actions, their remarks are applicable with very little
alteration to the problem of appraising decision processes
by the decisions resulting from them.

Horsburgh (1968, p. 42) claims first
(interpreting Gandhi) that "to undertake to justify oneself
by results is to fall into presumptuousness since results
can never be guaranteed". For our purposes this argument
may be translated thus: if the rationality of decisions
produced by some process cannot be guaranteed then it is
presumptive to try to justify such processes by the
decisions they produce.

This argument seems to rest on an unwarranted
rejection of nondemonstrative or inductive reasoning.
Granted that the rationality of the decisions produced by a
certain process cannot be guaranteed, one still might have a
good reason in the form of strong inductive evidence that

the decisions produced will be rational. Provided that one
has some criterion or standard by means of which the
rationality of   a   given   decision   may   be   assessed
(independently of the process generating it), one can and
most people do obtain such evidence in a   fairly
straightforward way.   For   example,   new   members   of
organizations generally invest a considerable amount of time
trying to discover reliable information channels about
various aspects of their new environment. After a while
they develop workable rules of thumb on how to obtain good
advice about this or that, from whom, when and at what cost.
As Blau and Scott (1962) and others (e.g., in Hare, Borgatta
and   Bales   (1955))   have   shown   us,   a   number   of
socio-psychological   variables   are   involved   in   the
consultation processes that occur in organizations; but the
rationality of the advice received is also   important.   All
consultants   or   advisors   tend   to   be characterized,
intuitively at least, by something very much like a batting
average, and rational consultees or advisees use these rough
characterizations   in   much   the   same   way   that baseball
managers use batting averages. (Marschak (1959))   Thus,
unless one has quite general and persuasive arguments
against any sort of induction by enumeration, it must be
granted that there is nothing especially presumptuous about
the attempt to justify decision processes by assessing the
decisions they produce.

        Second, Horsburgh (1968, p. 42) asserts "that to
commit oneself unreservedly to an end when it may prove to
be unrealizable is to be prepared to do anything without
legitimate assurance of its being justified by one's end".
For   our   purposes   this   becomes: If one is committed
unreservedly to a kind of decision that might be impossible
to make, then one is committed to doing anything without
legitimate assurance of its being justified by such a
decision.

        I think that this argument is a useful ignoratio
elenchi.   In   the   first   place it reminds us of the
foolishness of pursuing ends without taking account of the
costs of pursuit. Clearly the costs of producing some ends
might be so high in comparison to the benefits receivable
from the production that it would be irrational to produce
them. As Oppenheim (1964, p. 219) puts it,

        "Means have consequences other than the goal,
        and the negative utility of the former may
        outweigh the positive utility of the latter.
        A rational actor must therefore predict...
        the total outcome of each alternative
        action open to him in the given situation."

Second, it suggests one of the criticisms that I have
leveled agains maximization policies, namely, that they tend

to be too weak or too strong (See IX 6.). And third, it reminds us that one ought to consider the potential costs of failure. Here, however, the pragmatist's problem is exactly analogous to those confronted by anyone interested in testing new theories, production or sales techniques, and so on. Sometimes the potential costs of failure for action are so high that wisdom is on the side of lethargy. This is precisely the strength of the "piecemeal social engineering" (Popper (1945)) and "disjointed incrementalistic" (Braybrooke and Lindblom (1963)) proposals for policy changes. Granting all of these points, however, the argument before us is not a sound argument against appraising processes or means by their products or ends. It is merely an argument against cost-ignoring and unsatisfiable commitments. If these suggestions are deleted from it, the remainder would be nothing more than the unjustified rejection of induction by enumeration considered in the preceding argument.

Third, Horsburgh (1968, p. 42) presents the moral argument "that, since results cannot be commanded, but methods can, our responsibilities have mainly to do with methods rather than with results". I believe Horsburgh is alluding here to the view often espoused by contemporary philosophers that while human actions can (logically) typically, if not always, be commanded, mere physical happenings (e.g., cloud bursts) cannot be commanded. Thus, on this view one might command and hold someone responsible for using a certain method insofar as that is tantamount to commanding and holding that person responsible for performing a certain action but one cannot command or hold someone responsible for the results of such action. For our purposes the argument would run thus: If decisions cannot be commanded but the use of processes can, then one is mainly responsible for the latter rather than the former.

The key word in this argument is 'mainly'. With it the argument has some plausibility, but without it, it is extremely dubious. It will surely not do to accept the general principle that individuals should never be held responsible for the results of their actions. After all, some kinds of results are for all practical purposes certain to follow some kinds of actions. Similarly, it will not do to entirely discount the decisions generated by certain processes as if the former were completely independent of the latter. The fact is that there are frequently law-like relations between various kinds of processes and the decisions they tend to produce, e.g., leaders who make it a habit of making decisions for followers without ever consulting them tend to make more biased (self-serving) decisions than leaders who are committed to consultation processes. Hence, some qualifying term like 'mainly' must be inserted in the conclusion of the present argument to give it any plausibility at all. Nevertheless, the specific

version of the argument that is of interest to us is not
sound because decisions c<u>an</u> be commanded.   It is, as I
insisted in Chapter <u>IV,</u> perfectly sensible to order,
persuade, bribe or force one to make decisions and it is
sensible to hold one more or less responsible for decisions
more or less freely made.

A fourth argument against the a posteriori
evaluation of decision processes has been suggested by
Niehans (1959) and received the support of Shackle (1961).
(Compare also Dror (1968).) Niehans (1959, p. 87) claims
that

> "...the outcome of a decision is as much the
> result of the ensuing state of nature as of the
> decision principle. It is impossible, therefore,
> to find out from <u>ex post</u> outcomes of unique
> decisions if the <u>decision</u> principle was good in
> view of the very uncertainty of the outcomes
> <u>ex ante</u>. How should we ever find out whether
> the satisfactory outcome was due to our clever
> decision theory and not to our good luck?"

It should be noticed first that Niehans
specifically refers to decision principles, unique decisions
and outcomes of decisions. In my terminology he is talking
about features of some kinds of decision processes (decision
principles), overt and covert decisions, and the
dependencies of the latter. Moreover, while he is concerned
to demonstrate the impossibility of appraising certain
features of decision processes, namely, decision principles
(e.g., the principle enjoining the maximization of expected
utility) on the basis of results <u>following</u> decisions, I
have been focusing on the decisions themselves as results.
As I have already insisted, it is usually difficult to draw
anything but a very fuzzy line between any sort of human
action like, for example, an overt decision and its
consequences. (See also Dror (1968).) So, in fact two
appraisers might find themselves examining precisely the
same aspects of some situation under different descriptions.
On the other hand, one who is committed to the examination
of the consequences of acts as well as to the acts
themselves is probably going to have more to examine than
one who is merely committed to the examination of the acts
themselves. So, it is quite possible that an
act-with-consequences-appraiser is going to gather
information leading to a quite different appraisal from that
obtained by an act-appraiser (i.e., assuming that they agree
on what the act is and what its consequences are). Although
such possibilities do not affect the issue of primary
interest to us here (i.e., whether any a posteriori
evaluation is possible), one ought to be aware of the fact
that Niehans's focus of attention is not exactly the same as
mine when we use the term "results". Here I am focusing on

decisions themselves as the results of processes because
that seems to be the least troublesome and cumbersome
approach to take.

In response to Niehans's argument, I would say
first that the main problem to which he is calling our
attention is that of uniqueness. It is closely related to
the problem of unique events that was discussed earlier
(VIII 4) as an infelicity of frequency theories of measuring
probabilities.   Like the frequentists, pragmatic appraisers
thrive on similarities, because the latter are necessary for
the construction of large reference classes relative to
which long run frequencies may be measured.   The more
products (decisions) examined from some decision process,
the more reliable can be one's a posteriori assessment of
the process.

Confronted by allegedly unique situations, a
pragmatist has roughly the same kinds of alternatives that a
frequentist has.   In the first place, a pragmatist can take
the line Niehans suggests and admit that the pragmatic
appraisal of processes used to generate unique decisions is
impossible on the basis of arguments like Niehans's.   That,
of course, would seriously limit the prospects of a
posteriori evaluation. More importantly, however, it would
not be warranted by arguments like Niehans's.   Contrary to
the assumption of the latter, in the absence of some reason
for regarding either a process or a situation in which it is
used as especially responsible for a particular decision,
one is not logically required to attribute the decision to
the process alone or to the situation alone. Rather, one is
required to attribute it to the complementary activity of
both process and situation.   Thus, although there is no
reason for attributing the decision to one antecedent rather
than the other, there is a good reason for attributing it to
both.   Consequently, a second alternative naturally arises
for the pragmatist, namely, to regard the value of the
unique decision as the value of the process and situation
generating it.   This makes it possible to obtain some
measure of a pragmatic evaluation of the process, albeit a
precarious one.

Finally, it could be said that the kind of
uniqueness required to make long run a posteriori evaluation
virtually impossible is so rare that the pragmatist's
proposal is not seriously threatened by it.   After all,
insofar as situations and decisions can be described with
general terms at all, they must be similar to other things
in which the terms apply. For example, a sentence like

(1)   The man in the corner by the window in room 203
             of the physics building of the University of
             Guelph decided to touch the ceiling with his nose
             at noon on June 23, 1977.

could be used to describe a unique situation and decision insofar as it involves only one particular person, in a particular place, at a particular time, making a particular decision to perform a particular and even peculiar action. Nevertheless, it is full of general terms (e.g., 'man', 'corner', 'window', etc.) that indicate similarities between the state of affairs it may be used to describe and others. Each of these similarities represents a reference class relative to which some long run frequencies might be obtained. These then, suggest a third way to deal with the uniqueness problem, namely, to try to find non-unique features of unique situations and decisions that will provide useful reference classes on the basis of which long run appraisals may be made. In other words, given one-of-a-kind situations and decisions, one tries to analyze them into aggregates of several kinds of features that are not one-of-a-kind. Without having specific allegedly unique situations and decisions to examine, there is no way of telling just how often this third approach will lead to worthwhile appraisals. However, armed with this strategy and the possibility of precariously evaluating situations and processes together, we seem to have all that is required to rescue the pragmatist's program from Niehans's attack. Uniqueness presents a difficult problem, but not a fatal objection. (See also Hovland, Lumsdaine and Sheffield (1949) and Suchman (1967) on "program" and "variable" testing.)

A final objection to the a posteriori evaluation of decision processes is that there are characteristics of such processes themselves that can and ought to be assessed independently of any decisions reached by them. Much of the work of formalistic theories like Arrow (1951), Black (1958) Murakami (1968) and Farquharson (1969) must be guided by the premiss of this argument. For example, these theorists assume, correctly I think, that democratic group decision processes ought to be egalitarian whatever the consequences. If it were to turn out that the circumstances and/or composition of any group were such that egalitarian processes always or nearly always led to irrational decisions or generally disastrous results, then that would be unfortunate (just plain bad luck) for the groups involved and for democrats generally. But it would be logically irrelevant to the question of whether or not democratic processes ought to be egalitarian This question can only be answered (affirmatively) by a priori analysis (i.e., by consideration of the meaning of the term 'democratic'). Any a posteriori synthetic assessment of the benefits and costs of egalitarianism is logically beside the point.

This argument seems strong enough to destroy any hope one might have had for using only a posteriori assessments for every kind of feature of decision processes. Even the limited pragmatism envisioned here cannot provide

an adequate instrument of appraisal for all the features of
processes that are built into them in an a priori and
analytic fashion. Thus, whenever one sets out to assess a
decision process, one must try to distinguish those
characteristics that are from those that are not amenable to
a priori evaluation. And so far, of course, it seems that
neither the a priorists nor the pragmatists have been
especially concerned with or careful about this distinction.
Granting this much, however, it does not follow that the
objection before us shows that all a posteriori evaluations
of every kind of feature of decision processes are
impossible.   More precisely, it does not show that one
cannot or should not appraise a process by its products,
i.e., it is completely innocuous against the pragmatists'
program.

4   THE CASE AGAINST A PRIORI EVALUATION

        If my analysis in the last section has hit its
mark, then the logical viability of a posteriori evaluation
of decision processes has been sustained against some
serious objections. In this section then, I shall try to do
as much for a priori evaluation. In particular, I shall
attempt to save the program of a priorists like Arrow, Black
and so on against three specific criticisms.

        In the first place, because processes are
partially defined in terms of their ends or products, it
might be thought that it is logically impossible to assess
the former apart from the latter. On the contrary, however,
such separate appraisals are quite commonplace wherever
there are alternative processes leading to a single kind of
product.   To take a trivial but decisive example, it is
frequently possible and preferable to use   multiplication
instead of addition to arrive at precisely the same solution
to arithmetical problems. Much of the business of ordinary
life as well as the more esoteric investigations of time and
motion, systems and cost-effectiveness analysts is devoted
to the problem of finding easier (less costly) ways to
achieve certain ends. (Horngren (1962))

        A second objection to the a priori evaluation of
decision processes is that it makes the decisions actually
reached and the consequences attached to them totally
irrelevant to the appraisal of the processes. (See, for
example, March and Simon (1958) on the "displacement of
goals".) Clearly, however, there are typically causal
connections between such processes and their products, and
any a priori rejection of all such dependencies would be
unwarranted.

This argument is evidently analogous to the fifth objection considered against a posteriori evaluation. It shows that it would be a mistake to assume that one could use only a priori assessments for every kind of feature of decision processes. This, of course, is what many self-styled "practical" decision theorists have been insisting for years. The following remark is an excellent example of the general attitude of theorists to the a priorists.

> "The paradox of voting, as it has been called, is a minor difficulty in voting that people with a mathematical turn of mind enjoy toying with". (Dahl and Lindblom (1953, p. 422))

Obviously, however, the argument presented here does not show that all a priori evaluations of every kind of feature of decision processes are impossible. We have already seen counter-instances of this thesis. Again, this argument, like many of the others presented, merely warns us against undue reliance upon a single kind of evaluation strategy for all kinds of features of decision processes.

A similar sort of objection may be raised against that type of a priori evaluation that makes decision situations (including decision-makers) irrelevant to the appraisal of decision processes. Such processes can only be used by someone (or some group) in some situation or other, and this or that process may be more or less rationally suited for a given environment. For example, as Argyris (1957, 1964) and others (e.g., in Costello and Zalkind (1963)) have shown us, highly democratic group processes may be counter- productive on the whole and from most points of view, for certain kinds of individuals and situations. Again, however, all this argument establishes is the impossibility of using only a priori assessments for all kinds of features of decision processes. Some a priori evaluation is still feasible.

5   ADVANTAGES OF A PRIORI AND A POSTERIORI EVALUATION

Having defended these two general approaches to the evaluation of decision processes against allegedly fatal criticisms and having indicated their actual limitations, I shall now state their major advantages. As one might expect, some of these may be discovered by noticing the benefits more or less concealed in some of the objections already examined.

a)   A priori evaluation. The fact that results, situations generally and even decision-makers may be irrelevant to the appraisal of a decision process can be a distinct advantage from a logical point of view. It not only tends to give an appraiser fewer variables to contend with, but those that remain tend to be individually fairly stable - if not, as Plato thought, eternal and unchangeable. Second, a priori evaluation is typically less expensive from economic, technological and physical points of view than a posteriori evaluation, as proponents of "thought experiments" attest. Third, the availability and legitimacy of a priori evaluation allows many people to assess processes just as they are often naturally inclined to assess them, namely, by reflecting upon their merits without putting them to work. And finally, this sort of evaluation does not raise the spectre of uniqueness problems. Granted that such problems are not in principle unsolvable or peculiar to a posteriori evaluation, the fact that they do not even arise for a priori evaluation means that it is logically invulnerable to a breakdown resulting from them. In this respect then, a priori evaluation is superior to a posteriori evaluation. (See also Kerr (1976).)

b) A posteriori evaluation. This approach to the assessment of decision processes has at least three important advantages. In the first place, it is in complete agreement with the intuition of many people, that in one way or another the results of decision processes do provide some indication of the value or rationality of the processes themselves. Second, it correctly gives processes the aura of fallibility and corrigibility that is a psychologically necessary condition for individuals to entertain ideas about improving them. And third, it goes a step further in encouraging experimentation with novel processes or features of processes in order to produce higher relative frequencies of more rather than less rational decisions.

6   RATIONALITY OF PROCESSES: FIRST APPROXIMATION

Supposing that the case for using some mix of a priori and a posteriori evaluation strategies to determine the rationality of decision processes has been satisfactorily made, we may proceed immediately to a first approximation of an explication of the concept of a rational decision process.

To begin with, let us assume that we are process appraisers who know for any given process to be assessed, (i) what features are amenable to a priori and a posteriori evaluation, and how to make the assessments; (ii) what counts as a rational decision emerging from that process; and (iii) what dependencies are likely to be attached to any of the decisions arising from that process in any specified spatio-temporal region. Then, if 'p' is a placeholder for the names or descriptions of any decision process,

(1)   P is rational = the estimated resulting benefits
                             df
                of using P reveal a tendency to balance or outweigh
                the estimated resulting costs for some recipient
                populations (to be specified) in some regions of
                analysis (to be specified).

(2)   P is irrational = the estimated resulting costs
                              df
                of using P reveal a tendency to outweigh the
                estimated resulting benefits for some recipient
                populations (to be specified) in some regions of
                analysis (to be specified).

and

(3)   P is more rational than P' = P and P' are
                                           df
                rational and the estimated resulting B/C ratio
                of using P reveals a tendency to be greater than
                that of P' for some recipient populations (to be
                specified) in some regions of analysis (to be
                specified), or else P is rational and P' is
                irrational.

        Most of the terms in (1) require some
explanation, which I shall outline briefly immediately and
develop more thoroughly in the remaining sections of this
book.

        First, in view of my defense in previous sections
of the necessity of mixing a priori and a posteriori
evaluations in order to obtain satisfactory assessments of
decision processes, "using p" must not be taken as a
recommendation that only a posteriori evaluations should be
used. The fact is that any benefit or cost that is attached
to P could only be obtained as a result of using P, because
unused processes do not have any effects at all.

        Second, the phrase "reveal a tendency" is
supposed to indicate two requirements, one pertaining to
evidence and the other to what is to be evidenced. Fairly
hard evidence rather than, say, hunch or hearsay is demanded
in the interests of intersubjective testability and
confirmability, while the identification of tendencies as
well as mere occurrences is demanded as a means of taking
some account of the benefits and costs of dependencies
beyond given regions of analysis. Dror's (1968, p. 60)
claim that "a change between past and present net output is
insignificant and misleading unless it indicates a trend
that can be extrapolated into the future" is probably too
strong (since information about a present state of affairs
may be accurate and significant for certain purposes), but
it is in the spirit of the proposal being made here.

Third, I speak of "estimated" benefits and costs
because one seldom has the resources to do anything but
estimate benefits and costs, and it would be self-defeating
to offer an explication which made the actual   determination
of   the   rationality   of a decision process virtually
impossible. (Knight (1921), Merton (1936), Dror (1968))
Problems related to the subjectivity, objectivity, accuracy
and consistency of estimations of "benefits" and "costs" are
discussed in Chapter XIII, but the senses in which the
former may be said to "balance or outweigh" the latter are
primarily the ones designated when people talk about various
kinds of considerations balancing or outweighing others.
For example, we talk of considerations of needs, morality
and self-satisfaction balancing or outweighing preferences,
monetary gain and public acclaim, respectively. To take a
rather famous example, consider the following quotation from
Cannabis: A Report of the Commission of Inquiry into the
Non-Medical Use of Drugs (Commission (1971, pp. 282-283).)

> The criminal law may properly be applied, as a
> matter of principle, to restrict the availability
> of harmful substances, to prevent a person from
> causing harm to himself or to others by the use
> of such substances, and to prevent the harm
> caused to society by such use. In every case the
> test must be a practical one: we must weigh the
> potential for harm, individual and social, of the
> conduct in question against the harm, individual
> and social, which is caused by the application of
> the criminal law, and ask ourselves whether, on
> balance, the intervention is justified.   Put
> another way, the use of the criminal law in any
> particular case should be justified on   an
> evaluation and weighing of its benefits and
> costs."

However one feels about the Commission's final
assessment concerning the use of criminal law for drug
control, it is clear that members of the Commission were
committed to the view that they had to weigh and balance
diverse considerations or, as they said, "benefits and
costs."

Similarly, Olson (1976, p. 375) claimed that

> "...cost-benefit analysis is ultimately a recipe
> for rational behavior. If ... we consider not
> only those costs and benefits that are reflected
> in markets, but all of those that are relevant to
> the decision at issue, cost-benefit analysis in
> its most elemental form becomes equivalent to a
> logically careful weighing of the advantages and
> disadvantages of a stipulated alternative. ...On
> this interpretation, cost-benefit analysis merely

says that only those options that are on balance
advantageous should be chosen, and accordingly is
only a sophisticated form of common sense."

It is precisely this fairly common capacity for weighing and
balancing diverse benefits and costs that I am claiming is
essential for rational decision-making. (A rough idea of
the scope of the literature on issues related to the
weighing of benefits and costs may be found in Rothenberg
(1961), Prest and Turvey (1965), Hinrichs and Taylor (1969),
Fishburn (1973), Wendt and Vlek (1975), and Jungermann and
de Zeeuw (1977). I have not attempted to address these
issues directly in this book, although Michalos (1970d) and
the article in the Appendix are indirectly relevant.)

        Fourth, it should be noticed that the requirement
that estimated resulting benefits should "balance" or
"outweigh" resulting costs represents a genuine alternative
to the maximizer's and satisficer's proposals. (See IX
6-8.) (1) does not require a decision-maker to seek out the
single "best" course of action from any set of alternatives
and it does not allow one merely to satisfy oneself that the
value of a process or decision is "good enough".   In other
words, (1) provides an objective "standard of quality" (Dror
(1968)) that is not impossible to realize.

        In effect this requirement is close to the
"survival quality" standard discussed at length by Dror
(1968) and strongly recommended by Grauhan and Strubelt
(1971). According to the latter,

        "The fact that an individual can deliberately
        commit suicide shows that the more conscious he
        is about his own choices, the more clearly he has
        to choose existence first in order to choose any
        other goal.   It is not by chance that even the
        proponents of a procedural concept of rationality
        give as the only material standard of appraisal,
        the   survival quality... .   The pathological
        choice par excellence would be, in the last
        resort, the choice of self- destruction.   In this
        conception the elements of rational and
        pathological choice are mutually   exclusive."
        (Grauhan and Strubelt (1971, p. 254))

        Dror (1968) criticizes the survival quality
standard on the grounds that mere psycho-physical survival
does not entail worthwhile existence. What is required,
according to Dror, is not merely the preservation of people,
but also the preservation of their ideals or values.   For
example, most of us would want to have "survival plus
freedom" instead of just survival. It seems to me that a
distinction between existence simpliciter and worthwhile
existence is of fundamental importance. Therefore, I have

tried to accommodate this view. (See Rescher (1973b) and Michalos (1974) for contrasting views on exactly what values have survival value.)

Another writer who has come very close to articulating the requirement proposed here is Ladd (1964). "I think," he tells us, "that when we call an action "irrational", we usually mean that, although it is an effective means to the end sought (and thus rational in the broad sense), the outrageous price that has to be paid for using that particular means is completely ignored by the agent, that is, the means are unsuitable." (Ladd (1964, p. 141). See also Stein and Denison (1960) and V. Taylor (1970).)

The requirement that estimated resulting benefits should "balance" or "outweigh" resulting costs may be regarded as opposed to certain maximization policies in another way. According to utility maximizers like Davidson, Suppes and Siegel (1957) and Luce and Raiffa (1957), following von Neumann and Morgenstern (1944), rational choice is logically impossible in the presence of cyclical preferences, because there is no alternative to which no other is preferred, i.e., there is no "best" or maximally efficient alternative. On the contrary, the question of cyclical or non-cyclical preferences is here logically irrelevant to the rationality of processes, decisions or choices, because the rationality of any alternative is not viewed as a function of its status in comparison with others but as a function of its own net output.

Fifth, the qualifying term "resulting" which appears before "benefits" and "costs" marks a distinction between, as it were, the direction and the net outcome of the B/C ratio change. Suppose, for example, that an alteration in a particular decision process lowers its typical B/C ratio from 4 to 3. In that case it is still a rational process according to (1), but it is less rational than it was, according to (3). In other words, the net outcome of the B/C ratio change is such that the modified decision process is still rational, but the direction of the change is unfavorable or destructive. Generally speaking, according to (1) to (3) the B/C ratios of prime importance for the determination of rationality are resulting or net outcomes rather than transitional ratios. The significance of this position for relations between rationality, morality and distributive justice shall be sketched in the next Chapter.

Sixth, since one cannot be expected to search for benefits and costs indefinitely, appropriate spatio-temporal "regions of analysis" must be determined. Different cuts of space-time may yield quite different estimates of benefits and costs. For example, business practices that are very

profitable in the short- run may turn out to be disastrous
in the long-run. Problems related to the selection of
appropriate regions of analysis are considered in Chapter
XII.

          Finally, by "recipient populations" I mean the
classes of all those individuals who will be counted as
recipients of the benefits and costs produced by any
activity, where 'individual' is interpreted as broadly as
'decision-maker',   i.e.,   it   denotes   persons,   clubs,
corporations, committees, nations, etc. Generally, if there
are N individuals in a certain region of analysis, then
there are 2^N -1 mutually exclusive possible recipient
populations. For example, if you and I are the only
individuals in some region under consideration, then the
three possible recipient populations are

          you <u>and</u> I

          you <u>and</u> not I

     not you <u>and</u> I

The next Chapter is devoted entirely to the question of the
kind of recipient population required for rational
decision-making.

          Using a mix of a priori and a posteriori
evaluation techniques to determine the rationality of
decision processes is tantamount to appraising processes on
the basis of estimated benefits and costs attached to the
processes themselves (when they are used), to the decisions
emerging from the processes and to the complementary
activity of the processes and the decisions. That is, some
benefits and costs will be largely the result of using a
process no matter what kinds of decisions are produced by
it, some will be largely the result of the process usually
yielding certain kinds of decisions, and some will be the
result of the joint activity of the process and its usual
products. Furthermore, given the facts that the boundaries
between decisions and their consequences are typically vague
and that the unintended and unexpected consequences of a
process may well have more significant benefits and costs
than the products themselves, a complete assessment of the
benefits and costs of using a process should include an
estimate involving all the dependencies of the process, its
products and the results of the complementary activity of
the process and its products in a given region of analysis.
(Compare Dror (1968) on "integrated schemes" of evaluation,
Merton (1936) and MacRae (1968).)

          In the presence of these general sources of
benefits and costs then, it becomes apparent that and how
certain <u>prima facie</u> irrational decision processes can

actually be rational. For example, if 'p' is interpreted as a dictatorial group decision process which, because of the special attributes of a particular dictator and his constituency, regularly happens to yield estimated resulting B/C ratios greater than one, then the kind of evaluation envisioned would identify P as rational although a purely a priori evaluation (e.g., a la Reddiford (1975)) would probably regard P as irrational. Again, using the kind of evaluation envisioned here, the process of regularly consulting an agreeable and inexpensive agent who seldom has good advice might be rational, provided that there are significant by-products of the consultation process. For example, sessions with a consulting agent (e.g., business associate, friend, relative, priest, psychiatrist, etc.) might be such that although they typically fail to produce useful advice regarding any given decision, they do give one extremely beneficial relaxation or relief from mental and physical strain.

7   RATIONALITY OF DECISIONS: FIRST APPROXIMATION

It has been argued that the decisions actually produced by a decision process constitute an important source of information for the evaluation of that process. What is required now is a provisional analysis of the rationality of such decisions. The general guidelines of this analysis have already been drawn by my explication of decision acts and objects on the one hand and the rationality of decision processes on the other.

As explained in Chapter VI, there are no decisions without decision objects. Hence, although it is necessary for a thorough analysis of decision-making to distinguish such acts from their objects, such a distinction is not normally necessary for a thorough analysis of the rationality of decisions. One can, of course, imagine someone being so relieved to have made any decision at all in some situation that the great bulk of the benefit accruing to him no matter what happens is a product simply of his act of deciding. But my guess would be that sheer decisiveness with little or no regard for the content or objects involved is seldom assessed or significant enough to warrant assessment. Normally, I should think, it is the rationality of deciding-something-or-other that merits attention.

Following the provisional explications in 6(1) to 6(3), we may say that if 'D' is a placeholder for names or descriptions of practical or cognitive decisions then

(1)   D is rational   =   the estimated resulting benefits
                         df

of D reveal a tendency to balance or outweigh the estimated resulting costs for some recipient populations (to be specified) in some regions of analysis (to be specified).

(2)   D is irrational $=$ the estimated resulting costs
                              df
of D reveal a tendency to outweigh the estimated resulting benefits for some recipient populations (to be specified) in some regions of analysis (to be specified).

and

(3)   D is more rational than D' $=$ D and D' are
                                       df
rational and the estimated resulting B/C ratio of D reveals a tendency to be greater than that of D' for some recipient populations (to be specified) in some regions of analysis (to be specified), or else D is rational and D' is irrational.

Since the only difference between 6(1) to 6(3) and (1) to (3) are that the latter have 'D' in place of 'p' and lack 'using', (1) to (3) do not require additional explanations.

CHAPTER XI

Recipient Populations: Benefits and Costs for Whom?

1 INTRODUCTION

In this Chapter I examine the strengths and weaknesses of two _prima facie_ plausible views concerning the recipient populations required for rational decision-making, and attempt to eliminate one of the views in favor of the other. In other words, I examine the question: Whose benefits and costs should be considered when one is assessing the rationality of a decision process or a decision? The next Section contains a precise statement of the problem and an elucidation of the view to be rejected, which I call 'egoistic rationality'. In Section Three, I offer a critique of egoistic rationality. Insofar as this Section is successful, egoistic rationality should be substantially, if not totally, discredited. Section Four is devoted to an exposition of the view that I call 'consensual rationality'. Five objections to this view are met in the following Section and in the sixth Section its principal advantages are reviewed. Insofar as these two Sections are successful, consensual rationality should be substantially, if not totally, vindicated.

In the final Section second approximations of explications of 'rational decision process' and 'rational decision' are given.

Although the entire discussion is carried on with specific reference to the decisions of "individuals " interpreted as persons, it is obviously applicable to decision processes and "individuals" interpreted in the broader sense cited earlier.

2   SIZE AND COMPOSITION

The question,

(1)   What recipient population   is   required   for rational decision-making?

is divisible into two others, namely,

(2)   What   is   the   size   of the recipient population required for rational decision-making?

and

(3)   What   is   the   composition   of   the   recipient population required for rational decision-making?

It has already been noted that if N individuals are affected by some decision made in some region of analysis, then there are 2^N -1 different sets of individuals that are candidates for the required recipient population. For example, if 'T', 'R' and 'H' are the names of all the individuals affected by some decision and '-T' '-R' and '-H' are short for 'not T', 'not R' and 'not H', respectively,   then   the 2^N -1 = 7 different   candidates   for the required recipient population are as in Figure I

FIGURE I: POSSIBLE RECIPIENT POPULATIONS

	Composition	Size
T . R . H	1 }	N
T . R .-H	2	
T .-R . H	3	N-1
-T . R . H	4	
T .-R .-H	5	
-T .-R . H	6	N-2
-T . R .-H	7	

        If the answer to question (2) is N then question
(3) is evidently superfluous, i.e., if everyone is to be
counted then there is no point in asking which persons in
particualr are to be counted. On the other hand, if the
answer to (2) is any number less than N (and, trivially,
greater than zero) then some justification for the selection
of one composition rather than another is in order. If, for
example, a recipient population of size N-2 is selected then
one has three mutually exclusive and exhaustive alternatives
and one ought to be able to provide some warrant for the
selection of one of these over the others. (Barry (1965))

        Most people who talk about rational action   seem
to hold that the size of the recipient population required
for rational decision-making is fundamentally N-(N-1) = 1.
Indeed, not only is there general agreement on the size, but
a single kind of composition is also recommended. In
particular, most people seem to assume that rationality only
demands that one looks after one's own interests, one's own
benefits and costs. The interests of others, it seems to be
assumed, should only be considered insofar as they affect
one's own. In this respect then, people seem inclined to
extend Aristotle's view of one type of wisdom, which he
called 'practical', to rationality generally. According to
Aristotle, "... the mark of a man of practical wisdom [is]
to be able to deliberate well about what is good and
expedient for himself". (1140a) Similarly, Sumner has
claimed that

        "Something becomes a reason for me to do a
        certain action only if it can somehow be related
        to my interests ... . In general the locutions
        'That is no reason for me to do it' and 'I have
        no reason to do it' are taken to be, roughly
        speaking, disclaimers of interest.

        The term 'interest' here is of course a dummy
        one; it need not be specifically interests which
        are at stake. Instead, it might be likes,
        dislikes, wants, desires, aversions, needs,
        tastes, inclinations, enjoyments, cravings and
        other items of this sort." (Sumner (1968, p.
        389))

Thus, in terms of Figure I, those who hold this view would
say that if T makes a decision, the required recipient
population is basically that with composition 5 on Figure I.

It can become composition 1 only if the benefits and costs
to R and H affect T's. Hereafter I shall refer to this
apparently widely espoused view of the size and composition
of recipient populations required for rational
decision-making as 'egoistic rationality'. More precisely,
following 7(1) in Chapter X, we may say that if 'D' is a
placeholder for the names or descriptions of cognitive or
practical decisions, then

(4)   D is egoistically rational   =   the estimated
                                          df
           resulting benefits of D reveal a tendency to
           balance or outweigh the estimated resulting costs
           for the individual making D in some region of
           analysis (to be specified).

Egoistic rationality is obviously the
rationalistic counterpart of ethical egoism, the view that
morality only demands that one look after one's own
interests - especially in the presence of conflicts with the
interests of others. If 'moral' is substituted for
'rational' in (4), the latter can serve as a rough
definition of an egoistically moral decision.

Unlike egoistic rationality, ethical egoism has
never been very popular. Usually, it is regarded as "the
devil's doctrine" and people defend it only as "devil's
advocates". (see, for example, the essays in Gauthier
(1970); the exception is Olson (1965) about which I shall
have more to say shortly.) Egoistic rationality, on the
other hand, seems to have all the blessings of common sense
and scientific theory. Taken together the two views give
rise to the following four possible combinations.

ethical egoism and egoistic rationality (no conflict)

ethical egoism and non-egoistic rationality (conflict)

non-egoistic ethics and egoistic rationality (conflict)

non-egoistic ethics and non-egoistic rationality (no conflict)

As indicated at the right of each of these
combinations, two of them permit conflicts to arise between
the demands of morality and rationality because of the fact
that different recipient populations are involved, and two
do not. One must emphasize permit rather than say, require,
demand or force conflicts to arise, because a given ethical
egoist might as a matter of fact always prefer to be
benevolent, self-sacrificing, nice to people and so on.
However, the fact than an ethical egoist can be this sort of
person does not show that being this sort of person is
required, prescribed or even encouraged by ethical egoism,
and that is what will be crucial for our discussion.

Because most people seem to accept egoistic rationality and some non-egoistic form of ethics (e.g., the Golden Rule, Kant's Categorical Imperative, Aristotle's Golden Mean or Universal Utilitarianism (Leys (1952)), they find themselves confronted by the possibility of just such a conflict. For example, an individual like T in Figure I might find himself in a situation in which his egoistic rationality requires him to focus his attention on the benefits and costs for composition 5, while his non-egoistic ethics requires him to focus his attention on the benefits and costs for composition 1; and the resulting assessments may be significantly different. If T were an ethical egoist then he could not fall into such a predicament, and this fact may constitute part of an explanation for people ever bothering to play "devil's advocate" for ethical egoism, i.e., if the position could be vindicated then a necessary condition of one kind of human problem would be eliminated. The adoption of a non-egoistic view of ethics and rationality could also eliminate the condition in question and, as I shall try to show, this approach would be better than the other.

3 A CRITIQUE OF EGOISTIC RATIONALITY

There are at least five prima facie plausible, but defective, reasons for recommending the recipient population cited in 2(4), i.e., for recommending egoistic rationality. The first three are adapted from Olson's (1965) defense of ethical egoism. I shall present each argument in turn, followed by my objections and comments. Then I shall introduce two distinct disadvantages.

(i) In order to convince anyone that egoistic rationality should be rejected, one must appeal to "intuition" or "faith". However, the latter appeal has the effect of undermining "habits of rationality and rational self-control". Since one certainly does not want these undermined, one must abandon the tainted appeals and accept egoistic rationality. (Olson (1965, p. 9))

The main infelicity of this argument is that its first premiss is false. As prisoner's dilemma enthusiasts have emphasized for years, it is quite possible for egoistically rational individuals to bring about their own destruction. (See, for example, Luce and Raiffa (1957), Rapoport (1966) and Gauthier (1967).) Thus, no appeal to faith or intuition is required to prove that egoistic rationality can be self-defeating. Furthermore, the second premiss assumes without warrant that "habits of rationality and rational self-control" are antithetical to faith and intuition. Although it is possible to have misplaced or misguided faith and intuition (Michalos (1970a)), it is undoubtedly the case that faith and intuition are

significant resources in the arsenal of rational
decision-makers. (Dill, Hilton and Reitman (1962), Vickers
(1965), Dror (1968, 1971) and Conklin (1974).) Hence, this
first argument fails on two counts.

(ii) Insofar as "...an individual has been led
to perform a socially undesirable act because the prevailing
system of rewards and penalties renders that act in his own
best all-round interests," there is probably something
wrong with the "social institutions" in his society.
Insofar as such an individual can be convinced that his act
is wrong, the defective "social institutions" can be
vindicated. But it is surely wrong to contribute to the
preservation of faulty institutions. Thus, instead of
trying to persuade the individual who acts "in his own best
all-round interests" that such action is wrong, one ought to
praise him as a guardian of social justice. (Olson (1965,
pp. 9-11))

The first premiss of this argument is a recurrent
theme in Olson's book. "In a reasonably well-ordered
society", he believes, "most socially undesirable behaviour
is not in the best interests of the individual agent himself
and would automatically disappear if the individual were
rationally to pursue his best interests." (Olson (1965, p.
62.)) This is apparently a double-edged claim to the effect
that in a "reasonably well-ordered society" the penalties
for "socially undesirable behaviour" would be so high and
the rewards so low that an egoistically rational agent would
never be inclined to such behaviour. While this seems to be
an admirable ideal, I think it is seriously misleading in
two respects. In the first place, it assumes that in a
"reasonably well-ordered society" there are no or, at any
rate, few serious conflicts of interest. In other words, it
assumes that in such a society life never or seldom has the
character of a zero-sum game. Such a society would seem to
presuppose a world of complete or nearly complete abundance,
with all the problems that entails. (See IX 3.) At the
very least the world would have to have enough benefits of
one sort or another to be able to adequately compensate any
individual for any loss suffered in someone else's interest.
If, for example, T and H each need an aspirin for a headache
and there is only one aspirin available, then in a
"reasonably well-ordered society" either T or H must have
something yielding a benefit worth as much as that conferred
by the aspirin which he must forego. Needless to say, I
find the idea of this sort of "society" fanciful.

Secondly, supposing that individual and public
interests are commensurate in a "reasonably well-ordered
society", there is as much reason to put forward argument
(ii) as there is the following argument leading to a
contradictory conclusion. Insofar as an individual has been
led to perform a self-sacrificing act because the prevailing

system of benefits and costs makes that act in the "public's" best all-round interests, there is probably something wrong with the "social institutions". It is wrong to try to persuade such an individual that such acts are wrong because that tends to preserve faulty institutions. Hence, acts of self-sacrifice should be encouraged. Thus, if (ii) proves anything, it proves too much, i.e., an argument with a similar structure may be designated to "prove" exactly the opposite of what (ii) is supposed to prove.

(iii)   Again, Olson claims that

> "In distributing praise and blame according to how a man acts or fails to act in his own best long-range interests, we oblige ourselves to take the interests of other individuals into fuller consideration than we would if we distributed praise and blame in some other fashion, thereby eliminating a very considerable source of friction and bitterness in human relationships." (Olson (1965, p. 12))

In short, by recommending egoistic rationality, one contributes toward a "fuller consideration" of the interests of all people. Why? Because one establishes a "relationship of mutual respect" with others and creates "conditions that favor a reasonable and co-operative endeavor to reconcile differing interests... ." (Olson (1965, p. 12))

    The trouble with this argument is that most of the evidence we have from all the social sciences shows that egoistic rationality does not produce the happy conditions Olson alleges. The records of international, industrial and interpersonal relations clearly bear witness to the fact that overt self-serving tends to breed ruthless competition and a lack of concern for individuals as "ends in themselves". As Grauhan and Strubelt observe,

> "The processes by which individuals, groups and societies restrict their consciousness of self to themselves alone raise the potential for destructive choices with respect to the excluded, i.e., for pathological choices in a comprehensive sense of system rationality." (Grauhan and Strubelt (1971, p. 259); see also Niebuhr (1932), Coase (1960) and Deutsch (1963).)

(iv) An individual's decision-making ability happens to be one of his primary resources for the specification and procurement of his preferences and needs. Thus, the rejection of egoistic rationality would be tantamount to a rejection of a necessary condition of self-determination and self-reliance. (Fried (1970))

In response to this argument it should be noticed that egoistic rationality is rather more than necessary for self-determination and self-reliance. It not only gives one the opportunity to look after oneself but it obliges one to look out for oneself alone in conflict situations. That is, in conflict situations, egoistically rational decision-making is not merely self-determining but selfish. This may be demonstrated as follows. Suppose again that T and H each need an aspirin for a headache and there is only one aspirin available. So each man can have relief only at the other's expense. Unless they are ethical egoists, it is clear that in the given situation they ought (morally) to consider the benefits and costs that their decisions will create for one another. But it is precisely in this kind of situation that an egoistic rationalist ought (rationally) to consider only his own benefits and costs, and the benefits and cost accruing to others only insofar as they affect his own. However, such behaviour is plainly selfish, because the decision-maker knows or believes that although his gain will be someone else's loss and vice-versa, he simply refuses to consider the interests of others. (Nowell-Smith (1954)) Thus, egoistic rationality seems to be personally more advantageous than non-egoistic rationality only when it is indistinguishable from egoistic immorality (=selfishness). In other words, it is "obviously smart" for T or H to look after his own affairs rather than the affairs of everyone affected by his decision only when looking after his own affairs is tantamount to looking out for himself alone.

The upshot of the argument in the preceding paragraph is that in conflict situations (i.e., situations such that one individual or group can only obtain a certain benefit or avoid a certain cost at another's expense) egoistic rationality is logically incompatible with non-egoistic morality. Contrary to the impression that one might receive by reading some contemporary literature on rational decision-making (e.g., Harsanyi (1972)), egoistically rational decision-making is not generally neutral or logically independent of non-egoistic morality. Those who hold that in conflict situations one ought (rationally) to look after one's own interests are committed to the view that in such situations one ought to act immorally, i.e., selfishly. In such situations, there is simply no difference between self-interested and selfish action.

(v) It could be argued that since an individual typically has a greater amount of reliable information about what is really beneficial and costly to him than he has about anyone else, the chances of erroneous evaluations concerning costs and benefits should be reduced by keeping recipient populations to a bare minimum. That minimum is exactly what is recommended by egoistic rationality.

At this point one should remember what Socrates told Thrasymachus, namely, that men do not always know what is in their own best (or worst) interests. The general recognition of this state of affairs accounts for the fact that people often consult others (e.g., doctors, lawyers, dentists, plumbers, etc.) in order to determine their interests. Moreover, the literature of social science is replete with evidence of interpersonal activity providing fundamental features of self-perception and self-evaluation. (See, for example, the Appendix.) Thus, the most one can say for this final argument is that although it has some prima facie plausibility, it seems to involve misleading oversimplification.

Having shown that apparently plausible arguments in defense of egoistic rationality are at best defective and at worst self-defeating, there are two additional criticisms to be considered. Both of them are adapted from Kalin's (1970) discussion of ethical egoism.

(i) Since it may not be to the advantage of an individual to give advice to another person on how to further the latter's own interests, an egoistic rationalist should always be prepared to withhold or distort his views in his own interests. Hence, "interpersonal reasoning" tends to become characterized as competitive bargaining, with co-operative group problem-solving being virtually eliminated. (The differences between these two kinds of processes and the dilemmas arising from their coalescence are examined in detail in Walton and McKersie (1966).)

(ii) Finally, since it may not be to the advantage of an individual to encourage another person to act in an egoistically rational fashion, egoistic rationality should be practiced in the classic Machiavellian tradition, i.e., an egoistic rationalist ought to preach self-sacrifice to his brethren while secretly pursuing his own selfish ends. In other words, for an egoistic rationalist the good life is a life of deception!

4   CONSENSUAL RATIONALITY

If 'D' is a placeholder for the names or descriptions of cognitive or practical decisions then

(1)   D is consensually rational $\underset{df}{=}$ the estimated
resulting benefits of D reveal a tendency to balance or outweigh the estimated resulting costs for every individual affected by D in some region of analysis (to be specified).

Again it is assumed that (1) would be unpacked along the lines of 7(1) in Chapter X. (Compare Kerr (1976) on 'relevant publics'.)

Lest there be any misunderstanding, it is perhaps worthwhile to point out immediately that although (1) does require a favorable B/C ratio (estimate) for every individual affected by any decision, it does not require exactly the same ratio for every individual, i.e., (1) does not require equal distribution. Nevertheless, insofar as (1) has a mild distribution requirement built into it, it escapes a standard objection to cost-benefit approaches to rational decision-making. (For example, see Fischhoff (1977, p. 179.)

If should also be noted that insofar as (1) does have implications concerning the distribution of the benefits and costs attached to decisions, the implications are not equivalent to those of the famous Pareto Principle. In the terminology employed here, the latter principle would state roughly that a decision D is consensually rational if and only if the estimated resulting B/C ratio of D for each individual affected by D in some region of analysis is at least as high as any alternative decision for the given situation. (Rescher (1966b)) The great difference between this kind of consensual rationality and that specified by (1) may be elucidated with an example. Suppose T wants to make a consensually rational decision to adopt or reject a new policy. He estimates the resulting B/C ratios attached to the decisions to adopt or reject the policy as follows.

	Adopt	Reject
T	1	2
R	1	1/2
H	1	1/2

According to (1), the decision to adopt the new policy is consensually rational. However, this decision is not consensually rational according to the Paretian proposal, because T would not be better off if the new policy were adopted.

Generally speaking, I am in complete agreement with Coase (1960, p. 35) when he insists that "nothing could be more 'anti-social' than to oppose any action which causes any harm to anyone." So, (1) has been designed accordingly. It gives us an explication of rationality that accommodates moral principles a bit more easily than some notable alternatives, although it is not itself a principle of morality or distributive justice. (Compare the "difference principle" of Rawls (1971).)

5   THE CASE AGAINST CONSENSUAL RATIONALITY

At least five objections may be raised against consensual rationality as it is defined by 4(1). I shall present each of them along with what I take to be more or less satisfactory replies.

First, in a world in which most individuals (in a broad sense) seem to be or at least try to be egoistically rational, there is very little to be gained by consensual rationality. If, for example, most people are really looking out for themselves, then they are not likely to be the innocent victims of the decisions of others.

This objection is faulty on two counts. In the first place, it presupposes that everything that happens to any individual is a result of the latter's own action. But this is obviously false, as the existence of natural catastrophes demonstrates. Furthermore, it assumes that if most individuals can look after themselves, the few that cannot may be ignored. That such an assumption is indefensible on non-egoistically moral grounds is indisputable. But it is equally indefensible on the grounds of consensual rationality. In fact, the assumption is only rational in the sense of some form of non-consensual rationality, e.g., egoistic rationality. However, it would be question-begging to criticize consensual rationality because it is not rational in some non-consensual sense. Thus, this first objection to consensual rationality involves both a falsehood and a _petitio principii_. (See also Emmet (1976).)

Second, anyone committed to consensual rationality in this world is probably only stacking the cards against himself, because he is trying to make decisions that yield favorable B/C ratios for everyone affected and the latter are merely trying to make decisions with similar ratios for themselves.

In a sense this argument has some merit. Given the abundance of egoistic rationalists in the world today, there seems to be no way to avoid the conclusion that a consensual rationalist is likely to end up with fewer of some kinds of things than one might like, e.g., less money and all the things it can buy. On the other hand, he is also likely to end up with more of some other kinds of things, e.g., friends, trust and respect. Thus, in another sense, the argument is unsound. It certainly cannot be maintained without question-begging that it is irrational (or rational) _simpliciter_ to prefer to risk losing, say, the things money can buy to friendship. (See, however, Fried (1970).) Hence, the most that could be established with this argument is that the adoption of consensual rationality is not without some cost, which no one has ever doubted.

Third, it is an implausible consequence of consensual rationality that if everyone cannot survive or prosper as a result of some decision, then it is not rational for anyone to survive or prosper. For example, suppose there is a conflict situation such that no available decision yields a favorable resulting B/C ratio for everyone affected, but some decision does yield such a ratio for some individuals. In such cases a decision that would, say, save as many as possible could not be consensually rational.

The first point to be noticed about this objection is that insofar as it hits consensual rationality, it hits egoistic rationality too. That is, it is an implausible consequence of egoistic rationality that if a decision-maker himself cannot survive or prosper as a result of his decision then it is not rational for anyone else to survive or prosper. If, for example, R and H are in a situation such that only one of them can obtain a favorable resulting B/C ratio and R can only have it as a result of H's decision while H can only have it as a result of R's decision, then neither R nor H can make an egoistically rational decision. But if they are committed to egoistic rationality, then they can not make a rational decision at all in such situations. Nevertheless, it seems that it would have been rational in some respectable sense to allow one of these individuals to survive or prosper.

The "respectable sense" of rationality involved in these situations seems to be essentially related to some form of maximization principle. However, as I have already tried to show, the search for a satisfactory maximization policy (i.e., one that does not require too little or too much) is bound to be abortive. Although it is tempting to introduce a rule of thumb based on such a policy in order to meet the special problems in given conflict situations, one is never able to sharpen the rule of thumb satisfactorily for situations that are not given but constructed. Hence, it seems to me that a more plausible line to take with respect to given conflict situations is to say that it seems rational in some respectable sense to save as many as possible because the more one saves, the closer one's decision comes to being consensually rational. For example, if one were confronted by the alternatives of making a decision yielding a favorable resulting B/C ratio for 99 of 100 affected individuals or making a decision yielding such a ratio for only 10 of 100 individuals, the former would be preferable because it is more nearly rational in the consensual sense. The fundamental difference between a consensual rationalist and what we might call a 'maximizing consensual rationalist' does not lie in the kinds of decisions that they would typically end up making. It lies instead in the way those decisions would be described. The decision yielding a favorable B/C ratio for 99 of 100 affected individuals would be rational for a maximizing consensual rationalist but irrational for a consensual rationalist. Still, both rationalists would make that decision in the given situation. While the consensual rationalist's view of the decision in question here certainly sounds extraordinary, it is no more extraordinary than some of those to which a maximizing consensual rationalist would be committed, e.g., like those at the end of Chapter IX 7.

A fourth objection to consensual rationality is that it is by no means clear that anyone could (in every sense) determine whether or not the resulting B/C ratio attached to any decision for every individual affected by it is favorable. It has already been emphasized that people are not especially reliable appraisers of their own interests, and the same may be said a fortiori with respect to their ability to appraise the interests of others. Thus, requiring everyone to accurately assess the impact of his decision on everyone affected by it in order to determine its rationality is tantamount to severely reducing the chances of anyone ever making a decision that could be known to be rational. Indeed, the greater the estimated number of affected individuals, the smaller would be the probability of anyone making such a decision.

I would be the first to admit that consensual rationality could well be more demanding than most other apparently plausible kinds of rationality with respect to its informational requirements. However, this does not seem to be a fatal objection, for several reasons. In the first place, there are more or less reliable ways to determine the interests of others, e.g., direct consultation, elections, survey research, empathic understanding, experimentation, etc. Consensual rationality does not preclude the use of these and other means. Second, it is sometimes possible to assess the benefits and costs of decisions for others with more accuracy (objectivity) than one can assess one's own benefits and costs. Third, we are not demanding complete certainty of assessments but only more or less accurate estimates. And finally, it is possible to place some limits on informational requirements by limiting the size of regions of analysis or the scope of decisions. (This is developed more fully in the next Chapter.)

Finally, Kass (1971) has presented a lucid and thought-provoking indirect attack on consensual rationality via the responsibilities of those who act in behalf of others. He is primarily concerned with the duties of physicians to their patients, but everything that he says has profound implications for anyone else, e.g., public officials, lawyers, industrial employees , and so on. The following paragraphs summarize his position.

"We must learn to desist from those useless
technological interventions and institutional
practices that deny to the dying what we must owe
them - a good end. These purposes could be
accomplished in large measure by restoring to
medical practice the ethics of allowing a person
to die.

But the ethic of allowing a person to die is
based solely on a consideration of the welfare of
the dying patient himself, rather than on a
consideration of benefits that accrue to others.
This is a crucial point. It is one thing to take
one's bearings from the patient and his interests
and attitudes, to protect his dignity and his
right to a good death against the onslaught of
machinery and institutionalized loneliness; it is
quite a different thing to take one's bearings
from the interests of, or costs and benefits to,
relatives or society. The first is in keeping
with the physician's duty as the loyal agent of
his patient; the second is a perversion of that
duty, because it renders the physician, in this
decisive test of his loyalty, merely an agent of
society, and ultimately, her executioner. The
first upholds and preserves the respect for human
life and personal dignity; the second sacrifices
these on the evershifting alter of public
opinion." (Kass (1971, p. 701). See also
Blackstone (1975).)

Insofar as one assumes, apparently with Kass,
that a "loyal agent" ought to act in the interests of his
client in case these interests conflict with others, one is
almost certainly presupposing that clients (and people
generally I suppose) are (whether or not they ought to be)
egoistic rationalists. If acting in a client's behalf
means or implies acting as the agent himself would act if he
were able, and if it is assumed that a client would act
egoistically rationally if he were able, then it clearly
follows that a "loyal agent" should act precisely as Kass
claims. Thus, even if one abandons egoistic rationality for
oneself, one is committed to it insofar as one acts as the
agent of another.

If Kass's line can be sustained then it will be
virtually impossible to make any headway against egoistic
rationality, because most people spend a great deal of their
lives as the agents of others, i.e., most people are not
self-employed. Fortunately, Kass's line cannot be
sustained, for two reasons. In the first place, it involves
the fallacy of special pleading. (Michalos (1970a)) If
egoistic rationality is problematic, dangerous or offensive
when it is practiced for oneself, it is equally problematic,

dangerous or offensive when it is practiced for others _for
the very same_ reasons. It would be question-begging to
assert at this point that egoistic rationality is
problematic, dangerous or offensive in order to undermine
Kass's position. But it is certainly legitimate to insist
that considerations like those presented above in Section
Three have merely been ignored in Kass's argument. Second,
the first premiss of that argument as formulated in the
preceding paragraph is doubtful. By using 'would' instead
of 'should' in it, one tends to free an agent from any
principles or norms that are not accepted by his client.
Thus, for example, if an agent's client happens to be a
giant corporation whose operating principles do not include,
say, the preservation of a neighborhood grocery, then that
agent, insofar as he is loyal, might well destroy the
grocery without any pangs of conscience. Needless to say,
examples like this could easily be multiplied. Hence,
unless one is prepared to permit people to commit all kinds
of immoral acts under the guise of "Loyal Agency", the
second premiss of Kass's (reformulated) argument must be
rejected; and with it, the argument itself. (For a more
thorough analysis of this subject, see Michalos (1977).)

6   THE CASE FOR CONSENSUAL RATIONALITY

          If my analysis in the preceding Section has hit
its mark, then the concept of consensual rationality has at
least been spared an ignominious early death. Some
advantages of this concept over egoistic rationality
primarily and maximizing consensual rationality secondarily
have already been suggested, but there are five others that
deserve to be mentioned.

          In the first place, as suggested at the end of
Section Two, if one happens to hold a non-egoistic view of
morality (as most people do) then the adoption of consensual
rationality eliminates the possibility of a conflict arising
between the demands of morality and rationality merely
because of the fact that different recipient populations are
involved.

          Second, consensual rationality is impartial and
objective in the sense that it regards every individual
affected by a decision as having a claim to a favorable
resulting distribution of benefits and costs. This does not
mean that everyone is (rationally) entitled to the same
ratio (or to an equal distribution of costs and benefits),
but only that everyone is entitled to at least a
self-sustaining share of any benefits and costs attached to
any decision affecting them. In other words, according to
this view of rationality, the idea of a welfare state is
essentially rational. (Compare Rescher (1972).) Although

most people have been willing to grant that it is a morally
good idea to look after people who cannot look after
themselves, implicit assumptions of egoistic rationality
have made the idea difficult to defend on rational grounds
alone. Consensual rationality eliminates this impediment.

        Third, as non-egoistic moralists, most people are
probably favorably disposed to the idea that consensually
rational decisions ought (morally) to be given a fair
hearing, if not some kind of support. No doubt this is one
of the main reasons for policy makers typically referring to
their policies as "for the benefit of all concerned" or "in
the interests of everyone". (Gross (1966))   Although such
remarks frequently disguise what might be called
'institutional egoistic rationality' insofar as the
referents of "all concerned" and "everyone" are merely
supposed to be everyone in a certain select group of
individuals (e.g., as in Brandt (1963)), the rhetoric of
consensus tends to make policies prima facie more palatable.
(See also MacRae (1970).)

        Fourth, in the course of a brief discussion of a
pair of concepts like those considered in this Chapter,
which Rapoport refers to as 'individual rationality' and
'collective rationality', he offers the following argument
for the latter. "It is", he claims, "incorporated in every
disciplined social act, for instance in an orderly
evacuation of a burning theatre, where acting in accordance
with 'individual rationality' (trying to get out as quickly
as possible) can result in disaster for all, that is, for
each 'individually rational' actor." (Rapoport (1974, p.
18)).   Thus, the idea of consensual rationality is inherent
in social acts whose reasonableness is generally granted.
(See also Katz (1972), Gauthier (1975) and, in opposition,
Harsanyi (1972).)

        Finally, I would like to mention again the
suggestion made in response to the second objection to
consensual rationality in Section Five. It was pointed out
there that a consensual rationalist would probably have more
friends and generate more trust and respect than an egoistic
rationalist.   It seems to me that in spite of the
entrenchment of the idea of egoistic rationality in western
civilization, most people are reluctant to attribute wisdom
to people perceived as merely egoistically rational. There
is an old Negro spiritual that Martin Luther King, Jr. was
fond of, which went something like this: "We are all in the
same boat brother; so you can't rock one end without rockin'
the other." Like the author of these lines, a wise person
and a consensual rationalist would have at least one thing
in common. They would both have a feeling for and a
commitment to the unity of humanity. Can we afford to ask
less of a rational human being in the twentieth century?

7 RATIONAL DECISIONS AND PROCESSES: SECOND APPROXIMATION

In the light of my investigation so far, we may
state the following second approximations.   If 'D' is a
placeholder for the names or descriptions of practical or
cognitive decisons,

(1)   D is rational = the estimated resulting benefits
                         df
             of D reveal a tendency to balance or outweigh
             the estimated resulting costs for every individual
             affected by D in some region of analysis (to be
             specified).

If 'p' is a placeholder for the names or descriptions of
decision processes,

(2)   P is rational = the estimated resulting
                           df
             benefits of using P reveal a tendency to balance
             or outweigh the estimated resulting costs for
             every individual affected by the use of P in some
             region of analysis (to be specified).

Second approximations toward explications of irrational
decisions and processes, and comparatively rational or
irrational decisions and processes may be routinely
constructed from (1) and (2) following Chapter X 6(1) to
6(3) and 7(1) to 7(3).

CHAPTER XII

Estimates, Regions, Costs and Benefits

1   INTRODUCTION

In this Chapter the final formulations of my explications of 'rational decision' and 'rational decision process' are presented. I begin by examining the problem of specifying the degrees of accuracy and consistency of estimates required for rational decision making. In Section Three the question of adequate regions of analysis is considered. Following that, there is a Section in which concepts of 'costs' and 'benefits' are explicated. In the last four Sections important species of benefits and costs are discussed in the context of describing a general classificatory scheme for costs and benefits.

2   ACCURATE, CONSISTENT AND REASONABLE ESTIMATES

Supposing that one accepts the provisional explications of 'rational decision' and 'rational decision process' in terms of estimated resulting benefits and costs which I refer to briefly as 'favourable B/C ratios', a question that immediately arises is:

(1)   What kind of an estimate is required for rational decisions and processes?

This could be regarded as a request for any one of several different kinds of answers. First, it could be a request for information concerning the accuracy of estimates of B/C ratios, i.e., what social scientists and statisticians often refer to as the 'validity of estimates'. Again, it might be a request for information concerning the consistency of estimates of B/C ratios in relevantly similar situations, i.e., what social scientists and statisticians often refer to as the 'reliability of estimates'. And finally, it might be a more general request for information concerning the reasonableness or rationality of estimates of such ratios. All three of these kinds of answers will receive attention in this Section.

A question like (1) naturally arises because it would obviously be a mistake to say that any old estimate of benefits and costs is adequate for rational decision-making. There are certainly wise, foolish, careful, careless, skillful, amateurish, etc. estimates. In fact, a thorough analysis of the concept of an estimate would reveal a set of ancillary concepts and problems precisely analogous to those involved in the present investigation of rational decision-making. For example, one would have to distinguish and examine overt and covert processes and acts of estimation, objects of estimation, estimation situations, and so on. Rather than attempt a complete examination of these issues, I shall merely pursue those that are especially pertinent to our main problem.

Having rejected the idea that one estimate of a B/C ratio is as good as another, it might be thought that an estimate is adequate provided that anyone using it sincerely believes that it is adequate. Unfortunately, this view is practically indistinguishable from the former, because it would generate the same outrageous range of permissible kinds of estimates. Sincere belief in the adequacy of an estimate has exactly the same status as sincere belief in the adequacy of a mathematical proof or a scientific explanation. On the one hand, one is inclined to say that a sequence of sentences is a good, adequate or satisfactory mathematical proof or scientific explanation if and only if some normal person is convinced or understands it, respectively. According to this view, there cannot (logically) be a proof that no one believes proves anything or an explanation that no one finds enlightening. On the other hand, one is inclined to say that a sequence of sentences is a good, adequate or satisfactory mathematical proof or scientific explanation if and only if any normal person ought to be convinced by or understand it, respectively. According to this view, there might well be a proof which ought to be persuasive or an explanation which ought to be enlightening, although no one is in fact persuaded or enlightened. Similarly, on the one hand one is inclined to say that an estimate is good, adequate or satisfactory if and only if some normal person believes it is; and on the other, it is satisfactory if and only if any normal person ought to believe it is.

For ease of reference, explications of satisfactory proofs, explanations and estimates in terms of what _is_ the case may be called 'descriptive', while explanations in terms of what ought to be the case may be called 'normative'. (Compare Brandt (1963).) For our purposes, the latter kind of explication is certainly required. That is, the estimates required for rational decision-making must be such that any normal person ought to believe that they are good, adequate or satisfactory.

One apparently plausible move to make at this point is to require that the estimates in question must be obtained by methods that tend to be accurate and consistent. That is, the estimating techniques employed by a rational decision-maker must be such that they tend to obtain estimates that accurately represent states of affairs that they are supposed to represent and these estimates must be consistently obtainable from the same kind of data. Granted that this _is_ a plausible move, it does not take us very far, because there are degrees of accuracy and consistency, So the question now becomes:

(2)   How accurate and consistent should one make the estimates required for rational decision-making?

This question can be answered in at least three significantly different ways, none of which is particularly satisfying. In the first place, one might suggest a maximization policy, e.g., estimates should be as accurate and consistent as one can make them. For reasons already reviewed, however, it is unlikely that such a policy could be satisfactorily specified. Alternatively, one might suggest that estimates should be accurate and consistent enough so that the accurately and consistently estimated resulting B/C ratio of using such levels of accuracy and consistency in some region of analysis is favorable. The trouble with this answer is that it drives us straight back to a question like (2). In other words, it drives us to an infinite regress of explications of 'rational estimates'. What is worse, however, is the fact that anyone in doubt about the meaning of 'rational decision' is not going to be enlightened by an explication in terms of rational estimates, because the concept of an estimate probably cannot be analyzed adequately without some reference to decisions. Thus, this alternative is as problematic as the first. Finally then, one might do what statisticians and social scientists usually do, namely, simply stipulate certain preferable levels of accuracy and consistency. Obviously, the more plausible one attempts to make any level sound, the greater the danger of falling into one or the other of the first two alternatives; and the less concerned one attempts to be about the plausibility of any preferred level, the greater the danger of falling into arbitrariness or unthinking adherence to the "done thing". Like many people, I would work with this third alternative usually and continue to try to find a way to make the second alternative satisfactory.

Given the disappointing conclusion of the preceding paragraph, it is tempting to consider the possibility of deleting any reference to estimates from our explication of rational decision-making. I have already suggested some reasons for resisting this temptation in Chapter X. 6. Here it may be further noted that the net effect of such an excision would be to make the rationality of decisions logically independent of the beliefs of decision-makers, whether those beliefs are actually held or ought to be held. It would follow then that rational decision-making has nothing to do with the assessment one actually makes or ought to make of the benefits and costs of using some process, or making some decision. Whether one's assessments were slipshod or careful, or, indeed, whether one ever tried to assess one's situations at all, it would not matter. Such considerations would be logically irrelevant to an appraisal of the rationality of decisions. However, since these consequences are certainly intolerable, estimates cannot be eliminated from our explication.

In conclusion then, third approximations of explications of 'rational decision' and 'rational decision process' may be obtained from 7(1) and 7(2) in Chapter XI by inserting 'accurately and consistently' in front of 'estimated'.

3   REGIONS OF ANALYSIS

The question

(1)   What is the size of a region of analysis required for rational decisions and processes?

cannot be answered in a quite general way by a priori analysis. It depends heavily on the kinds of decisions, processes and situations with which one is confronted, including especially one's objectives, resources and restrictions. This is granted by virtually all writers who consider the question. (See, for example, Diesing (1955), Horngren (1962), Prest and Turvey (1965), Dror (1968), Hinrichs (1969) and Petersen (1977).) If, for example, a certain level of accuracy and consistency of estimates is regarded as absolutely necessary for rational decision-making, then the region of analysis selected for any given situation may be largely determined by the estimating techniques at one's disposal. Again, if most of the costs of deciding to become a physician are borne during medical school and internship while most of the benefits are received in the years following these periods, then a region of analysis used in the evaluation of such a decision certainly ought to be large enough to include both the costly and the beneficial years. While there may well be some difficulty drawing a line to the beneficial years short of retirement, no one will doubt the wisdom of _not_ drawing a line on the last day of internship.

One might, of course, say that a region of analysis should be just large enough so that the estimated resulting B/C ratio of using that region is favorable. But by now the inherent incompleteness and, therefore, worthlessness of such a remark should be apparent. Since benefits and costs cannot be counted forever, some appropriate particular region must be chosen in which one's efforts should be concentrated. Thus, we are driven back to (1) again.

Alternatively it might be said that a region of analysis should be just large enough to include all the data that are relevant to a given decision. (Dror (1968) seems to prefer 'most' to 'all' in the present context, but in order to avoid questions like 'Does that mean 51 or 52 per cent?' and 'How about 68 per cent of the data?', I have opted for 'all'.) Undoubtedly no one is going to claim that a relevance requirement is irrelevant, but it does tend to be useless in the absence of specific guidelines. More precisely, consider the various kinds of possibilities and points of view that were roughly outlined in Chapter VII, and suppose that we could decide on an appropriate spatio-temporal region of analysis for some decision. For example, suppose we were committed to an analysis of all the relevant data arising in the period of one week in an area consisting of the total physical plant of some university. Is one rationally required to investigate such a region from all other points of view in search of relevant data or would one typically be able to eliminate certain points of view a priori as irrelevant? In other words, supposing that we had a plausible answer to (1) from a physical point of view,

(2)   What kind of _composition_ of other points of view should be _required to_ specify a region of analysis for rational decisions and processes?

As in the case of recipient population compositions, if there are N possible points of view then there are 2^N -1 candidates for the required region composition. Moreover, given the general limitations cited above concerning the specification of regions of analysis, the fact of the matter seems to be that most people do tend

to eliminate certain compositions a priori. (March and
Simon (1958)) I would like to suggest, however, that this
practice should not be countenanced, because it is
tantamount to the elimination of the possibility of
discovering benefits and costs which a priori one might
imagine do not exist. That is, it is tantamount to letting
one's presuppositions, predilections, conjectures or
theories be entirely decisive in the search for facts about
the benefits and costs of decisions. Granted that alleged
facts are permeated with theoretical elements in varying and
largely inscrutable ways, some theoretical constructions are
demonstrably more open to some kinds of facts than others.
For example, decisions concerning birth control and housing
for certain groups which are made with no means of taking
account of moral, religious, social and esthetic benefits
and costs, are closed to certain kinds of facts to which
they could and should be open. Hence, in place of the a
priori elimination of certain compositions, roughly
following Prest and Turvey (1965), I would recommend
beginning with the most inclusive composition known for any
selected spatio-temporal region, and eliminating points of
view only after inspection reveals them to be barren of
benefits and costs.

          If the position outlined in the preceding
paragraph is sound, we now have some guidelines as to the
sort of conceptual net that ought to be cast over any given
region of analysis in order to capture all the data that are
relevant to a given decision. Nevertheless, no answer to
our original question (1) has been offered that would take
us beyond the first sentence of this Section. However,
apart from specific situations, I do not think much more can
be said that would not be so general or "cookbookish" as to
be worthless for our purposes. At this point then, I shall
merely present the following final formulations of my
proposals.

          If 'D' is a placholder for the names or
desciptions of practical or cognitive decisions:

(3)   D is rational = the accurately and consistently
                       df
          estimated resulting benefits of D reveal a
          tendency to balance or outweigh the accurately
          and consistently estimated resulting costs for
          every individual affected by D in a
          situation-determined region of analysis.

(4)   D is irrational = the accurately and
                          df
          consistently estimated resulting costs of D
          reveal a tendency to outweigh the accurately and
          consistently estimated resulting benefits for
          every individual affected by D in a
          situation-determined region of analysis.

and

(5)   D is more rational than D' = D and D' are
              rational and the accurately and consistently
              estimated resulting B/C ratio of D reveals a
              tendency to be greater than that of D' for every
              individual   affected   by   D   and   D' in a
              situation-determined region of analysis, or else
              D is rational and D' is irrational.

          The   construction   of   the analogues for decision
processes may be carried out by routine substitutions and is
therefore omitted.

4   COSTS AND BENEFITS

          With the help of some familiar explicata, it is
possible to   provide plausible explications of our ordinary
concepts of costs and benefits.   First, if x is a
placeholder   for   the   names   or   descriptions   of
decision-makers, and a and b are placeholders for the names
or descriptions of objects, states of affairs, persons,
actions, beliefs or attitudes; then I propose that

(1) a is a cost to x for b $=$ x wants, likes or
                                          df
              needs a and b, but x's possession of either
              mutually excludes x's possession of the other.

          This explication uses the definition of 'wants'
given in Chapter III 3(3), 'likes' given in III 2(10),
'needs' given in IV 2(5) and 'mutual exclusion' given in
VIII 6(II).   Since the latter is a causal notion, (1) seems
to capture Knight's (1921) widely accepted insight that all
costs are opportunity costs.   That is, something is regarded
as a cost if and only if paying it causes one to give up
something else.   If nothing must be given up, then no costs
are borne.

          For 'benefit', I propose that if x and a are
interpreted as above, then

(2) a is a benefit to x $=$ x wants, needs or likes,
                                     df
              and gets a.

This explication uses the notions of wanting, liking and
needing specified in (1).   (I assume that the ideas of
getting and having possession of something are innocuous
primitives.)

(1) and (2) may be used to explicate a naturalistic concept of value. If x and a are interpreted as above, then

(3) a is valuable (has value, is a value, etc.) to x $\underset{df}{=}$
     a is a cost or a benefit to x.

In Michalos (1976a) I have called the view of value that is explicated in (3) 'naturalistic subjectivism'. According to this view, values are essentially a function of human feelings and inclinations. Needless to say, this is a fairly old view of the nature of value, and its strengths and weaknesses are well-known. The most thorough development of the position may be found in Perry (1926), although Dewey (1939) and Lewis (1946) had worthwhile insights about it.

5   FIXED AND VARIABLE COSTS AND BENEFITS

Cost accountants customarily insist upon at least a rough distinction between the fixed and variable costs of any enterprise. Fixed costs are more or less unavoidable and stable costs that are attached to any particular kind of enterprise, while variable costs are more or less avoidable and unstable. For example, the total costs of driving to work every day might include exactly and unavoidably a twenty-five cent toll-bridge charge (a fixed cost) plus from zero to fifty cents worth of extra gasoline occasionally for being caught in a traffic jam (a variable cost).

The distinction between variable and fixed costs is a rough one insofar as what is counted as fixed or variable depends greatly upon (in our terminology) the size and composition of one's region of analysis. Generally, the larger and more complex the region, the smaller the variability. (Horngren (1962)) A driver might, for example, regard the variable cost cited above as a fixed cost if he were interested in determining his total cost of driving to work this year. Here, as everywhere else, variability is partially a function of one's units or bases of measurement.

A distinction between fixed and variable benefits is evidently as viable as that between fixed and variable costs. Thus, we may say that the fixed benefits of an enterprise are more or less "unavoidable" and stable benefits attached to it, while variable benefits are more or less "avoidable" and unstable. For example, a fixed benefit accruing to our hypothetical driver for using a certain toll-bridge might be the pleasure he receives from the friendly smile of a toll-clerk, while a variable benefit might be a certain time-saving.

The "enterprise" of particular interest to us is still decision-making and, more precisely, decision processes and their products, practical and cognitive decisions. Thus, we want to know something about the structure of fixed and variable costs and benefits of decision processes and decisions.

6   METHODS, MATERIALS AND PERSONNEL BENEFITS AND COSTS

On the basis of my analysis of possibilities and points of view from which any feature of a decision situation can be examined (VII 4), it is apparent that many kinds of fixed and variable costs and benefits might be attached to any decision process or decision. Broadly speaking, these will include the full range of monetary and non-monetary or social costs as these terms are generally used in the current literature. (See, for example, Coase (1960), Bauer (1966), Suchman (1967), Dror (1968) and A.I. Goldman (1970).) What is perhaps less obvious is the fact that three other useful subdivisions may be distinguished. There are fixed and variable costs and benefits of methods, materials and personnel. It is usually the case that some of these subdivisions are more significant than others for certain points of view, processes and decisions, e.g., one seldom has moral materials except in a loose, indirect or derivative sense. But in my review of each of these three classifications I shall not examine all possibilities.

Methods costs and methods benefits are all those costs and benefits that fall upon a recipient population as a result of a decision-maker using a decision process or making a decision in a particular way, or with a particular technique or method. Clearly the benefits and costs of employing some processes or making some decisions will vary with the method, manner or fashion in which the processes are employed or the decisions made. For example, a simple group decision process like majority rule by a show of hands can become excessively costly if it is used in a manner which militates against a discussion of the issues that is logically coherent and generally tolerable physically (it doesn't take too much time and energy too often), economically (it does not cost too much in dollars and cents) and socially (it does not lead to breakdowns in the social fabric of the group, i.e., to cliques and schisms). Similarly, the benefits of using such a process tend to increase when it is used in a manner that is acceptable logically, morally, legally and so on.

Material costs and material benefits are all those costs and benefits in the form of raw material and equipment that fall upon a recipient population as a result of a decision-maker using a certain decision process or

making   a certain decision.   For example, the material costs
of using certain   processes   and   making   certain   decisions
concerning   the quality of life in some region might involve
highspeed computers (technological material),   cash   outlays
(economic   material)   and   fuel   and   power   of   one sort or
another to keep technological   artifacts   running   (physical
material).   The   material benefits of using these processes
and making these decisions   might   include   more   attractive
housing   (esthetic   material),   more   cash on hand (economic
material) and more time and   energy   for   hobbies   (physical
material).

        Personnel costs and personnel benefits are easier
to illustrate than to define.   Roughly speaking they are all
those   benefits   and costs that tend to be distinctive of and
inhere in human beings.   For example, the personnel costs in
terms   of   education   and   experience   for   using   certain
processes and making certain decisions might include that of
a   lawyer   (legal   personnel   cost),   minister   (religious
personnel cost)   or   psychiatrist   (psychological   personnel
cost).   That   is,   one   might   want   or   need   to bring the
education   and   experience   of   one   or   another   of   these
professionals to bear on a certain problem, and not merely a
certain   method   or   some particular material.   On the other
hand, the   use   of   certain   processes   and   making   certain
decisions   may   yield   personnel   benefits   in   the   form of
increased   legal,   moral   or   political   education   and
experience.

7   PERSUASION AND PROTECTION COSTS AND BENEFITS

        All of the kinds of costs and benefits considered
so   far   may arise as a result of decision-makers attempting
to bargain with or persuade   others   to   act   in   a   certain
fashion,   or   to   protect   recipient populations against the
action of others.   I refer to the former kinds of   costs   as
'persuasion'   or   'bargaining   costs'   and   to the latter as
'protection   costs'.   Buchanan   and   Tullock   (1962)   have
examined the relations between such costs and group decision
processes   requiring   various proportions of group agreement
in order to produce a decision that would be binding on   the
whole   group.   They concluded (not entirely correctly as we
shall   see shortly) that if all other things   are   equal,   as
the   necessary   proportion   increases,   persuasion   costs
increase while protection   costs   decrease.   That   is,   the
persuasion   costs required for a simple majority are smaller
than those for an absolute majority, the latter are   smaller
than   those   for two-thirds and the latter are still smaller
than those required for unanimity.   On the other   hand,   the
protection   costs   required   with unanimity are smaller than
those with two-thirds which   are   smaller   than   those   with
simple majority rule.

What should be emphasized first about Buchanan and Tullock's analysis is that bargaining or persuasion costs seem to vary more with the peculiar <u>qualities</u> of group members than with their quantity. As every school teacher knows, the cost of "selling" a particular idea to three different classes of roughly the same size can vary considerably. What is vitally important to these costs is the past experience, training, industry, interest, ability, temperament, manners, etc. of both students and teacher. Similarly, the crucial variables involved in the bargaining and persuasion costs required for a particular group to employ a particular procedure are those that reflect these qualities. Buchanan and Tullock insist that one cannot answer the question, "What proportion of a group must agree in order to bind the whole group to their decision?", until one knows what issue is before them. I would suggest that the question cannot be answered until one also knows what personal qualities (education, temperament, experience, etc.) are required and possessed by the group members.

Second, although it must be granted that the cost of protecting an individual against <u>some</u> of the activities of others decreases as the decisive proportion increases, the cost of protecting an individual against some of these activities must increase. Moreover, the latter increase cannot be regarded as a product of bargaining or persuasion. For example, consider the training costs for members of some decision-making group. Generally, the larger the group, the higher the training costs. Furthermore, in one way or another, each member must obtain protection against losses resulting from the activities of group members in their training programs. Training costs usually include some for raw materials, textbooks, reference libraries, teachers, administrators, rooms, furniture, etc. and the quantity and total costs of these resources must increase with the number of trained people required. Therefore, the amount of protection costs one must incur in order to be covered against losses arising from the use of these resources must also increase with the required number of trained people. (Within limits, of course, we may reduce some of the costs per individual by training more people at the same time, but this does not alter my claim with respect to total costs.) Similarly, as more resources of any sort are required, more protection is required , and more resources are usually required whenever the size of the decisive proportion increases. Hence, contrary to the view suggested by Buchanan and Tullock, some protection costs vary in the <u>same</u> direction as bargaining costs with respect to the decisive proportion.

While the benefits attached to persuasion and protection will almost certainly vary with the proportion of a group required to produce a decision that is binding on the whole group, there seems to be no good reason to expect that   the variation will take any one particular form rather than another.   If support for a decision were counted as   a benefit,   then   it   would be trivially true that the greater the required proportion, the greater the   benefits   attached to   any decision that happens to be made.   But it would be a mistake to regard support as a benefit because   support   for certain   decisions   might   well   be   costly   rather   than beneficial.   I think, therefore, that the most that   can   be said   about   persuasion   and protection benefits is what was said above.

8   RETENTION, INSURANCE AND PREVENTION COSTS   AND   BENEFITS

The   problem   of protecting recipient populations from the "external effects" of other people's decisions   has been   given   considerable   attention by political scientists and   philosophers.   The   protection   costs   incurred   might involve   expenses   arising   from   three   kinds of protective devices,   namely,   devices   of   prevention,   insurance   and retention.   Following   Denenberg   et al.   (1964), it will be worthwhile to review these alternatives in turn.

When members   of   recipient   populations   protect themselves   against losses due to the decisions of others by maintaining enough assets to be able   to   sustain   any   loss arising from those decisions, they are protecting themselves by retention of the risk.   That is, rather than transferring the   risk   of   loss   to someone else (taking out insurance), they are retaining   it   themselves.   For   example,   a   very conservative   city   council   that   proposes   urban   renewal programs whose   estimated   costs   are   always   less   than   a certain   set   and   safe amount of immediately available cash could be regarded as protecting itself by retention   against losses   resulting   from   faulty programs.   Even if a program should turn out to be a total loss, the council   would   have enough   cash   to meet its other commitments.   Similarly, the council might direct its planning board to use a   particular decision   procedure   in   selecting programs, without seeking outside help to protect itself against losses resulting from the application of that procedure.

As I have parenthetically suggested, when members of recipient populations protect themselves   against   losses resulting   from   the decisions of others by transferring the risk of such losses to someone   else,   they   are   protecting themselves   by   insurance.   The advantage of insurance over retention is primarily the reduction of assets that one must maintain more or less secure and, therefore,   more   or   less idle   and   unproductive.   With insurance one obtains needed protection for a relatively small price, which allows one to use the remainder of one's assets   for   other   things.   For example,   when   a   traveler   buys the low cost single flight

insurance before he puts himself in the hands of numerous
airline employees, he is transferring the risk of loss that
he or his family might suffer as a result of one or more of
those employees making a faulty decision. Moreover, he is
transferring the risk of loss that might result from a
breakdown of any of the naturally fallible routine and
emergency procedures employed by airlines.

        The most thorough way for members of recipient
populations to protect themselves against losses resulting
from the decisions of others is through <u>prevention</u>, i.e.,
the elimination of the sources of risk. For example, the
city council might cut off all renewal programs and the
prospective flyer might cancel his trip. If less drastic
tactics are preferred, the council might try to slow down
urban deterioration by strengthening its building and
maintenance codes and their enforcement. Concomitantly,
clean-up programs could be initiated with teach-ins,
contests, prizes and other sorts of incentive-producing
techniques.

        Again, the other side of the coin of the costs of
retention, insurance and prevention consists of all the
benefits of these devices. The general advantage of
insurance has already been cited. Prevention is even more
advantageous where it is feasible, because it allows one to
escape even temporary losses with whatever ancillary
inconveniences they might generate. When retention is
genuine and not merely the product of one's inability to
obtain insurance or to discover a satisfactory program of
prevention, it is obviously a sign of self-sufficiency.
Self-sufficiency then, is its distinctive benefit.

CHAPTER XIII

The Ethics of Belief: A Synthesis

1   INTRODUCTION

The question addressed in this Chapter has an illustrious philosophic history going back at least to W.K. Clifford's (1886) classic paper, "The Ethics of Belief." Briefly put, the question is: Is there an ethics of belief? In terms of the discussion in this book, the question is: Is cognitive decision-making subject to moral appraisal? Granted that one might be morally praiseworthy or blameworthy for deciding to do something (i.e., for making a particular practical decision), the question is: Is one ever morally praiseworthy or blameworthy for deciding that something is or is not the case? Clifford answered this question one way and James (in James (1956)) answered it in another way. In this Chapter I show that the views espoused by these men were two sides of a single coin. More importantly, the positive thesis defended here is that insofar as one engages in an activity designed to discover truth or avoid falsehood, one is engaged in an activity which is essentially moral, i.e., it is not morally neutral. Thus, for example, the scientific enterprise is not morally neutral or value-free, but essentially moral. (That does not mean, of course, that every particular act of every particular scientist is essentially moral.)

In the next Section I explain the difference between positive and negative moral maxims. The cases for and against a negative ethics of belief are presented in

Sections Three and Four. In the fifth and sixth Sections
the cases for and against a positive ethics of belief are
developed. Following this, in the final Section I offer a
critique of apparently plausible but faulty objections to
any version of an ethics of belief.

2   POSITIVE AND NEGATIVE MORAL MAXIMS

        'Moral' and 'ethical', as most philosophers know,
may be contrasted with their complements 'nonmoral' and
'nonethical' or with their contraries 'immoral' or
'unethical'. In the case of contraries, goodness and
badness are attached to the connotations, but not in the
case of complements. In the latter, 'moral' is contrased
with things like political, psychological, technical and so
on. Lewis (1969) divided the moral or ethical into a wider
class of principles dealing with action generally and a
narrower class dealing with what we usually regard as
morality proper. The wider class of moral concerns seems to
be coextensive with what some people call 'praxiology'
nowadays. (See, for example, Kotarbinski (1965) and
Michalos (1972).) At any rate, the only thing that hangs on
this distinction is one's understanding of Lewis's ethics of
belief. In his view, "...cognitive correctness is itself a
moral concern, in the broad sense of 'moral'. (Lewis (1969,
p. 163), emphasis added) Hence, little more will be said
about his view here.

        It is the narrower sense of 'moral' that is of
primary interest in this Chapter. I take it that something
is morally good if and only if it is good from a (narrow)
moral point of view, good on moral grounds or good for moral
reasons. Such a view, such grounds or reasons would include
maxims like "One ought to be fair-minded and treat people
fairly or justly" (Principle of Justice), "One ought to be
honest and speak the truth as one sees it, deceive no one."
(Principle of Honesty or Integrity), and "One ought to be or
do good rather than evil." (Principle of Benevolence). We
need not be concerned with the justification or the
operationalization of these principles, so long as we all
find them acceptable. i.e., we believe that violations are
prima facie, at least, morally wrong. However, it should be
noticed that each one is formulated as a prescription for
being a certain sort of person as well as for acting in a
certain way. This was done following the fairly standard
view that morality concerns both character and action.

        One other distinction is necessary before we can
lay out our central set of options. The following quotation
from James will serve as an introduction.

"There are two ways of looking at our duty in the matter of opinion... We <u>must</u> <u>know</u> <u>the</u> <u>truth</u>; and we <u>must</u> <u>avoid</u> <u>error</u>... they are two separable laws ... We may regard the chase for truth as paramount ... or we may, on the other hand, treat the avoidance of error as more imperative, and let truth take its chance. (James (1956, p. 17))

Roughly speaking, the distinction James is suggesting is the sort that obtains between so-called affirmative action and equal opportunity employers, or between a mother who urges her son to try to find honest work and one who tells him to at least stay out of trouble. In other words, one might subscribe to a <u>positive</u> ethical maxim of cognitive decision-making such as "One ought to pursue the truth and believe it.", or a <u>negative</u> maxim such as "One ought to avoid falsehood and <u>disbelieve</u> (or at least withhold belief from) it." Accordingly, we have four options. One might hold that there <u>can</u> be logically coherent and plausible

(1) positive and negative moral maxims of cognitive decision-making

(2) positive but not negative maxims

(3) not positive but negative maxims

(4) neither positive nor negative maxims.

Moreover, since the maxims would provide the backbone of a moral code, anyone accepting the fourth position would be opposed to an ethics of belief on logical grounds and anyone favouring such an ethical system would accept one or the other three positions.

3 THE CASE FOR A NEGATIVE ETHICS OF BELIEF

By the phrase 'negative ethics of belief', I mean an ethical code based on a negative maxim like "One ought to avoid falsehood and disbelieve (or at least withold belief from) it." or "One ought to avoid believing anything on insufficient or inadequate evidence." Strictly speaking, these two maxims are not equivalent unless it is assumed that <u>the</u> <u>only</u> way to avoid falsehood is to withhold belief in propositions for which one has inadequate evidence. In fact, in Clifford's (1886) classic defense of such an ethics, this assumption is frequently, if not always, made. I will say more about these maxims later.

Clifford offers several different but closely related arguments which are as intriguing as they are vague.

For those to be considered below, it may be assumed that the relation of belief to action is at most contingent, i.e., the fact that someone believes something does not logically imply that he will act in certain ways, but certain actions are as a matter of fact often correlated with certain beliefs. That is almost certainly a weaker assumption than Clifford would have preferred, but it is strong enough to do the job. (See Clifford (1886, p. 342).) I also assume, though Clifford does not make the distinction, that it is prima facie duties or obligations that are our concern, rather than duties or obligations simpliciter. Finally, since he pretty clearly shifts from talking about holding a belief to acquiring it in the first place (i.e., the act of deciding that), I will try to straighten out his views with paraphrasing. The first argument we will consider (3.1) is not sound, but it is used so often in one form or another by Clifford that it is worthwhile to get it out in the open and dispose of it. The other three arguments in this Section (3.2 to 3.4) seem to provide good reasons for the maxim of avoiding falsehood.

Clifford's most frequently used argument runs as follows. (Clifford (1886, p. 342))

3.1 Because we are social beings, beliefs tend to be held in common. For any task men pursue in common with others, each man has a moral obligation to hold up his own end. If one holds a belief on insufficient evidence, one neglects that duty.

To neglect a duty is to violate the Principle of Justice. Hence, it is morally wrong to hold a belief on insufficient evidence. (See also James (1956, p. 140) and Tomas (1957, p. 16).)

Clifford (1886, pp. 342-343) spells out the first premise of 3.1 thus:

"And no one man's belief is in any case a private matter which concerns himself alone. Our lives are guided by that general conception of the course of things which has been created by society for social purposes. Our words, our phrases, our forms and processes and modes of thought, are common property, fashioned and perfected from age to age; an heirloom which every succeeding generation inherits as a precious deposit and a sacred trust to be handed on to the next one, not unchanged but enlarged and purified, with some clear marks of its proper handiwork".

Ignoring the flowery parts of this passage, it seems unobjectionable, as do the first, second and fourth premises. It is really only the third premise that might create problems. Why should holding a belief on insufficient evidence count as neglecting one's duty to contribute a fair share of the labour necessary to sustain a collective good? Presumably what is required here is the assumption that the structure of beliefs held by a community is bonded together by sufficient evidence also held jointly. Then, anyone holding a belief without sufficient evidence would, as it were, be guilty of trying to hold only the structure without holding the foundation too. Altering our metaphor slightly, imagine a tent held up by several people with one hand on ropes holding the roof on and the other hand on ropes holding the floor taut. Then one who dropped his floor rope would be guilty of jeopardizing the shape of the tent. Similarly, one who holds beliefs on insufficient evidence only does part of what one is required to do to keep the total shape of our beliefs intact.

Plausible as this argument may sound, I think it is question-begging insofar as it requires the assumption that the structure of beliefs held by a community must be bonded together by sufficient evidence -- held jointly or not. To see that this is so, one need only ask: Why is sufficient evidence required to bond the structure of beliefs together? Why not merely some significant evidence or, indeed, some nonevidential reason like faith or hope? That, of course, is roughly the sort of question James put to Clifford in "The Will to Believe". (James (1956)) Clifford would be assuming here precisely what has to be demonstrated, namely, that if one has a good reason for believing any proposition to be true then one must have sufficient evidence for it, i.e., sufficient evidence is the only warrant for believing a proposition to be true.

Another argument suggested by Clifford arises from the following. "Habitual want of care about what I believe leads to habitual want of care in others about the truth of what is told me". (Clifford (1886, p. 345))

That is,

3.2   When one is careless about the reasons one has for the beliefs one holds, others tend to become careless about the reasons for the views they express toward one.

As others become careless, they tend to supply one with falsehoods; so one becomes surrounded by "a thick atmosphere of falsehood and fraud".

To surround a person with "falsehood and fraud" is to violate the Principle of Honesty.

Hence, it is morally wrong to be careless about the reasons one has for the beliefs one holds.

Beginning with the first two premises of 3.2, Clifford also suggests the following finish.

3.3 To encourage others to surround a person with "falsehood and fraud" is to violate the Principle of Benevolence.

Hence, it is morally wrong to be careless about the reasons one has for the beliefs one holds.

The difference between 3.2 and 3.3 is that the former focuses on the evil of drowning a person in "falsehood and fraud" while the latter focuses on the evil of encouraging people to perform such an act. It's wrong to do it and to help people to do it.

Although I have not run any controlled experiments to determine whether the effects posited in the first premise of 3.2 and 3.3 occur always, usually or hardly ever, casual observation seems to suggest that the effects occur often enough not to be swiftly discounted. There is, of course, plenty of evidence on the pressures for and likelihood of individual conformity to group norms which is at least indirect support for this premise. (Hare, Borgatta and Bales (1955)) The second premise is also basically empirical, though it presupposes that in fact careless thinkers have more false beliefs than careful thinkers. If this is not true, then one of the main reasons one might have for being a careful thinker is lost. I presume it is true. Similarly, I presume the final premises of 3.2 and 3.3 are unobjectionable.

Again, Clifford (1886, p. 342) argues

3.4 Insofar as one holds beliefs dogmatically one is less inclined to give issues a fair hearing.

Insofar as one is less inclined to give issues a fair hearing, one is inclined to violate the Principle of Justice.

Hence, it is morally wrong to hold beliefs dogmatically.

As the first premise is formulated, it is virtually analytic. To hold beliefs dogmatically is just to automatically reject contrary views and arguments, and that is certainly not compatible with fairness. Unless one insists that "fair-mindedness" can only apply to the adjudication of conflicting interests among people, the second premise is also unobjectionable. I should think, however, that the burden of proof would be on the insister in this case. Accordingly, the conclusion of 3.4 strikes me as true.

A couple of pages later Clifford asserts that "Every time we let ourselves believe for unworthy reasons we weaken our powers of self-control, of doubting, of judicially and fairly weighing evidence". (Clifford (1886, pp. 344-345), emphasis added.) This suggests a variant of 3.4 in which the error is not in holding the belief but in deciding that it is true.

4   THE CASE AGAINST A NEGATIVE ETHICS OF BELIEF

As indicated earlier, James sought to discredit what he took to be Clifford's position. In fact, Clifford unwittingly presented arguments in defense of at least two different basic maxims for a negative ethics of belief. Furthermore, as will be explained shortly, it is only the maxim linking belief to sufficient evidence that James opposed, not the maxim against belief in falsehoods. In the following passage James suggests three reasons for finding

> "...it impossible to go with Clifford. We must remember that these feelings of our duty about either truth or error are in any case only expressions of our passional life ... he who says 'Better go without belief forever than believe a lie!' merely shows his own preponderant private horror of becoming a dupe ... but I can believe that worse things than being duped may happen to a man in this world: so Clifford's exhortation has to my ears a thoroughly fantastic sound. ... In a world where we are so certain to incur errors in spite of all our caution, a certain lightness of heart seems healthier than this excessive nervousness on their behalf". (James (1956, pp. 17-19))

The first suggestion, that "these feelings of our duty" are "only expressions of our passional life", seems to be tantamount to the admission that we have reached a level of analysis at which the giving of reasons necessarily gives way to the expression of attitudes. That hardly seems plausible even for James, since he does try to present reasons for his view. His second suggestion is that considering the evils which may fall upon a person in this world, believing a falsehood is among the least of our worries. I suppose this should only be taken lightly, since the consequences of some beliefs turning out false might be the overturning of one's whole orientation toward life, one's whole Weltanschauung, and that could be serious indeed. Finally, he suggests that we are so prone to error that one ought to maintain "a certain lightness of heart" toward it -- rather than become what Lyndon Johnson used to call "a nervous Nellie". I imagine neither James nor anyone else knows how prone to error most people are, but again, I would think that the claim must be taken lightly at best.

Taking these arguments together, I do not think we get to the heart of James's position. The latter comes out most clearly in the following passages.

> "There are ... cases where a fact cannot come at all unless a preliminary faith exists in its coming. And where faith in a fact can help create the fact, that would be an insane logic which should say that faith running ahead of scientific evidence is the 'lowest kind of immorality' into which a thinking being can fall. ... a rule of thinking which would absolutely prevent me from acknowledging certain kinds of truth if those kinds of truth were really there, would be an irrational rule". (James (1956, pp. 25-28))

Thus, for example, one cannot have trusted friends unless one believes that they are trustworthy without sufficient evidence, i.e., without evidence that would guarantee their fidelity. Since a maxim proscribing belief on insufficient evidence would "absolutely prevent" one from deciding that a friend was trustworthy without serious testing, such a maxim should be rejected.

What James has hit upon in this passage is a species of prudential or pragmatic reasoning leading to belief. Schematically it might be represented thus:

PRAGMATIC SCHEMA

1.   p $\begin{cases} \text{only if} \\ \text{usually only if} \\ \text{probably only if} \end{cases}$ x believes that p.

2.   x would like it to be the case that p.

3.   So, x believes that p.

This pragmatic schema is roughly similar to traditional maxims of practical reasoning, e.g.,

> If performing action z is (usually, probably) a necessary condition of it being the case that p and x wants the latter, then x ought (rationally, prudentially) to perform action z.

For example,

> If believing that I can outrun Newberry is
> (usually, probably) a necessary condition of my
> being able to outrun him, and I want to be able
> to outrun him, then I ought (rationally,
> prudentially) to believe that I can. (See also
> Rescher (1969c) and Norris (1975).)

However, the conclusion of our schema is not that
one ought to do something, but that one believes something.
Although the premises do, I think, provide good grounds for
the practical conclusion, it is the cognitive conclusion
that is most interesting. For here we have not evidential
i.e., straight deductive or (narrowly) inductive) grounds
for believing that something is the case, but purely
pragmatic, prudential or teleological grounds. We have good
reasons for belief, but not good evidence! That I find at
once exciting and frightening. It is exciting because such
grounds have been almost entirely neglected by
epistemologists so far as I know, and it is frightening
because no one knows what one might have good pragmatic
reasons for believing. Some people, of course, have tried
to pull the Almighty Himself out of this hat!   I wish I
could pursue all the niceties of pragmatic schemata, but
that is both beyond me and the plan of this book. So I will
return directly to James.

What surprises me about James's approach here is
that he does not try to rest his case on moral grounds,
following Clifford, for instance. Instead, he complains
that it would be "an insane logic" and an "irrational rule"
which would proscribe belief without sufficient evidence.
But why, after all, isn't it just plain morally wrong to
prevent people from deciding that their friends or, indeed,
their fellow citizens are trustworthy prior to tests?
"Don't trust anyone until he has proven worthy." is the
sort of maxim which, if followed, would virtually destroy
the social fabric of any community. One must trust the
butcher not to color the meat, the doctor to conscientiously
prescribe therapy, the mechanic to fix exactly what is
broken, the teacher to try to put decent ideas into our
children's heads, and so on. Without such trust there can
be no community, no social or moral life, no friendship and
no love. A maxim with these consequences must be pronounced
morally offensive, and that seems to be as strong an
objection as one could raise against it.

In James's final shot against the negative maxim,
he says, "...if we believe that no bell in us tolls to let
us know for certain when truth is in our grasp, then it
seems a piece of idle fantasticality to preach so solemnly
our duty of waiting for the bell." (James (1956, p. 30)) In
other words, there is no logical point in proscribing the

acceptance of beliefs on insufficient evidence because no one knows when evidence really is sufficient. One might as well tell people not to believe anything at all or, on the contrary, to believe whatever they please.

Although I think it must be admitted that there is no single, all purpose, sure-fire criterion of sufficiency for evidence, it is hardly the case that we are entirely at sea in this area. For all sorts of everyday occurrences as well as for scientific research and judicial proceedings we are able to reach widespread agreement about what counts as sufficient evidence. Case by case, the problems are by no means insurmountable, although in general and in the abstract they may be.

5   THE CASE FOR A POSITIVE ETHICS OF BELIEF

Briefly and roughly the conclusion reached in the preceding two Sections is that there is a negative ethics of belief, i.e. cognitive decision-making can be morally right or good, wrong or bad. Furthermore, it was shown that James clearly saw that there is a difference between such a view and what I have called a positive ethics of belief, and he evidently opted for the latter. From what was said in the preceding Section and the following remarks we may formulate the sort of argument he would want to use.

> "The importance to human life of having true beliefs about matters of fact is a thing too notorious. We live in a world of realities that can be infinitely useful or infinitely harmful. Ideas that tell us which of them to expect count as the true ideas in all this primary sphere of verification, and the pursuit of such ideas is a primary human duty. The possession of truth, so far from being here an end in itself, is only a preliminary means towards other vital satisfactions. ... Our obligation to seek truth is part of our general obligation to do what pays." (James (1955, pp. 134, 150); emphasis added.)

That is,

5.1   We have a moral obligation to try to preserve human life. "The possession of truth ... is only a preliminary means ... toward that end."

The pursuit of truth is often if not always necessary for its possession. Hence, "the pursuit of such ideas is a primary human duty."

In short, we are obliged to pursue that course of action which, often enough, is necessary to obtain a morally prescribed end.

The first premise of this argument follows immediately from the universally recognised Right to Life. The second premise strikes me just about as it struck James, namely, as "a thing too notorious." The third premise is phrased as it is to avoid the objection that one might after all just stumble upon the truth. Of course one might, but I do not believe that is the usual or most promising way to find it. Given these premises then, there does not seem to be any escape from the conclusion. That is, James has given us one good reason to accept a positive ethics of belief.

As James laments elsewhere, he and other pragmatists paid dearly for all their references to payments, cash value, practical consequences, working and utility. The cost, he suggests, was in the form of the "solemn attribution of ... rubbish to us ..." (James (1909, p. 212)) I will not review the literature on the nature of the pay-offs actually or usually envisioned by pragmatists generally or James in particular. However, I should point out that if the reference to payment in the last sentence of the quoted paragraph above is understood in terms of the preservation of human life, then that sentence is roughly only a truncated version of the argument set out for him.

Another argument in favor of a positive ethics of belief runs as follows.

5.2   If there is a moral obligation to speak the truth as one sees it then there is a similar obligation to try to see it as it is. There is a moral obligation to speak the truth as one sees it (Principle of Honesty). Hence, there is a moral obligation to pursue the truth, i.e., to try to see the world as it is.

This argument clearly stands or falls with the first premise. Suppose it is false. If one has no obligation to try to find the truth, then the obligation to speak the truth is pointless. "Believe whatever you like for whatever reasons you like but always say what you believe." is a silly commandment because there is no virtue, intellectual or moral, in speaking falsehoods or in some kinds of reasons. That is, not all reasons are good reasons and not everything one likes is worth sharing. Thus, an unconditioned command to say whatever you believe cannot be a moral maxim, though it may be good psychotherapy. Consequently, the first premise of this argument must be accepted and with it, the argument itself.

6   THE CASE AGAINST A POSITIVE ETHICS OF BELIEF

It might be argued that because, for example, a little philosophy makes one an atheist or at least an agnostic, one has no obligation to pursue the truth. Better to be a dogmatic believer than a doubter or a disbeliever. I do not doubt at all that one could imagine cases in which blatant dogmatism has short run results that are preferable to the results of disbelief or agnosticism. But to admit that is to admit nothing more than that the obligations and duties we are discussing are necessarily prima facie in character. It is a big step from this to the conclusion that we have a prima facie obligation to be dogmatic because sometimes dogmatism has more benefits than costs. If that line of argumentation were accepted then we would have similar obligations to lie and steal as well. In fact, the moral realm might be turned virtually up-side down. Accordingly, I reject this line without reservation.

7   THE CASE AGAINST ANY ETHICS OF BELIEF

At this point everything that I have to say in favor of an ethics of belief based on a negative and a positive maxim has been said. In the remaining paragraphs of this Section then, I will present apparently plausible objections to the position defended above and try to show that they are unacceptable.

7.1   The idea of an ethics of belief or of cognitive decision-making being moral or immoral is just so much self-serving sop. Only an academic mind or worse, a philosophic mind, would seriously entertain the notion that deciding that something is the case or holding on to a belief once acquired could be a moral act. No one else would be inclined to try to get moral credit for thinking straight.

Reply. This objection is obviously just an argumentum ad hominem. Of course an ethics of belief would have special relevance for academics of all kinds, philosophers, scientists or whatever. But that does not make the idea true or false, sound or silly. Our critics will have to aim higher.

7.2   Suppose it is granted for the sake of argument that there is, as some ancient philosophers might have said, moral virtue in intellectual virtue. It still would not follow that cognitive decisions are moral or immoral. Recall, for example, Lewis's view that the sense of 'moral' involved is wide rather than narrow. Alternatively, consider the following remarks by Thomas Aquinas.

"Other intellectual virtues [wisdom, science and art] can, but prudence cannot, be without moral virtue. The reason for this is that prudence is right reason about things to be done, and this not merely in general, but also in the particular, where action takes place. ... Consequently ... in order that he be rightly disposed with regard to the particular principles of action, viz., the ends, he needs to be perfected by certain habits, whereby it becomes connatural to man, as it were, to judge rightly about the end. This is done by moral virtue, for the virtuous man judges rightly of the end of virtue, because such as a man is, such does the end seem to him.Consequently the right reason about things to be done, viz., prudence, requires man to have moral virtue". (Pegis (1945, p. 447))

In other words, Aquinas holds that morality can play a role in decision-making only insofar as beliefs are related to overt actions, i.e., only in the realm of what he calls 'prudence'. In that realm there is moral virtue in intellectual virtue, but that is only possible because the decisions made are not merely cognitive.

Reply. Aquinas's view may be true, but it is question-begging to merely assert it in this manner. After all, what has to be shown is not that one can classify so-called intellectual virtues so that cognitive decisions never have any moral import, but that such a classification does justice to all the relevant facts or arguments. This sort of a justification has not been provided.

7.3 If cognitive decision-making has moral import then all good scientists, philosophers and mathematicians must be morally good. If that doesn't destroy the thesis once and for all, what else can?

Reply. This argument is a non-sequitur. One might just as well argue that anyone who performs morally good actions is morally good. What if he is also performing morally bad actions on the side? For example, he might be murdering people for money and giving all the money to his favorite charity. Or, what if he performs morally good but trivial actions and one or two morally horrendous and highly significant actions? For example, he might regularly pay his grocery bills until one day he murders his grocer and every one else in the store. Clearly, the first premise of 7.3 will have to be tightened up in order to have any plausibility.

7.4 If cognitive decision-making has moral import then a mathematician doing his sums correctly (with no inclination or opportunity to share his results with others) is doing something that is morally right or good. That is, granted that he is not neglecting some duty or doing anything else on the side which is morally reprehensible, we must say that there is moral virtue in what he is doing. That is just an outrageous departure from common sense and ordinary usage. Imagine trying to persuade a man on the street that an accountant correctly multiplying 3728 by 261 is doing something that is as morally significant as telling his neighbour the true product!

Reply. In fact, of course, the last sentence is misleading. Insofar as both acts have moral significance they are in the same class, but it does not follow that each act has the same amount of moral virtue. The fact that all moral acts are praiseworthy does not imply that they are all equally praiseworthy. Whether or not finding the correct product would be as morally praiseworthy as truthfully giving the information to one's neighbor is a debatable question. Would giving the information to a total stranger merit more praise than giving it to a friend? I don't think one can answer such questions without considerable development of the cases.

For its relevance, if not for the beauty of the prose, the following passage for Lundberg's (1968) classic The Rich and the Super-Rich is worth repeating.

"... in the process of being educated there is always the danger that the individual will acquire scruples, a fact dimly sensed by some of the neo-conservatives who rail against the school system as "Communistic". These scruples, unless they are casuistically beveled around the edges with great care, are a distinct handicap to the full-fledged money-maker, who must in every situation be plastically opportunistic. But a person who has had it deeply impressed upon him that he must make exact reports of careful laboratory experiments, must conduct exact computations in mathematics and logic, must produce exact translations and echoes of foreign languages, must write faithful reports of correct readings and must be at least imaginatively aware of the world in its diversity, and who has learned these lessons well, must invariably discover that some element of scrupulosity -- even if he hasn't been subject to moral indoctrination -- has been impressed on his psyche. If he enters upon money-making in a world bazaar where approximate truths, vague deceptions, sneak maneuvers, half promises and even bald falsehoods are the widely admired and heavily rewarded order of the day he must make casuistic adjustments of his standards. The very process of laboriously making the adjustment, even if he succeeds, puts him at a disadvantage vis-a-vis the unschooled, who need waste no

energy on such adjustments, who pick up anything
lying around loose as easily as they breath.
Some educated people can't make even a partial
adjustment to the market bazaar, and their
disgraceful bank accounts show it. They are, as
even their wives sometimes kindly inform them,
failures, though they are doing something
conceded to be useful such as instructing
children or enforcing the law. They can inscribe
after their names a big "F" and go stand in a
corner under a dunce cap as the propaganda
dervishes scream about success". (Lundberg
(1968, pp. 107-108))

The rest of 7.4 is straightforward, but
answerable. If one believes, as I and many others do, that
it is logically possible, say, to dedicate one's life to
learning and leave the comfort of human communities (with
all that such a severance implies) and be or become a good
person by doing just that, then there is nothing outrageous
or extraordinary about the thesis being defended here. In
short, the thesis of the moral significance of cognitive
decision-making must be not only logically coherent but true
as well.

7.5 Price (1966, p. 113) objected to the idea of
an ethics of belief on the following grounds. "If we are to
be allowed, "he wrote, "or even encouraged, to blame
[people] for the way they direct their thoughts, as well as
for their actions, there will be a perfect orgy of moral
indignation and condemnation, and charity will almost
disappear from the world".

Reply. This is an implausible moral argument
resting on equally implausible empirical grounds. With
respect to the latter, I am not aware of persuasive evidence
that would suggest that an "orgy of moral indignation" would
be generated by people committed to an ethics of belief.
With respect to the former, one must recall argument 5.2
above. Insisting that people behave in certain ways
without insisting that they also have good reasons for their
behaviour is tantamount to treating people like machines.
After all, it is not mindless behaviour that makes us human,
but the fact that this behaviour is accompanied by
appropriate thoughts and feelings.

Appendix:
Decision-Making in Committees*

1   INTRODUCTION

This paper has two aims, one fairly general and the other fairly specific. The general aim is to provide a basis for logical and empirical investigations of a particular type of group-decision procedure. The type is distinguished by the fact that inequalities in the "weight" of the individual voters and their votes are permitted. For reasons which will become clear shortly, if such procedures are practicable at all, they would seem to be so only for small groups, say, of two to fifteen people. Since most committees contain less than fifteen members, if such procedures are practicable at all, they should be practicable for committees. Hence, our discussion is oriented toward decision-making in committees.

The more specific aim of this paper is to introduce and critically evaluate certain prima facie plausible solutions to the problem of selecting an acceptable group-decision procedure. We begin with a precise statement of the problem in Section Two. In Section Three five informal necessary conditions of adequacy for proposed solutions are introduced. Section Four introduces the notion of "weights of influence" and defines seven fundamental types of distributions. This is followed by a presentation of six more or less plausible "voting schemes" that involve the application of various "weights of influence." In Sections Six and Seven the constructive work

of Sections Four and Five is examined in the light of our
adequacy conditions. The upshot of this examination is,
unfortunately, that none of the six schemes appears
extraordinarily attractive.

2   THE PROBLEM

        Very often individuals are called upon to share
their decision-making capacities with others. They are
asked to serve on committees. There are many reasons for
establishing a committee, e.g., to keep people busy (Idle
hands get into trouble!), to give them a sense of
"belonging", to keep them interested, to fix responsibility,
to separate problems and solutions (divide and conquer), and
so on. Some committees are supposed to solve problems or
make decisions. They frequently plan conventions, parties,
and dances, i.e., they choose locations, entertainment,
refreshments. They select textbooks, candidates for new
positions, visiting professors, office furniture, etc.

        To avoid difficult epistemological problems which
for present purposes need not be solved, we shall assume
that a decision is made if and only if a person or group of
people come to accept a certain sentence. The sentence
would normally be in the imperative or in the indicative
mode. Since committees are social organizations with their
own rules, norms, procedures, etc., ordinarily a committee
makes a decision if and only if there is a sentence which is
accepted by the committee according to its operating rules.
The operating rules of many committees are such that when
there are conflicts of interest, the decision of the
committee might not be similar to those of any of its
members, e.g., a "compromise candidate" may become the first
choice of a committee in which no member ranked him first.

        Given the sense of "a committee decision"
explained in the last paragraph, the primary question we
shall attempt to answer in this paper is: How should the
various decisions (with respect to some issue) of the
members of a committee be amalgamated for the committee
decision to be determined in the most acceptable fashion?[1]
Three points must be made immediately about this question.
In the first place, although it is a normative sort of
question, it cannot be answered by logical analysis and
intuition alone. What we ought to do to reach more (rather
than less) acceptable committee decisions depends, among
other things, on the composition of and the issues
considered by this or that committee. That is to say,
proposals for optimal group decision-making must be guided
by some knowledge of the behavior, skills, resources,
preferences, ambitions, etc., of human beings in fairly
well-defined circumstances. Such knowledge is not only

usually meager, it is also usually difficult to obtain. In
the second place, it should be noted that in this paper the
term "acceptable" will be used in a very broad sense to
designate characteristics or dispositions frequently
referred to by such (equally vague) terms as "competent",
"wise", "good", "skillful", "enlightened", "rational", and
so on. For the purposes at hand this usage is innocuous and
convenient. Finally, it should be emphasized that we are
primarily concerned with the procedures, methods, or means
used to arrive at committee decisions, not with the
products, ends, or committee decisions themselves.[2]
Although in practice a peculiar committee decision often
leads us to question the procedure used to obtain it (just
as we might have suspicions about an argument schema which
yielded a bizarre conclusion from ostensibly true premises),
it is important to distinguish the former from the latter,
the decision from the decision procedure.

3   CRITERIA OF ADEQUACY

        Lest we become dizzy chasing our own tails,
something should be said about the necessary conditions of
adequacy that might be applied to the amalgamation
procedures offered as solutions to our problem. The
following five are consistent (jointly satisfiable) and seem
fairly plausible, although I suspect that they are neither
independent nor in any technical sense complete.[3] As we
shall see later, they are considerably stronger than they
appear.

(3.1) The procedures must be free from coercion in the
sense that committeemen are not forced to cast their votes
contrary to their preferences. This is to guarantee each
voter the opportunity to use his influence (the "weight" of
his vote) exactly as he sees fit.

(3.2) The procedures must be self-consistent or logically
coherent. This is merely a formal requirement excluding
inconsistent procedures from which contradictory decisions
could be obtained.

(3.3) The procedures must be practicable or manageable.
Practicability is bound to be relative to people and issues,
so this is bound to be a pretty unstable criterion. But if
a procedure is so complicated that for every group of people
and every sort of issue some other procedure is simpler and
equally effective, then our procedure would have to be
regarded as relatively (relative to the other procedure)
worthless. Hence, only those procedures that are manageable
for most (normal) people and some (realistic) issues will be
accepted. If as a matter of fact most issues confronting
most committees do not merit a more subtle decision

procedure   than,   say,   majority rule by a show of hands, then
our proposal(s) might   still   be   acceptable   and   valuable,
i.e.,   we   only   require practicability (which I am assuming
means some kind of superiority)   for   some   fairly   realistic
issues.[4]

(3.4)   The   procedures   must be efficient in the sense that
they   take   account   of   all   of   the   relevant   information
available   to   a   committee   for a given decision at a given
time.   What is required is not   an   everlasting   search   for
relevant data, but the elimination of procedures that cannot
process   or   make   use of relevant data already possessed by
committeemen.[5]

(3.5)   The   influence   of   each   committeeman   should   be
proportionate   to   his   relative competence. This condition
requires a more lengthy explanation and some defense, and   I
shall begin with the former.

        We   suppose a committee decision is to be reached
by "combining" the decisions of all   its   members.   If   the
committee   operates   on democratic principles, each member's
decision   influences   the   final   outcome   (the   committee
decision) in exactly the same way.   Each member receives one
vote   and if it is cast at all, it carries as much weight or
has   as   much   influence   formally   (or   legally,   or
arithmetically)   on   the   final outcome as every other vote.
(Informally or in fact, of course, every group seems to have
leaders and followers, and both types of   people   influence
each   other   in   more   or   less subtle ways.) The committee
decision itself then is usually determined by   the   majority
of   the   voters.   3.5 implies that this democratic procedure
is acceptable if and only   if   every   voter   is   exactly   as
competent   as   every other.   According to 3.5, each member's
vote should carry only   as   much   weight   or   have   as   much
influence   on   the   committee   decision   as   his   competence
merits.   Moreover, since the composition of and   the   issues
confronted   by committees vary, 3.5 suggests that the status
of   a   committeeman's   competence   should   be   regarded   as
relative to both of these variables.

        In   view of the vast amount of literature devoted
to the problem of equality, my defense of 3.5 will   probably
seem   much   too   brief and primitive.[6]   It is as follows.   As
the influence of a committeeman increases,   the   chances   of
committee decisions being similar to his increase (provided,
of   course, that other things are equal and stable).   As the
competence (ability, rationality, etc.) of   a   committeeman
increases,   the   chances   of   his   decisions being "correct"
increase.   Hence, as   the   influence   and   competence   of   a
committeeman   increase,   the   chances of committee decisions
being "correct" increase.   Similarly, it is easy to see that
as   the   influence   and   incompetence   of   a   committeeman
increase,   the   chances   of   committee   decisions   being

"incorrect" increase. According to 3.5, acceptable procedures must contain some provision for the distribution of influence according to relative competence. Therefore, insofar as this condition is met, the chances of committee decisions being "correct" will be increased and the chances of them being "incorrect" will be decreased. While this is not a guarantee that a committee will make "correct" decisions (or even more "correct" decisions more often), it does seem to be a necessary condition of adequacy for an acceptable group-decision procedure.[7]

Notice that the argument we have just presented does not commit us to the view that in all, most or even some situations there is a "correct", more or less "correct", etc., decision which is known or even, practically speaking, could be known by certain committeemen. Of course in certain fields (e.g., logic and mathematics) there are independent and explicit criteria of "correctness" for the solutions of most problems. So in these fields one frequently can and does know whether or not his decision is "correct"." However, in many of the most interesting and important fields (e.g., human welfare, morality, law, religion, etc.) one seldom has such knowledge. But it does not follow that there are no "correct", "incorrect", etc., decisions to be made with respect to the various sorts of evaluative problems that arise in these fields. Indeed, following a long line of different types of "objectivists" and a somewhat shorter line of naturalists,[8] I believe that in one way or another evaluative problems (including problems of conflict of interest, etc.) can be analyzed in ways which permit one to make decisions that are "correct", more or less "correct", etc., and occasionally to know which are which. If it should turn out that a naturalistic theory of value is untenable, then it might well be necessary to make a sharp division between procedures that are applicable to evaluative problems and those that are applicable to nonevaluative problems. In that case, the argument presented above would be applicable only to procedures designed for non-evaluative problems. Nevertheless, until "all the returns are in", I shall continue to line up with the naturalists.

4   WEIGHTING VOTERS

Even if one is persuaded by this argument for 3.5, which I am, it does not take us very far. For it is one thing to say that we ought to distribute influence according to relative competence and it is quite another to know how to do it.[9] The remaining paragraphs of this Section will be devoted to the latter problem, i.e., the problem of implementation. Suppose we have a committee with $\underline{n}$ voting members:

$$M_1 , M_2 , ..., M_n$$

Each member's vote will be assigned a weight of influence (or, for short, a weight) W which satisfies the following condition:

(4.1)   The weight of every committeeman's vote will be a real number greater than or equal to zero, i.e.,

$$W_i \geq o(i = 1,2,...n)$$

In view of 3.5 it is imperative that the weight of every member's vote is proportionate to his relative competence. The crucial question is: How are we going to measure relative competence? Clearly the usefulness of our amalgamation proposals will be severely curtailed unless a fairly plausible answer to this question is produced. The solution offered here is not new[10] and it is at best fairly plausible. Its greatest virtue is its apparent ease of application, i.e., it is relatively convenient.[11] We shall explain it with the help of a concrete example.

Consider a committee with three members:

$$M_1 , M_2 , M_3$$

The committee is supposed to select an appropriate logic text for use in a freshman course. The usual (democratic) procedure is to give each committeeman one vote which he may cast as he sees fit. He may vote for this or that text, or abstain altogether. Following this democratic tradition, each of our committeemen will also be given exactly one vote. However, instead of asking each member to cast his vote on some question before the committee (e.g., the selection of a logic text), we shall ask each of them to distribute the weight of his vote (which is unity) among each of the committeemen. The distribution of a given member's vote should be such that it indicates the relative competence of every voter in the judgment of that committeeman.

More precisely, we are asking first that each member weakly order every voter in accordance with his relative competence. That is, every committeeman is supposed to try to decide for all of the members whether

(i) M_i is more competent than M_k or M_k is more competent than M_j, or M_i and M_k are equally competent ,

and

(ii) if M_i is at least as competent as M_k and M_k is at least as competent as M_j , then M_i is at least as competent as M_j .

And second we are asking that every member try to assign a number to every voter in accordance with his rank order to serve as an indicant[12] of his relative competence. These numbers will be called "initial weights of influence" (or, "initial weights"). Moreover,

(4.4)   Every initial weight will be a real number $\underline{w}$ in the closed interval from 0 to 1, i.e.,

$$0 \leq w \leq 1$$

and the sum of the assignments that may be given by every committeeman will be 1.

The following matrix illustrates a possible result of 4.2.

FIGURE I

	M_1	M_2	M_3	W_i
M_1	1	0	0	1
M_2	$\frac{1}{3}$	$\frac{1}{3}$	$\frac{1}{3}$	1
M_3	$\frac{1}{2}$	$\frac{1}{2}$	0	1
W_i	$1\frac{5}{6}$	$\frac{5}{6}$	$\frac{1}{3}$	3 =n

Here M_1 has assigned himself an initial weight of 1 and left nothing for M_2 or M_3 . We may assume then, that in the opinion of M_1 the other members of the committee do not know anything about logic texts. Or, to put the point another way, we may assume that M_1 believes the committee decision has a better chance of being "right" if it is similar to his own decision. M_2 believes his opinion is worth no more and no less than the others. So he distributes his initial weight equally among all the voters. M_3 figures that M_1 knows about as much as M_2 about logic texts and he (M_3) just does not know anything. So he distributes his initial weight equally between M_1 and M_2 .

If a committee has $\underline{n}$ members then it has $\underline{n}$ votes to be distributed or, withheld. Then, by definition:

> (4.3) The weight of every committeeman's vote equals the sum of the initial weights assigned to him by all members of the committee, i.e.,

$$W_i = \Sigma w_{ji} \quad (i \text{ and } j = 1, 2, \ldots, n)$$

> for the jth committeeman according to each (ith) member.

In Figure I, the weight of M_1 equals the sum of the initial weights in the column below M_1, namely, $1^5/_6$. The weights of M_2 and M_3 are $^5/_6$ and $^1/_3$, respectively. The sum of these weights is $\underline{n}$ =3, which happens to equal the maximum number possible for this group because no one withheld any of his inital weight.[13]

Notice the efficiency of the voting procedure prescribed for these committeemen in comparison to the usual (democratic) procedure. For example, consider M_3 's position. Given the usual procedure if M_1 and M_2 disagreed on a text then M_3 would have to either abstain altogether or else go along with M_1 or M_2. But in both cases he would be merely making the best of a bad situation. His "real" judgment is that M_1 's views are about as reliable as M_2 's. However, the voting procedure forces him to act as if he had nothing at all to contribute (i.e., he abstains) or else to act as if he preferred the view of M_1 or M_2. In short, the usual procedure suppresses that modicum of competence that the committee recognizes in M_3. On the other hand, our procedure of weighting voters takes account of M_3 's ability. It allows him to make a contribution that reflects his own best judgment. It is not a judgment about the question at issue (i.e., about the best logic text), but about the relative ability of the other members of the committee to judge that issue. It is what many writers regard as a typically administrative decision.[14] It is a decision about the ability of certain personnel to judge a certain issue, rather than a technical decision about the issue itself. The legitimacy and usefulness of administrative decisions can hardly be doubted, since it is difficult to imagine a highly complex organization such as an industrial corporation, university, or government agency without many people responsible for such decisions, viz, the administrators or managers. Therefore, if all other things are equal, then insofar as the procedure we are recommending provides a more efficient treatment of such decisions than the usual procedure, the former should be regarded as superior.

According to 4.1-4.3, the weight of each committeeman's vote must be a real number in the closed interval from o to $\underline{n}$, i.e.:

$$o \leq W_j \leq n \ (j=1,2..,n)$$

If every committeman distributes his initial weight in equal amounts among all of the members of a committee then each one will receive an initial weight of $1/\underline{n}$ from every member. Since there are $\underline{n}$ members, the result of such a distribution will be a <u>democratic weighting</u> with every committeeman's weight:

$$W_j = 1(j=1,2,..n)$$

Formally, this result is indistinquishable from an <u>anarchic weighting</u> in which everyone keeps all of his initial weight. The different attitudes of democrats and anarchists toward legitimate government are reflected by the different paths leading to the equalitarian weights. The democrat assigns each committeeman the same weight and, therefore, is obliged to use numbers of supporters as a legitimizing criterion. The anarchist assigns only himself a weight, and, therefore, is obliged to use his own preferences as a legitimizing criterion.

If every committeeman distributes his initial weight such that the weight of a single member, say M_d is

$$W_d = n$$

the result will be a <u>delegatory weighting</u>. In effect the complete responsibility for the commmittee decision has been delegated to M_d. If the latter could be born into the position, there would be some justification for regarding this pattern as a <u>monarchic weighting</u>.

If the distribution of initial weights is such that the total weight of fewer than half of the voters is greater than half of the total weight of the whole committee, the result is an <u>oligarchic weighting</u>. More precisely, if there are $\underline{m}$ committemen such that

$$\Sigma W_i > n/2 \ (i = 1,2,...,m)$$

although

$$m < n/2$$

the weighting is oligarchic. If the composition or membership of the set of $\underline{m}$ committeemen varies as the issues before the committee vary, it might be more appropriate to refer to the weighting as <u>polyarchic</u>. In practice, many organizations that operate formally with democratic weightings, operate informally with polyarchic or delegatory weightings.[15]

Finally, if the distribution of initial weights is such that the weight of a single member, say, M_O is

$$W_O = o$$

the result is a <u>disfranchising</u> <u>weighting</u>. Notice that no one can be disfranchised unless he chooses to be.

Obviously these weighting patterns are not mutually exclusive in pairs. While no pattern can be both oligarchic and democratic (or democratic and disfranchising), every delegated pattern must be oligarchic. Moreover, a priori there seems to be no good reason to suspect that the patterns defined here exhaust the interesting possibilities, i.e., these weighting patterns are probably not exhaustive.

More importantly, perhaps, it should be emphasized that it is not being claimed that the specification of the type of weighting pattern employed in a committee is sufficient to characterize the committee as, say, democratic. It is true, however, that the specification of the type of pattern is necessary for such a characterization.

5   WEIGHTED VOTING

Now that we have a procedure for weighting voters, the question is: How should the weights be used to reach committee decisions. This question can be neatly divided into the following two questions:

(A)   How should weights be applied by voters?

(B)   What proportion of the total weight ($\underline{n}$) available should be required for a committee decision?

The latter question (B) has received considerable attention by legislators and philosophers, and we shall not attempt to improve upon traditional discussions here.[16] Instead, we shall focus on the former (A) and try to present some options that have received little or no attention. In particular, we shall consider six voting schemes. For each of the schemes it will be assumed that the decision (item, solution, policy, candidate, etc.) which receives the greatest support or has the largest weight will be accepted as the committee decision. Roughly speaking, this assumption is equivalent to answering (B) with: a plurality or simple majority is required for a committee decision. This is not an especially profound or unproblematic answer, but it will be adequate for our purposes. Above all it should be remembered that (A) and (B) are quite different

questions and that success or failure with either does not
imply success or failure with the other.

Question (A) is vague. It might be answered by
such disparate remarks as: In accordance with their
consciences; with caution; happily; all together; in bits
and pieces; etc. The last two replies suggest the sense in
which we are interested. To begin with, we might apply
weights as follows:

> Total weight scheme: Each committeeman puts the
> total weight of his vote on a single decision
> (candidate, option, etc), or he withholds all of
> it.

For example, suppose the weights assigned to a five membered
committee are:

FIGURE II

	M_1	M_2	M_3	M_4	M_5
W_i	1	0.5	1.3	0.7	1.5

and there are three alternative decisions to consider

D_1 D_2 D_3

Then on the total weight scheme, the result of a vote might
be:

FIGURE III

	D_1	D_2	D_3
M_1	0	1	0
M_2	0.5	0	0
M_3	1.3	0	0
M_4	0	0	0.7
M_5	0	1.5	0
Total	1.8	2.5	0.7

That is, M_1 puts all of his weight behind D_2, M_2 puts all of his weight behind D_1; and so on. The result is that D_2 becomes the committee decision because it has the most support.

The   total   weight   scheme   is   perfectly straightforward.   Each man either applies all of his influence (i.e., the total weight of his vote) to a single decision or he withholds all of it. However, sometimes a committeeman regards certain alternative decisions as equally acceptable.   Or, faced with three or more options, he is frequently able to weakly order them. If any of the members of a committee is able to weakly order the various alternatives before him, then it would be useful (i.e., more efficient) to give him the option of dividing the weight of his vote according to his preferences. This involves two closely related assumptions. In the first place, it must be granted that weights of influence, which are already indicants of relative competence, may also be used as indicants of preferences. And secondly, it must be granted that people's preferences are comparable, e.g., if M_1 and M_2 rank D_1 above D_2 and the latter above D_3 , we would grant that they both "feel about the same" about the three decisions instead of insisting that, say, M_1 prefers D_1 to D_2 much more than M_2 prefers D_1 to D_2 and so on.[17] While the dual role of weights of influence seems harmless enough, we shall have more to say about the weak ordering and interpersonal comparisons of "utility" in Section 7.

Given the above assumptions, we might employ a:

Split weight option scheme: Each committeeman distributes the weight of his vote among the decisions in accordance with his preferences, or he withholds any part or all of it.

For example, consider the five-membered committee above, faced with the same three decisions. A possible result of the split weight option scheme for the voters in Figure II might be:

FIGURE IV

	D_1	D_2	D_3	W_i
M_1	0.5	0.5	0	1
M_2	0.5	0	0	0.5
M_3	0.8	0.5	0	1.3
M_4	0	0.2	0.5	0.7
M_5	0.5	1	0	1.5
Total	2.3	2.2	0.5	5=n

Here M_1 distributes the weight of his vote between two equally attractive (acceptable, plausible, preferred, etc.) decisions D_1 and D_2 ; M_2 keeps his vote intact; and so on. The result is that D_1 narrowly becomes the committee decision.

A major advantage of the split weight option scheme over the total weight scheme is that the former takes account of discernible preferential differences while the latter cannot take account of such differences. Or, to put this important point in a slightly different way, a committee decision based on the split weight option scheme is a function of more subtle or precise judgments than a committee decision based on the total weight scheme. Hence, the former scheme is more efficient than the latter.

Instead of allowing committeemen to divide their weights to indicate their preferences, we might provide each voter with an additional unit to distribute. More precisely, we might let each voter assign every decision (item, policy, etc.) a real number U in the closed interval from 0 to 1 called a "utility", with the sum of the utilities assigned by each member equal to or less than one. Here the term "utility" means nothing more than the value (desirability, satisfactoriness, etc.) of a decision according to a committeeman. An example of the result of such assignments might be

FIGURE V

	D_1	D_2	D_3	sum
M_1	0.5	0.5	0	1
M_2	1	0	0	1
M_3	0.7	0.3	0	1
M_4	0	0.3	0.7	1
M_5	0.4	0.5	0.1	1

If U_{ij} is the utility of the ith decision according to the jth member then the total weighted-utility of that decision for that member is:

$$U_{ij}W_j$$

Now we may define the:

> Total weighted-utility scheme: Each committeeman
> assigns every decision a total weighted-utility
> (i.e., the product of the total weight of
> influence of his vote and the utility he assigns
> to each decision).[18]

For example, given the utility assignments in Figure V and the weights of influence in Figure II, we have

Figure VI

	D_1		D_2		D_3	
M_1	(1)	(0.5)	(1)	(0.5)	(1)	(0)
M_2	(0.5)	(1)	(0.5)	(0)	(0.5)	(0)
M_3	(1.3)	(0.7)	(1.3)	(0.3)	(1.3)	(0)
M_4	(0.7)	(0)	(0.7)	(0.3)	(0.7)	(0.7)
M_5	(1.5)	(0.4)	(1.5)	(0.5)	(1.5)	(0.1)

---

total weighted-
utility sum

2.51	1.85	0.64

The result of applying the total weighted-utility scheme with the given numerical assignments is a clear victory for D_1.

Although the split weight option scheme is less cumbersome than the total weighted-utility scheme, it is easy to show that the two schemes are equivalent. Using the former, a committeeman M_j would distribute the weight of his vote W_j such that every alternative D_i receives a certain proportion of it, say, x_{ij} where

$$\Sigma x_{ij} \leq W_j \ (i=1,2\ldots,n)$$

for an n-membered committee. Using the latter, M_j would distribute his unit of utility U_j among the members in the same proportions.

So, for any member M_j and any alternative D_i :

$$\frac{x_{ij}}{W_j} = \frac{U_{ij}}{1} = U_{ij}$$

Hence:

$$X_{ij} = U_{ij} W_j$$

But x_{ij} is the index of M_j's support for D_i according to the split weight option scheme and $U_{ij} W_j$ is the same index according to the total weighted- utility scheme. Therefore, the two schemes are equivalent.

To obtain greater uniformity in our utility assignments, we might employ the sort of marking system introduced by Jean-Charles Borda.[19] We would assign 0 utility to the least preferred alternative, 1 to the alternative immediately above that, 2 to the third highest, and so on until we reach the end of the lot. Equally preferred alternatives are assigned the same number. For convenience, we shall call such indicants "Borda - utilities." The preferences ranked in Figure V would be indicated as follows in terms of Borda utilities.

FIGURE VII

	D_1	D_2	D_3
M_1	1	1	0
M_2	1	0	0
M_3	2	1	0
M_4	0	1	2
M_5	1	2	0

Notice that while alternatives with Borda-utilities of $\underline{n}$ have exactly $\underline{n}$ $\underline{ranks}$ below them, they may have more or less than $\underline{n}$ $\underline{alternatives}$ below them. For example, M_2 distinguishes two preference levels. So the top level has a Borda-utility of $\underline{n}$ =1, and there is one level but two alternatives below D_1 .

Now we may define a:

> Weighted Borda-utility scheme: Each committeeman assigns every decision a weighted Borda-utility (i.e., the product of the total weight of influence of his vote and the Borda-utility he assigns to each decision).

For example, given the Borda-utility assignments of Figure VII and the weights of influence of Figure II, we have:

Figure VIII

	D_1		D_2		D_3	
M_1	(1)	(1)	(1)	(1)	(1)	(0)
M_2	(0.5)	(1)	(0.5)	(0)	(0.5)	(0)
M_3	(1.3)	(2)	(1.3)	(1)	(1.3)	(0)
M_4	(0.7)	(0)	(0.7)	(1)	(0.7)	(2)
M_5	(1.5)	(1)	(1.5)	(2)	(1.5)	(0)

Weighted Borda-utility sum		
5.6	6	1.4

Hence, the result of applying the weighted Borda-utility scheme with the given numerical assignments is a victory for D_2 .

If we provide additional units such as utilities and Borda-utilities to be distributed and allow committeemen to split the weight of their votes, then we may define a:

> Split weight utility scheme: Each committeeman assigns every decision a split weight utility (i.e., the product of some or all of the weight of influence of his vote and the utility he assigns to each decision).

and a:

> <u>Split   weight   Borda-utility   scheme</u> :   Each
> committeeman assigns every decision a   split
> weight Borda-utility (i.e., the product of some
> or all of the weight of influence of his vote and
> the Borda-utility he assigns to each decision).

Using the Borda-utility assignments of Figure VI and the
weights of influence of Figure II, Figure IX   illustrates   a
possible result of applying the latter sheme:

FIGURE IX

	D_1	D_2	D_3
M_1	(1) (1)	(0.5) (1)	(0.5) (0)
M_2	(0.5) (1)	(0.2) (0)	(0.5) (0)
M_3	(1.3) (2)	(0.3) (1)	(0.8) (0)
M_4	(0.7) (0)	(0.7) (1)	(0.7) (2)
M_5	(1.5) (1)	(1) (2)	(0.5) (0)

Split weight
Borda-utility sum

5.6	3.5	1.4

Hence, the result of applying this scheme with the given
numerical assignments is a victory for D_2 .   (Notice that
every   committeeman   is   permitted   to   multiply   the
Borda-utility he assigns to each decision by a number no
greater than his total weight.)

By a line of argumentation analogous to that used
to   show   that   the   split   weight   option   and   total
weighted-utility schemes are equivalent, it may be   shown
that the split weight utility and split weight Borda-utility
schemes are both equivalent to the former two schemes.
Thus, in view of the unnecessary labor involved in the
additional   computations required for the application of the
latter three in comparison with the split weight option
scheme, there is no doubt that the other three schemes will
never be practicable.

The following matrix summarizes the six schemes
we have considered:

	No Additional Units Provided	Additional Units Provided
Use All or No Weight	total weight	{total weighted-utility {weighted Borda-utility
Use Some, All, or No Weight	split weight option	{ split weight utility {split weight Borda- {utility

The total weight scheme comes about by answering question
(A), (How should weights be applied by voters?) with "as a
whole" and not providing any additional units to be
distributed. If (A) is answered by "as a whole or in parts"
and no additional units are provided, the result is the
split weight option scheme. The remaining entries in the
matrix arise analogously.

6   OBJECTIONS AND REPLIES: WEIGHTING VOTERS

        The constructive work of this essay has now been
completed, and it is time to appraise our results in the
light of the adequacy criteria introduced in Section 3. Six
solutions to our basic problem (viz., How should the
decision (with respect to some issue) of the members of a
committee be amalgamated for the committee decision to be
determined in the most acceptable fashion?) were suggested
in Section 5. Each of these six employed the procedure for
weighting voters that was described in Section 4. So, if
there are no acceptable procedures for weighting voters,
then the practical value of the six schemes of weighted
voting must be nil. It will be convenient then, to consider
objections to the procedure for weighting voters prior to
and in isolation from objections to particular schemes of
weighted voting.

        How does our procedure for weighting voters fare
with respect to our five criteria, viz., 3.1 freedom from
coercion, 3.2 internal consistency, 3.3 practicability, 3.4
efficiency, and 3.5 influence proportionate to relative
competence? Taking the least problematic first, our
procedure seems (to me) to satisfy the conditions of freedom
from coercion, internal consistency, and efficiency. But
the other two requirements require some discussion.

        To begin with, it might be objected that our
procedure violates 3.5 because it begins with an
equalitarian distribution of influence in the form of a
single vote worth exactly one unit. That is, before
anyone's competence is estimated, every committeeman is
given a vote whose initial weight is equal to that of every
other. But according to 3.5, such a distribution is

permissible   only if the competence of every committeeman is
equal to that of every other. However, at this (first) stage
in   our   procedure   we   do   not   know   how   competent   any
committeeman   is.   Hence,   we   cannot   justify   an   opening
equalitarian distribution.   Moreover, if   we   could   justify
such   a   distribution   then the whole procedure of weighting
voters would be a waste of   time,   because   they   would   all
receive   the   same weight always.   But the first step in our
procedure   must   be   either   unjustified   or   justified.
Therefore,   it   must   either   violate   3.5 or trivialize the
whole procedure.

          This dilemma is more   apparent   than   real.   The
first   horn is problematic but the second horn is based on a
misunderstanding.   Let   us   take   the   second   horn   first.
Recall   that   in   our   procedure each committeeman is called
upon to make two different types of decisions,   one   on   the
abilities of the other members and the other on the issue(s)
before the committee.   Our opening equalitarian distribution
only   presupposes   that   every   committeeman   is   equally
qualified to make the   first   type   of   judgment.   If   this
assumption   is warranted then all that follows is that every
member's opinion about every   committeman's   judgment   about
the   issue(s)   before   the committee is equal to every other
member's opinion.   It does not follow   that   every   member's
opinion   about the issue(s) before the committee is equal to
every other member's opinion.   Hence,   the   whole   weighting
procedure   cannot   be trivialized by an opening equalitarian
distribution.   So much for the second horn.

          The   first   horn   of   the   dilemma   cannot   be
dispatched   so   swiftly.   Indeed, we must grant immediately
that we have no reason to suppose that the ability to   judge
the   ability   of   personnel   to judge more or less technical
issues is equally distributed among   all   or   most   people.
What we would like to substitute for an opening equalitarian
distribution   is   a   distribution   based   on   some   reliable
independent test.   But this raises the question: How should
we select such a test?   And this question seems to   lead   us
straight   to   Section 2 of this paper (which has finally led
us to the present   point)   or   to   an   infinite   regress   of
reliable   independent tests of reliable independent tests or
to some more or less arbitrarily final reliable   independent
test.   No   doubt   the last alternative will be preferred by
most people, and the   haggling   will   be   over   the   cut-off
point.   The   opening equalitarian distribution suggested in
our procedure is   merely   a   convenient   (admittedly   early)
cut-off   point   which   should be adequate for most purposes.
After all, even the usual democratic procedure (which   is
less   efficient   than   any   of   ours)   has been regarded as
adequate for most purposes.   If the   cost   of   an   erroneous
committee decision   is very high, we would expect much more
elaborate precautions to be taken to increase the chances of
arriving at a more acceptable opening distribution.[20]

Briefly then, my reply to the first horn of the dilemma is as follows. The objection is sound but not totally destructive. It reveals a defect in our procedure which becomes more or less serious as the cost of errors increases or decreases, respectively, and which further research should attempt to eliminate or reduce as much as possible.

Supposing we had solutions to these problems, would our procedure then be practicable (condition 3.3)? It seems that our procedure may be impracticable for at least eight reasons.

(1)   Committeemen may find the task of weakly ordering their colleagues in accordance with relative competence too complicated. Competence is very likely multi-dimensional and the dimensions may be extremely difficult if not impossible to compare. For example, a certain committeeman may be very good at identifying, say, the pedagogical strengths and weaknesses of a textbook (e.g., the organization and presentation of new material, definitions, illustrations, exercises, etc.) but very bad at recognizing factual or formal errors (e.g., that this was discovered by so-and-so then, that most people call this a such-and-such, that it is misleading to refer to this as that, etc.).

Should such a committeeman be assigned a high or a low weight? Should a committeeman who is good at both tasks be assigned a weight that is twice as great as that of a commiteeman who is only good at one? Are the two skills "really" equally important? Even if these problems could be solved, the cost of solving them may be too high given the benefits obtainable from our procedure and the availability of other procedures. That is, it is not merely this or that complication in the abstract that may be objectionable. Rather, it is the fact that in comparison with other procedures, the cost of untangling the complications in ours may be too high and the likely rewards too low to vindicate its application.

(2)   The determination of relative competence may produce disputes, factions, and enemies that might otherwise be avoided. For example, a member may not appreciate receiving a low weight from a voter to whom the former has just assigned a low weight. Since committee meetings will probably take more time with our procedure, we may expect greater fatigue, irritability, impatience, and ennui. Hence, even trivial issues may become highly problematic.

(3)   Our procedure may be regarded as too "brutal" because it does not provide any face-saving safeguards for perennial "light-weights". Even if the weights are never made public (which merely requires the help of a discrete and honest assistant, or a machine), it is bound to occur to

some people that in their own opinion the judgment of certain committeemen is almost always nearly worthless. What is worse, if the split weight option scheme is used and everyone must be informed of their colleagues' views about their relative competence, then perennial "light-weights" are going to be repeatedly embarrassed and probably embittered.

(4)   Our procedure may breed irresponsibility in those who, for a certain issue, have been assigned a fairly low weight. The low weight assigned to a committeeman may have the effect of a self-fulfilling prediction, i.e., everyone expects him to contribute very little; so he expends very little effort and, consequently, he has very little to contribute.

(5)   Committeemen may nullify the opportunity to determine the relative competence of their colleagues by employing a minimax loss strategy. According to this strategy, a voter should distribute his initial weight to insure himself the smallest possible loss. His options are to give away none of it, give away part of it, or give away all of it. Clearly, he can protect himself against any loss at all by simply keeping his vote all to himself.[21] However, if everyone employs this strategy, then the result is an anarchic weighting. And if enough people employ this strategy often enough, our procedure would have to be regarded as redundant.[22]

(6)   It is likely that committeemen will misjudge the relative competence of their colleagues. They will commit "errors of leniency" (i.e., avoid assigning extreme weights of 0 or 1), "logic" (i.e., assign similar weights for skills that seem to be "logically related"), "contrast" (i.e., assign weights roughly inversely proportional to those they assign themselves), and "proximity" (i.e., assign similar weights for skills that are considered at roughly the same time or in the same context).[23] They will fall prey to the "halo effect" (i.e., assign weights in accordance with their "general impression" of the individual rated)[24] and the "Matthew effect" (i.e, assign higher weights to the "biggest names" regardless of their particular competence in a given situation).[25] They will be influenced by "prestige considerations",[26] and, as the ambiguity of the situation increases, by social pressure to "conform".[27] Hence, instead of indicating relative competence, our weights will be meaningless numbers misleadingly suggesting precision and accuracy.

(7)   There is some evidence that less competent people are less influential than more competent people anyhow.[28] So an attempt formally to weaken the former and strengthen the latter is unnecessary.

(8)   If a committeeman believes that some other member of a committee is especially competent, then, rather than giving the latter some of his weight (losing formal influence and flexibility certainly and informal influence possibly), he would be wise to keep all of his weight and simply allow himself to be guided by the other member's decision. After all, from the former's point of view, the final result of giving the latter his weight to put behind a certain decision is no different from putting it in the same place under the other member's supervision. Hence, because committeemen have something to lose by distributing their weight and nothing to lose by keeping it, few or no distributions should ever occur.

Let us consider each of these objections in turn.

(1)   It must be granted that some people may find the task of weakly ordering their colleagues in accordance with relative competence virtually impossible. That is why our procedure does not require such an ordering from anyone. The ordering is requested, and if most people cannot satisfy the request most of the time, then our procedure cannot be expected to accomplish anything most of the time. Nevertheless, our procedure provides an opportunity to use whatever resources happen to be available, which seems to make it superior to procedures without this provision. Moreover, and fortunately, there is no evidence of a widespread human inability to perform such tasks. On the contrary, while it is difficult to appraise the relative competence of this or that scholar in a certain area, such appraisals are very common. Thousands of employers are required to do just that, and they are frequently promoted for doing it well and discharged for doing it poorly. Hence, the real question seems to be: Are the rewards of untangling the complications in our procedure high enough to justify the costs? And in the absence of a definite issue, committee, and alternative procedure this question seems to be unanswerable.

(2)   There seem to be good reasons for believing that our procedure will not create an inordinate number of disputes. In the first place, people frequently judge the merits of candidates for various positions of leadership, and our procedure is merely an extension of this common practice. In the second place, certain precautions may be taken to reduce the chances of disputes. For instance, one should avoid using our procedure in situations in which the likelihood of misunderstanding is known to be high, e.g., in meetings involving people with quite specific and, perhaps, antagonistic roles such as labor and management representatives,[29] or officers and enlisted men.[30] Perhaps committeemen might be impressed with the idea that they are all part of a single "team" and that the less energy they expend attacking each other the more they will be able to

expend on the issue before the committee. Again, the reward
and punishment structure might be designed to militate
against such phenomena, i.e., let the "payoffs" go to those
who do not get involved in disputes and factions, and the
penalties go to those who do.[31]

(3)   The third objection seems to suggest a nice
problem of balancing the demands of morality against those
of rationality. Fortunately, that is not the case.   The
problem is one of balancing the demands of one moral
prescription against those of another.   On the one hand,
committeemen   are   morally   obliged   to   try to avoid
embarrassing their colleagues.   On the other, they are
morally obliged to try to make as "correct" a decision as
possible. Hence, the question they must ask themselves is
this: Is the moral cost of embarrassing (and, perhaps,
embittering) some members greater than, equal to, or less
than the moral cost of making a less "correct" decision.   If
it costs more (i.e., seems to create more feelings of guilt)
to identify and isolate the "light-weights" than it does to
accept a slightly "incorrect" committee decision, then a
committeeman ought to accept the latter; otherwise he ought
to choose the former, unless the costs are equally balanced.
In the latter case he might flip a coin.

It would be a mistake to assume that
"lightweights" must be embarrassed or embittered. While
there is a wealth of evidence to support the view that they
will probably respond that way,[32]   there is also evidence
that the reaction of individuals to participation in or
exclusion from decision-making that affects their lives is
significantly influenced by their expectations.[33]   Hence,
someone who expects "the other fellow" to be responsible for
this or that may be perfectly happy to be assigned a lighter
weight. Moreover, it should be noted again that if the
variety of issues considered by a committee is large, the
probability that a certain committeeman will always be
judged a "light-weight" is small. Most people tend to be
specialists by inclination and aptitude. Hence, if the
issues before a committee vary, it is likely that no one
will be a perennial "light-weight", or "heavy-weight",
i.,e., the typical weighting will probably be polyarchic.[34]

(4) It seems that we might suggest with equal
plausibility that those committeemen from whom everyone
expects a great deal will be encouraged to work harder and,
consequently, will be able to contribute more than anyone
expects. But this reply merely reproduces the same
unwarranted assumption on which the objection is based.
That is, there is no reason to assume that committeemen must
be weighted long before the final vote on the issue is
taken.   Indeed, there is no doubt at all that the weighting
should immediately precede the voting and that both should
take place after a discussion of the issues. Moreover,

every committeeman should be given an agenda far enough in
advance of the meeting to provide some opportunity for him
to become familiar with the issues. Given these tactics and
the fact that our procedure allows committeemen to gain
complete control of a committee decision, it would seem to
be difficult for a person with average ability to justify an
attitude of impotence.[35]

        (5) The application of a minimax loss strategy is
not incompatible with the assignment of initial weights
according to judgments of relative competence, i.e., it does
not entail an anarchic weighting. If someone regards a less
"correct" committee decision as a greater loss than a
certain amount of personal influence on that decision, then
the minimax strategy would lead him to distribute his
initial weight in support of competence, rather than merely
in support of himself.   In effect, then, he would be
applying the strategy to the following alternatives:

        (a) Keep everything and obtain less "correct"
        committee decision.

        (b)   Distribute   part   and obtain more "correct"
        committee decision.

The second alternative might well represent the smallest
possible loss. The important unanswered question is: Will
enough people value "correctness" more than personal
influence to make our procedure effective?

        (6) The evidence for these suggestions is fairly
strong. So all we can do is try to devise ways to minimize
the effects of such propensities.[36]   One way to tackle the
problem is to construct a set of minimum standards according
to which initial weights must be distributed. For example,
in the case of the selection of a textbook, we might give so
many points for having taken so many courses, for having
taught so many, for having published so many related papers,
etc.   Other more reliable tests would have to be developed
for other types of issues. A second way to attack the
problem would be to have the committeemen present their
"credentials" with precise and standardized descriptions to
reduce vagueness and ambiguity.   This would reduce the
temptation to interpret perceptions in a more or less
arbitrary fashion.[37]

        (7) Insofar as events are bound to take place
exactly as we prefer with or without our (formal) efforts,
such efforts must be regarded as unnecessary. But the
ultimate triumph of wisdom over ignorance is hardly
inevitable. Hence, we seem to be obliged to take some steps
to "further the cause of rationality and good
decision-making." What I would like to suggest here is that
the formalization of influence in some situations might be a
step in the right direction.

(8) It seems clear that in some situations it
would be wiser to copy a more competent member's voting
behavior than to give him all or part of one's weight.
However, other situations, the latter strategy seems
preferable to the former. For example, suppose that one is
not only interested in the "correctness" of a committee
decision, but also in appropriately allocating the rewards
or punishments resulting from that decision. The
distribution of weights could be used as a basis for fixing
responsibility and for fairly allocating rewards and
punishments. Similarly, weight distribution provides an
explicit record of committeemen's views of one another's
competence which could be useful for the choice of operating
procedures and personnel. Again, it is often important to
know whether a committee decision has received a certain
amount of support on its own as it were or simply on the
strength of its supporters. After all, to return to a point
raised in Section 4, it is one thing to endorse a particular
alternative and quite another to endorse a particular person
who endorses that alternative. A ten -membered committee
decision with one knowledgeable supporter and nine
administratively competent but technically ignorant
supporters seems to have less support in some sense[38]
than the same decision with nine knowledgeable supporters
and one supporting administrator. While weight distribution
(according to the procedure suggested here) might not alter
the final number of points received for such a decision in
either case, it would provide some intuitively useful extra
bits of information whose value would tend to vary directly
with the error and implementation costs of any decision. Of
course, one could probably gather the extra information by
additional research of some sort, but weight distribution
always provides such information and always makes the subtle
difference in the kind of support received by any
alternative completely explicit.

7   OBJECTIONS AND REPLIES: WEIGHTED VOTING

After reviewing the objections and replies to the
procedure of weighting voters, it seems fair to say that as
yet neither a case for nor against it has been decisively
made. There are still a number of loose ends to be tied up,
some of which require empirical investigation more than
logical analysis. However, in this Section we shall assume
that our procedure for weighting voters is more or less
acceptable and ask: How do the various schemes of weighted
voting fare in the light of our five adequacy criteria?

Taking the least problematic point first, I think
that we may grant the internal consistency (condition 3.2)
of all six schemes. It is certainly true that if one
requires some sort of piecemeal comparison of alternatives

(e.g., pairwise comparison, triplewise, etc.) and assumes
that both individual and group systems of preferences must
be transitive, then all of these schemes are liable to
generate the so-called "paradox of voting" in certain
situations.[39] But it seems to me that there is no good reason
to expect group systems of preferences to be transitive or
to require piecemeal comparisons of alternatives. So the
"paradox" is something of a red herring.[40]

It may be recalled that in Section 5 we showed
that the total weight scheme is inefficient (violating 3.4)
in the sense that it is liable to be unable to take account
of available information. Similarly, the weighted
Borda-utility scheme must be inefficient because
Borda-utilities vary at regular intervals whether or not the
preferences of committeemen vary that way. For example, if
someone ranks D_1 above D_2 and the latter above D_3, then the
Borda-utility of D_1 is twice that of D_3 whether or not the
committeemen believes D_1 is twice as "good" as D_3. While
we are not bound to use the whole numbers 0,1,2,3, ..., as
Borda-utilities, we are bound to use some regularly
increasing set (e.g., $0, \frac{1}{3}, \frac{2}{3}, 1, ...; 0, \frac{1}{4}, \frac{1}{2}, \frac{3}{4} ...$) because it
is this very regularity that distinguishes this scheme from
the total weighted-utility scheme. Hence, whenever
committeemen have preferences that do not vary at regular
intervals, they will be unable to "feed" this information
into the weighted Borda-utility scheme. Hence, it too
violates 3.4. Since the split weight Borda-utility scheme
provides some means of breaking the rigid Borda-utility mold
(namely, by appropriately splitting one's weight), it does
not violate 3.4. Furthermore, for roughly the same reason,
neither do the other three schemes.

The total weight scheme seems to be free of any
peculiar problems of practicability (condition 3.3.)
However, as we saw in Section 5, the total weighted utility,
split weight utility, and split weight Borda-utility schemes
are all impracticable because the labor costs of applying
them are greater than the costs of applying the equivalent
split weight option scheme. Furthermore, with the exception
of the total weight scheme, they all presuppose (i) the
ability of some committeemen to weakly order their
preferences for various alternatives and (ii) the
interpersonal comparison of utility. Both of these
assumptions have been debated so exhaustively in the
literature that it seems very unlikely that anything novel
can be said here.[41] So, I shall restrict my "defense" to the
following brief remarks. In defense of (i) it should be
noted that people are frequently (though by no means always)
able to weakly order their preferences, and that this must
be regarded as favorable evidence for the view that, as far
as this problem is concerned, our voting schemes will
frequently be practicable.[42] In defense of (ii) it must be
admitted that the very fact that fairly stable wage and

price systems exist may be taken as evidence that some services and commodities must have roughly the same value for many people. That is, if people of roughly equal means are willing to pay the same price for a certain commodity or do the same work for the same salary, then it seems more likely that they are receiving the same rather than different amounts of satisfaction from the exchange. Hence, this second problem seems to be primarily one of constructing appropriate technical "devices" to obtain reliable measures of comparability.

The total weight scheme seems to violate condition 3.1, freedom from coercion, because it does not allow committeemen to distribute the weight of their votes in accordance with their preferences. They might, then, be forced to give more support to certain issues than they prefer or simply withhold all of their influence. Similarly, the weighted Borda-utility scheme is liable to be coercive when it is suppressing information.[43]

The split weight option scheme and its equivalents may be shown to violate 3.1 as follows. We have a three-membered committee in which each member has a weight of unity and a vote is to be taken to select one of four alternatives. If each member voted his "true" preferences, the result would be a victory for D_1, as follows:

	D_1	D_2	D_3	D_4	W_i
M_1	$\frac{1}{2}$	$\frac{1}{3}$	$\frac{1}{6}$	0	1
M_2	$\frac{1}{2}$	$\frac{1}{6}$	$\frac{1}{3}$	0	1
M_3	0	$\frac{1}{6}$	$\frac{1}{3}$	$\frac{1}{2}$	1
Total	1	$\frac{2}{3}$	$\frac{5}{6}$	$\frac{1}{2}$	

However, M_3 figures that "half a loaf is better than none" and that while his first choice is a lost cause, his second choice would win if he put all his weight behind it. By misrepresenting his preferences thus,

	D_1	D_2	D_3	D_4
M_3	0	0	1	0

he insures a victory for D_3, because the new total is

	D_1	D_2	D_3	D_4
	1	$\frac{1}{2}$	$1\frac{1}{2}$	0

Hence, for M_3 to insure a victory for his second choice given the split weight option scheme and the particular distribution of preferences of the other members of the committee, he must vote contrary to his preferences. So, the split weight option scheme and its equivalents violate 3.1; which means that all of our schemes are liable to be coercive.

Since the procedure for weighting voters is designed to guarantee the satisfaction of condition 3.5 and since it has rather precariously passed inspection, one might be inclined to say that the six schemes employing it are also provisionally acceptable on this score. Unfortunately, such an inference would not be warranted, because it is undoubtedly the case that all of these schemes are liable to violate 3.5. If, for example, every member of a three-membered committee has a weight of influence equal to unity going into an election and two of them abstain, the third member's weight of influence on the final outcome would jump from a third to one! But short of violating 3.1 there is no way to prevent such "anomalies" from arising. Hence, after all is said and done, we still do not have a scheme that will guarantee the satisfaction of 3.5. Indeed, we now know that it is impossible to construct such a scheme without violating 3.1. Thus, we have arrived at a conclusion that is analogous to Arrow's General Impossibility Theorem.[44] That is, it is impossible to construct a voting scheme such that for every individual under any circumstances, both freedom from coercion and the distribution of influence according to relative competence are guaranteed. Of course, given certain individuals and circumstances, influence may well be distributed according to relative competence without coercion. So 3.1 and 3.5 are certainly consistent. But no procedure can guarantee their joint satisfaction.

If we let "p" be short for "passes" and "f" for "fails", then the views presented in this Section may be summarized in the following matrix. The last line has been added to facilitate comparison with what we have been calling the "usual (democratic) voting procedure."

	Condition				
Voting Scheme	3.1	3.2	3.3	3.4	3.5
total weight	f	p	p	f	f
split weight option*	f	p	f	p	f
total weighted- utility*	f	p	f	p	f
weighted Borda-utility	f	p	f	f	f
split weight utility*	f	p	f	p	f
split weight Borda- utility*	f	p	f	p	f
usual procedure	f	p	p	f	f

* indicates equivalent schemes

As the table discloses, the weighted Borda-utility scheme is the weakest of the lot, and all of the others are equally acceptable. At any rate, they are equally acceptable provided that one regards each of the five adequacy conditions as equally important. If the conditions were weighted unequally then one of the voting schemes might prove to be superior to the others.

8   CONCLUSION

Insofar as we have succeeded in providing a more or less systematic basis for logical and empirical investigations of group decision procedures which permit formal or explicit inequalities among voters and votes, our more general task has been completed. Insofar as we have been able to throw some light on the relationships, strengths, and weaknesses of various more or less plausible solutions to the problem of selecting an acceptable group-decision procedure, our more specific task has been accomplished. Perhaps the most appropriate summary of our results on the latter score would be a loose paraphrase of a remark made by Sir Winston Churchill: "The usual (democratic) procedure is a very bad form of government, but it is every bit as good as all the others."[45]

*   I wish to thank the Editor and publisher of the
     American Philosophical Quarterly for permission to
     reprint this article from Vol. 7, 1970, 91-106.

1   The best introductory survey of recent work on
     amalgamation procedures is R. Duncan Luce and Howard
     Raiffa, Games and Decisions (New York, John Wiley and
     Sons, Inc. 1964), pp. 327-371

2   In Karl Mannheim's terms, our concern is with "means
     rationality" rather than "substantial rationality." Man
     and Society in an Age of Reconstruction (London,
     Routledge and Kegan Paul, 1940), pp. 51-53.

3   Readers who are familiar with the literature on
     "social-welfare functions" which arose out of Kenneth
     J. Arrow's classic Social Choice and Individual Values
     (New York, John Wiley and Sons, Inc., 1963) will notice
     that the five conditions introduced below differ from
     Arrow's. In part this is merely a result of the fact
     that Arrow's problem and primary concerns differ from
     mine. However, it is also partially the result of my
     rejection of some of his basic assumptions. Roughly
     speaking, the two sets of conditions are related as
     follows. My condition 3.1 implies his conditions of
     nondictatorship and nonimposition. Conditions 3.2 to
     3.5 are logically independent of his conditions of
     collective rationality, pair- wise comparisons, and
     Pareto optimality. Collective rationality and
     pair-wise comparisons are explicitly rejected in
     Section 7 (below) and I have nothing to say about
     Pareto optimality. Similarly, so far as I know, Arrow
     has been silent regarding conditions analogous to 3.3
     and 3.4, would probably reject 3.5, and accept 3.2.
     The most thorough discussion of Arrow's conditions is
     in Jerome Rothenberg, The Measurement of Social
     Welfare (Englewood Cliffs, N.J., Prentice-Hall, Inc.,
     1961).

4   There is some evidence that "group decision-making" in
     political parties through prima facie democratic
     processes is merely a "ritual" or "ceremonial"
     performing a legitimizing rather than a decion-making
     service; e.g., in Robert A. Dahl, Who Governs? (New
     Haven, Conn., Yale University Press, 1966), pp.
     112-114. My impression is that most of the university
     committees I have served on have been providing the
     same (perhaps important and necessary) service, a
     service that would not seem to require a very subtle
     procedure.

5   I include this remark for those who might expect this
     condition to generate problems similar to those of
     Carnap's inductive "principle of total evidence"; e.g.,

A.J. Ayer, "The Conception of Probability as a Logical Relation", in S. Korner (ed.), <u>Observation</u> <u>and</u> <u>Interpretation</u> <u>in</u> <u>the</u> <u>Philosophy</u> <u>of</u> <u>Physics</u> (New York, Dover Publications, Inc. 1957), pp. 14-17.

6   A review of this literature may be found in George L. Abernethy (ed.), <u>The</u> <u>Idea</u> <u>of</u> <u>Equality</u> (Richmond, Va., John Knox Press, 1959).

7   Cf ., "To have no voice in what are partly his own concerns is a thing which nobody willingly submits to: but when what is partly his concern is also partly another's, and he feels the other to understand the subject better than himself, that the other's opinion should be counted for more than his own accords with his expectations..." John Stuart Mill, <u>Considerations</u> <u>on</u> <u>Representative</u> <u>Government</u> (New York, <u>Harper and Brothers</u>, 1867), p. 181. More recently James W. Protho and Charles M. Grigg found that while roughly 96 per cent of the people in their survey (of registered voters in Ann Arbor, Michigan and Tallahassee, Florida) agreed that "every citizen should have an equal chance to influence government policy", there was nearly a "total absence of consensus" on the view that "in a city referendum, only people who are well informed about the problem being voted on should be allowed to vote." "Fundamental Principles of Democracy", <u>The</u> <u>Journal</u> <u>of</u> <u>Politics</u>, vol. 22 (1960), pp. 282-285.

8   This shorter line includes such illustrious names as M.R. Cohen, John Dewey, Herbert Feigl, R.W. Sellars, and most recently, Henry Margenau. The latter's <u>Ethics</u> <u>and</u> <u>Science</u> (Princeton, N.J., D. Van Nostrand Company, 1964) may be regarded as an outline of the sort of view I have adopted.

9   Mill's suggestion for "weighting" voters in a "universal but graduated suffrage" included the administration of "a trustworthy system of general examination", consideration of "the nature of a person's occupation", "successful performance" of a trade, "graduates of universities", and excluded "sex" or "any pecuniary qualification." <u>Op. cit.</u>, pp. 182-192. Some writers have admitted unequal "weightings" into their formal theories without tackling the problem of how such "weights" could be obtained; e.g., Germain Kreweras, "A Model to Weight Individual Authority in a Group", in S. Sternberg, V. Capecchi, T. Kloek, and C.T. Leenders (eds.), <u>Mathematics</u> <u>and</u> <u>Social</u> <u>Sciences</u> <u>I</u> (Paris, Mouton and Co., 1965), pp. 111-118; and William H. Riker <u>The</u> <u>Theory</u> <u>of</u> <u>Political</u> <u>Coalitions</u> (New Haven, 1962), pp. 257-258.

10   Roughly the same procedure was used by J. Sayer Minas
      and Russell L. Ackoff in "Individual and Collective
      Value Judgments," in Maynard W. Shelly, II and Glenn L.
      Bryan (eds.). Human Judgments and Optimality (New
      York, John Wiley and Sons, Inc., 1964), pp. 351-359. A
      considerably more complicated (though not necessarily
      more reliable) nine-step procedure may be found in my
      unpublished paper "Split Weight Option Voting."

11   A number of doubts about its "greatest virtue" are
      raised in Section 7.

12   "The difference between an indicant and a measure is
      just this: the indicant is a presumed effect or
      correlate bearing an unknown ... relation to some
      underlying phenomenon, whereas a measure is a scaled
      value of the phenomenon itself. Indicants have the
      advantage of convenience. Measures have the advantage
      of validity. We aspire to measures, but we are often
      forced to settle for less." S.S. Stevens,
      "Mathematics, Measurement and Psychophysics", Handbook
      of Experimental Psychology, ed. by S.S. Stevens (New
      York, John Wiley and Sons, Inc., 1951), p. 48.

13   To simplify the illustrations, no weight is withheld in
      any of them.

14   E.g., "In the field of organization, the knowledge on
      which what we call responsible control depends is not
      knowledge of situations and problems and of means for
      effecting changes, but is knowledge of other men's
      knowledge of these things ... the crucial decision is
      the selection of men to make decisions." Frank H.
      Knight, Risk, Uncertainty and Profit (New York, Harper
      and Row, Inc. 1965), pp. 292-299.

15   A classic description of a polyarchic system may be
      found in Dahl, op. cit.

16   An excellent review and criticism of some of the
      alternatives may be found in C.L. Dodgson (Lewis
      Carroll), "A Discussion of the Various Methods of
      Procedure in Conducting Elections" reprinted in Duncan
      Black, The Theory of Committees and Elections
      (Cambridge, Cambridge University Press, 1963), pp.
      214-222.

17   A suggestive graphic representation of this problem is
      given by Nicholas Rescher, "Notes on Preference,
      Utility and Cost", Synthese, vol. 16 (1966), p. 333.

18   This is basically the scheme recommended by Minas and
      Ackoff, op. cit., pp. 355-356.

19 "Mémoire sur les elections au scrutin", Histoire de
    l'Académie (1781). For a thorough examination of
    Borda's views see Black, op. cit., pp. 59-66, 156-159.

20 The relation between costs and precision in measurement
    is outlined in C. West Churchman, Prediction and
    Optimal Decision (Englewood Cliffs, N.J.,
    Prentice-Hall, Inc., 1964), pp. 116 ff.

21 Similarly, it has been argued that "A second vital
    reason for seeking the condition of political equality
    is a strategic calculation. Like so many important
    decisions, this one, too, is a calculated risk.
    Reduced to its boldest terms, our strategy comes to
    this: we cannot be confident of continued membership
    in an elite group whose preferences would be counted
    for more rather than less." Robert A. Dahl and Charles
    E. Lindblom, Politics, Economics and Welfare (New York,
    Harper and Row, Inc., (1963), p. 43.

22 Other possible strategies may be found in my Principles
    of Logic (Englewood Cliffs, N.J., Prentice-Hall, Inc.,
    1969), ch. 8.

23 Detailed discussions of these errors may be found in
    J.P. Guilford, Psychometric Methods (New York,
    McGraw-Hill Book Co., 1954), pp. 278-280.

24 Ibid., p. 279

25 Robert K. Merton, "The Matthew Effect in Science",
    Science, vol. 159 (1968), pp. 278-280.

26 Robert E. Lane, "Political Personality and Electoral
    Choice", American Political Science Review, vol. 49
    (1955), pp. 173-174.

27 E.L. Walker and R.W. Heyns, An Anatomy for Conformity
    (Englewood Cliffs, N.J., Prentice-Hall, Inc., 1962),
    pp. 92-95. Further problems may be found in Bernard R.
    Berelson, Paul F. Lazarsfeld, and William N. McPhee,
    Voting (Chicago, University of Chicago Press, 1962), p.
    232, and Paul F. Lazarsfeld, Bernard Berelson, and
    Hazel Gaudet, The People's Choice (Ithaca, N.Y.,
    Cornell University Press, 1960), pp. 80ff.

28 E.g., "The structure of interpersonal relations within
    legislative systems functions to place legislators with
    high degrees of skill and conscientiousness in the
    center of the legislative system and to increase their
    influence, and to isolate legislators with low degrees
    of skill and conscientiousness on the periphery of the
    legislative system and to decrease their influence."
    Stephen V. Monsma, "Interpersonal Relations in the

Legislative System: A Study of the 1964 Michigan House of Representatives", Midwest Journal of Political Science, vol. 10 (1966), p. 363. This article also contains a long bibliography. An instructive criticism of earlier attempts at formulating indices of "influence" may be found in Ralph K. Huitt, "The Outsider in the Senate", American Political Science Review, vol. 55 (1961), pp. 566-575.

29   Mason Haire found that "management and labor each sees the other as less dependable than himself ... and ... deficient in thinking, emotional characteristics, and interpersonal relations ... " in "Role-perception in Labor-management Relations: An Experimental Approach," Industrial and Labor Relations Review, vol. 8 (1955), p. 215.

30   Paul F. Lazarsfeld, "The American Soldier", Public Opinion Quarterly, vol. II (1966), pp. 383-386.

31   A number of other techniques are described in Richard E. Walton and Robert B. McKersie, "Behavioral Dilemmas in Mixed-motive Decision Making", Behavioral Science, vol. II (1966), pp. 381-384.

32   Lester Coch and John R.P. French, Jr., "Overcoming Resistance to Change," Human Relations, vol. 1 (1948), p. 532.

33   William R. Dill, "The Impact of Environment on Organizational Development", in Sidney Mailick and Edward H. van Ness (eds.), Concepts and Issues in Administrative Behavior (Englewood Cliffs, N.J., Prentice-Hall, Inc., 1962), p. 105.

34   This is suggested, but by no means proved, by Dahl's research in New Haven, Conn., op., cit., p. 228. A more extensive investigation by Robert E. Agger, Daniel Goldrich and Bert. E. Swanson suggests a number of other alternatives. The Rulers and the Ruled (New York, John Wiley and Sons, Inc. , 1964), pp. 478-537.

35   Robert E. Lane's investigation of the political attitudes of 15 "average" men led him to the conclusion that "people tend to care less about equality of opportunity than about the availability of some opportunity", Political Ideology (New York, The Free Press, 1962), p. 79.

36   Guilford introduces techniques to estimate some of the types of errors we listed. They obviously require the assistance of a trained statistician. Op cit., pp. 280ff.

37   There is no doubt at all that the (intentional and unintentional) ambiguity of politicians' claims is highly correlated with the erroneous interpretations of voters, e.g., see Berelson, Lazarsfeld, and McPhee, loc. cit.

38   The precise nature and plausibility of this "sense" is still rather vague to me.

39   An excellent review of the formal issues surrounding this paradox may be found in Yasusuke Murakami, Logic and Social Choice (London, Routledge and Kegan Paul, Ltd., 1968), chs. 5 and 6.

40   I am in complete agreement with Dahl and Lindblom, op. cit., pp. 422-424

41   I have entered the periphery of the arena in "Postulates of Rational Preference", Philosophy of Science, vol. 34 (1967), pp. 18-22, and "Estimated Utility and Corroboration", British Journal for the Philosophy of Science vol. 16 (1966), pp. 327-331.

42   It is worthwhile to note, I think, that the chances of performing this task seem to be increased by considering Bentham's seven aspects of the "satisfaction" attached to a particular decision, viz., intensity, duration, certainty, propinquity, fecundity, purity, and extent. On this point Wayne A.R. Leys' discussion in Ethics for Policy Decisions (Englewood Cliffs, N.J., Prentice-Hall, Inc., 1952) is very helpful, pp. 13-32.

43   A similar objection was raised by Condorcet against Borda's numbers in 1785, according to Isaac Todhunter. A History of the Mathematical Theory of Probabilty (New York, Chelsea Publishing Co., 1949), pp. 433-434.

44   Arrow, op. cit., pp. 46-60.

45   I would like to express my gratitude to Sidney J. Herzig, George Yoos, William Hughes, and especially Thomas A. Schwartz for their help and encouragement.

Bibliography

(Only works referred to in the text are included)

Alexis, M. and Wilson, C.Z. (1967). (ed) Organizational Decision-Making. Engelwood Cliffs: Prentice-Hall, Inc.

Alston, W.P. (1967). Motives and motivation. The Encyclopedia of Philosophy, (ed) P. Edwards. New York: MacMillan Co., 399-409.

Argyris, C. (1957). Personality and Organization. New York: Harper and Row Pub., Inc.

Argyris, C. (1964). Integrating the Individual and The Organization. New York: John Wiley and Sons, Inc.

Aristotle. Ethica Nichomachea. Trans. by W.D. Ross. Oxford: Clarendon Press, 1925.

Armstrong, A. (1971). On psychological impossibility. The Journal of Value Inquiry, 5, 81-89

Armstrong, W.E. (1939). The determinateness of the utility function. Economic Journal, 49, 453-467.

Arrow, K.J. (1951). Social Choice and Individual Values. New York: John Wiley and Sons, Inc.

Audi, R. (1973). The concept of wanting. Philosophical Studies, 24, 1-21.

Austin, J.L. (1961). Ifs and cans. Proceedings of the British Academy, 42, 109-132

Ayer, A.J. (1956). The Problem of Knowledge. Middlesex: Penguin Books Ltd.

Ayer, A.J. (1957). The conception of probability as a logical relation. Observation and Interpretation in the Philosophy of Physics. (ed) S. Korner. New York: Dover Pub., 12-17.

Ayer, A.J. (1959). (ed) Logical Positivism. New York: The Free Press.

Bachrach, P. and Baratz, M.S. (1970). _Power and Poverty_. New York: Oxford Univ. Press.

Baier, K. (1953). Good reasons. _Philosophical Studies_, 4, 1-15

Baier, K. (1958). _The Moral Point of View_. Ithaca: Cornell University Press.

Bales, R.E. (1971). Act-utilitarianism: account of right-making characteristics or decision-making procedure? _American Philosophical Quarterly_, 8, 257-265.

Barnard, C.I. (1938). _The Functions of the Executive._ Cambridge: Harvard University Press.

Barry, B. (1965). _Political Argument_. London: Routledge and Kegan Paul Ltd.

Bartley, W.W. (1962). _The Retreat to Commitment_. New York: Alfred A. Knopf.

Bartley, W.W. (1964). Rationality versus the theory of rationality. _The Critical Approach to Science and Philosophy_, (ed). M. Bunge. New York: Macmillan Co., 3-31.

Bauer, R.A. (1966). Detection and anticipation of impact: the nature of the task. _Social Indicators_, (ed) R.A. Bauer. Cambridge: M.I.T. Press, 1-67.

Benn, S.I. and Peters, R.S. (1959). _Social Principles and the Democratic State_. London: George Allen and Unwin, Ltd.

Berry, D.E. (1973). Health planning rationality. _Policy Sciences_ 4, 13-19

Black, D. (1958). _The Theory of Committees and Elections_. Cambridge: Cambridge University Press.

Blackstone, W.T. (1975). The American Psychological Association Code of Ethics For Research Involving Human Participants: An Appraisal. _The Southern Journal of Philosophy_, 13, 407-418.

Blanshard, B. (1961). _Reason and Goodness_. London: George Allen and Unwin Ltd.

Blau, P.M. (1955). _The Dynamics of Bureaucracy_. Chicago: University of Chicago Press.

Blau, P.M. and Scott, W.R. (1962). _Formal Organizations_. San Francisco: Chandler Pub. Co.

Brand, M. (1970a). Choosing and Doing. Ratio,   12,   85-92.

Brand, M. (1970b). (ed) The Nature of Human Action.
Glenview: Scott, Foresman and Co.

Brand, M. (1971). The Language of Not Doing.   American
Philosophical Quarterly, 8, 45-53.

Brand, M. (1972).   On Having the Opportunity. Theory and
Decision, 2, 307-313.

Brandt, R.B.   (1963).   Toward   a   Credible   Form   of
Utilitarianism. Morality and the Language of Conduct. (ed)
H. Castaneda and G. Nakhnikian. Detroit: Wayne State
University Press, 107-144.

Braybrooke, D. (1967). Economics and Rational Choice.   The
Encyclopedia of Philosophy .   (ed) P. Edwards. New York:
MacMillan Co., 454-458.

Braybrooke, D. (1968). Let Needs Diminish that Preferences
May Prosper. Studies in Moral Philosophy, (ed) N. Rescher.
Oxford: Oxford University Press, 86-107.

Braybrooke, D. and Lindblom, C.E. (1963). A Strategy of
Decision. New York: MacMillan Co.

Broad, C.D. (1930). Five Types of Ethical Theory.   London:
Routledge and Kegan Paul, Ltd.

Brown, D.G., (1968).   Action. London: George Allen and
Unwin, Ltd.

Buchanan, J.M. and Tullock, G. (1962).   The Calculus of
Consent. Ann Arbor: University of Michigan Press.

Bunge, M. (1961).   The Weight of Simplicity in the
Construction and Assaying of Scientific   Theories.
Philosophy of Science, 28, 120-149.

Cameron, N. (1947). The Psychology of Behavior Disorders.
Boston: Houghton Mifflin and Co.

Carnap, R. (1934).   On the Character of Philosophic
Problems. Philosophy of Science, 1, 5-19.

Carnap, R. (1950).   Logical Foundations of Probability.
Chicago: University of Chicago Press.

Charnes, A. and Stedry, A.C. (1966).   The Attainment of
Organization Goals Through Appropriate Selection of Subunit
Goals. Operational Research and the Social Sciences. (ed)
J.R. Lawrence. London: Tavistock Pub., 147-164.

Chisholm, R.M. (1968). Lewis' Ethics of Belief. The Philosophy of C.I. Lewis. (ed) P.A. Schlipp. LaSalle: Open Court Pub. Co., 223-242.

Churchman, C.W. (1961). Prediction and Optimal Decision. Englewood Cliffs: Prentice-Hall, Inc.

Clifford, W.K. (1886). Lectures and Essays. London: MacMillan and Co.

Coase, R.H. (1960). The Problem of Social Cost. The Journal of Law and Economics. 3, 1-44.

Cohen, J. (1960). Chance Skill and Luck. Middlesex: Penguin Books Ltd.

Cole, L. (1953). Human Behavior. Yonkers-on-Hudson: World Book Co.

Commission of Inquiry into the Non-Medical Use of Drugs (1972). Cannabis: A Report of the Commission of Inquiry into The Non-Medical Use of Drugs. Ottawa: Information Canada.

Conklin, K.R. (1974). Rational Action and Education. Philosophy of Education: Proceedings, 30, 165-174.

Costello, T.W. and Zalkind, S.S. (1963). (ed) Psychology in Administration. Englewood Cliffs: Prentice-Hall, Inc.

Dahl, R.A. (1960). The Analysis of Influence in Local Communities. Social Science and Community Action, (ed) C. Adrian. East Lansing: Michigan State Univ. Press, 230-247.

Dahl, R. (1965). Cause and Effect in the Study of Politics. Cause and Effect. (ed) D. Lerner. New York: MacMillan Co. 75-98.

Dahl, R.A. and Lindblom, C.E. (1953). Politics, Economics and Welfare. New York: Harper and Row Pub., Inc.

Daveney, T.F. (1964). Choosing. Mind. 73, 515-526.

Davidson, D. (1967a). Causal Relations. Journal of Philosophy, 21, 691-703.

Davidson, D. (1967b). The Logical Form of Action. The Logic of Action and Decision, (ed) N. Rescher. Pittsburgh: University of Pittsburgh Press, 81-95.

Davidson, D. (1969). The Individuation of Events. Essays in Honor of Carl G. Hempel. (ed) N. Rescher, et al. Dordrecht: D. Reidel, 216-234.

Davidson, D., Suppes, P. and Siegel, S. (1957). Decision-Making: An Experimental Approach. Stanford: Stanford University Press.

Davie, W.E. (1973). Being Prudent and Acting Prudently. American Philosophical Quarterly, 10, 57-60.

Denenberg, H.S., Eilers, R.D., Hoffman, G.W., Kline, C.A. Melone, J.J., Snider, H.W. (1964). Risk and Insurance. Englewood Cliffs: Prentice-Hall, Inc.

Deutsch, K.W. (1963). The Nerves of Government. New York: The Free Press.

Dewey, J. (1939). Theory of Valuation. Chicago: University of Chicago Press.

Diesing, P. (1950). The Nature and Limitations of Economic Rationality. Ethics, 61, 12-26.

Diesing, P. (1955). Noneconomic Decision-Making. Ethics, 66, 18-35.

Diesing, P. (1958). Socioeconomic Decisions. Ethics, 69, 1-18.

Diesing, P. (1962). Reason in Society. Urbana: University of Illinois Press.

Dill, W.R., Hilton, T.L. and Reitman, W.R. (1962). The New Managers. Englewood Cliffs: Prentice-Hall, Inc.

Dower, N. (1971). An Ambiguity in the concept of choice. American Philosophical Quarterly 8, 192-196.

Downs, A. (1957). An Economic Theory of Democracy. New York: Harper and Row Pub., Inc.

Dray, W.H. (1967). Holism and Individualism in History and Social Science. The Encyclopedia of Philosophy. (ed) P. Edwards. New York: MacMillan Co., 53-58.

Dror, Y. (1968). Public Policymaking Rexamined. San Francisco: Chandler Pub. Co.

Dror, Y. (1970a). Strategies for Administrative Reform P-4382. Santa Monica: Rand Corporation.

Dror, Y. (1970b). Law as a Tool of Directed Social Change: A Framework for Policymaking. P-4285. Santa Monica: Rand Corporation.

Dror, Y. (1971). Design for Policy Sciences. New York: American Elsevier Pub. Co. Inc.

Drucker, P.F. (1969). How to Make a Business Decision. Decision Theory and Information Systems, (ed) W.T. Greenwood. Cincinnati: South-Western Pub., 53-62.

Drucker, P.F. (1974) Management: Tasks, Responsibilities, Practices. New York: Harper and Row Pub., Inc.

Duncan-Jones, A. (1957). Utilitarianism and Rules. The Philosophical Quarterly, 8, 364-367.

Edgley, R. (1969). Reason in Theory and Practice. London: Hutchinson.

Edwards, E. and Tversky, A. (1967). (ed). Decision Making. Middlesex: Penguin Books Ltd.

Edwards, R.B. (1967). Is Choice Determined by the "Strongest Motive"? American Philosophical Quarterly, 4, 72-78.

Emmet, D. (1976). 'Motivation' in Sociology and Social Anthropology. Journal for the Theory of Social Behavior, 6, 85-104.

Englehardt, H.T. (1975). The Concepts of Health and Disease. Evaluation and Explanation in the Biomedical Sciences. (ed). H.T. Engelhardt and S.F. Spicker. Dordrecht: D. Reidel Pub. Co.

Evans, J. (1972). On Problems of Interpreting Reasoning Data: Logical and Psychological Approaches. Cognition, 1, 373-382.

Falk, W.D. (1945). Obligation and Rightness. Philosophy, 22, 129-147.

Farquharson, R. (1969). Theory of Voting. New Haven: Yale University Press.

Fischhoff, B. (1977). Cost-Benefit Analysis and the Art of Motorcycle Maintenance. Policy Sciences, 8, 177-202.

Fishburn, P.C. (1970). Intrasensitive Individual Preference and Transitive Majorities. Econometrica, 38, 482-489.

Fishburn, P.C. (1973). The Theory of Social Choice. Princeton: Princeton University Press.

Foa, U.G. (1971). Interpersonal and Economic Resources. Science, 171, 345-351.

Fox, J.T. (1969). Epistemology, Psychology and their Relevance for education in Bruner and Dewey. Educational Theory, 19, 58-75.

Fox, R.M. (1973). The Concept of Freedom in Sartre's Philosophy of Man. Philosophy in Context, 3, 56-70.

Frankena, W.K. (1958). Obligation and Motivation in Recent Moral Philosophy. Essays in Moral Philosophy, (ed) A.I. Melden. Seattle: University of Washington Press, 40-81.

Fried, C. (1970). An Anatomy of Values. Cambridge: Harvard University Press.

Friedrich, C.J. (1964). On Rereading Machiavelli and Althusius: Reason, Rationality and Religion. Rational Decision. (ed) C.J. Friedrich. New York: Atherton Press, 177-196.

Gallagher, K.T. (1964). On Choosing to Choose. Mind, 73, 480-495.

Gamson, W.A. (1968). Power and Discontent. Homewood: Dorsey Press.

Gauthier, D.P. (1967). Morality and Advantage. The Philosophical Review, 76, 460-475.

Gauthier, D.P. (1970). (ed) Morality and Rational Self-Interest. Englewood Cliffs: Prentice-Hall, Inc.

Gauthier, D.P. (1975). Reason and Maximization. Canadian Journal of Philosophy, 4, 411-433

Gewirth, A. (1964). The Generalization Principle. The Philosophical Review, 73, 229-242.

Gintis, H. and Bowles, S., (1975). The Contradiction of Liberal Educational Reform. Work, Technology and Education, (ed). W. Feinberg and H. Rosemont, Jr. Urbana: University of Illinois Press.

Goldman, A.I. (1970). A Theory of Human Action. Englewood Cliffs: Prentice-Hall, Inc.

Goldman, M.I. (1970). The Convergence of Environmental Disruption. Science, 170, 37-42.

Good, I.J. (1962). How Rational Should a Manager Be? Management Science, 8, 383-393.

Gore, W.J. and Silander, F.S. (1959). A Bibliographical Essay on Decision Making. Administrative Science Quarterly, 4, 97-121.

Gosling, J.C.B. (1969). Pleasure and Desire. Oxford: Clarendon Press

Grauhan, R.R. and Strubelt, W. (1971). Political Rationality Reconsidered: Notes on an Integrated Evaluative Scheme for Policy Choices. Policy Sciences, 2, 249-270.

Greenwood, W.T. (1969). (ed) Decision Theory and Information Systems, Cincinnati: South-Western Pub. Co.

Gross, B.M. (1964). The Managing of Organizations, Vol. II. New York: MacMillan Co.

Gross, B.M. (1966). The State of the Nation: Social Systems Accounting. Social Indicators, (ed) R.A. Bauer. Cambridge: M.I.T. Press, 154-271.

Hampshire, S. (1959). Thought and Action, New York: Viking Press, Inc.

Hancock, R. (1968). Choosing as Doing. Mind, 77, 575-576.

Handy, R. (1969). Value Theory and the Behavioral Sciences. Springfield: Charles C. Thomas.

Hare, A.P., Borgatta, E.F., and Bales, R.F. (1955), (ed). Small Groups. New York: Alfred A. Knopf, Inc.

Hare, R.M. (1952). The Language of Morals. Oxford: Clarendon Press.

Hare, R.M. (1963). Freedom and Reason. Oxford: Oxford University Press.

Harre, R. (1970). Constraints and Restraints. Metaphilosophy, 1, 279-299.

Harrison, J. (1952). Utilitarianism, Universalization, and Our Duty to be Just. Proceedings of the Aristotelian Society, 53, 105-134.

Harsanyi, J.C. (1969). Rational-Choice Models of Political Behavior vs. Functionalist and Conformist Theories. World Politics, 21, 513-538.

Harsanyi, J.C. (1972). Notes on the So-Called Incompleteness Problem and on the Proposed Alternative Concept of Rational Behavior. Theory and Decision, 2, 342-352.

Helmer, O. (1966). Social Technology. New York: Basic Books, Inc.

Hempel, C.G. (1950). Problems and Changes in the Empiricist Criterion of Meaning. Revue Internationale de Philosophie, 4, 41-63.

Hinrichs, H.H. (1969). Government Decision Making and the Theory of Benefit-Cost Analysis: A Primer. Program Budgeting and Benefit-Cost Analysis, (ed) Hinrichs, H.H. and Taylor, G.M. Pacific Palisades: Goodyear Pub. Co., Inc. 9-20.

Hinrichs, H.H. and Taylor, G.M. (1969). (ed) Program Budgeting and Benefit-Cost Analysis. Pacific Palisades: Goddyear Pub. Co. Inc.

Horngren, C.T. (1962). Cost Accounting Englewood Cliffs: Prentice-Hall, Inc.

Horsburgh, H.J.N. (1954). The Criteria of Assent to a Moral Rule. Mind, 63, 345-358.

Horsburgh, H.J.N. (1968). Non-Violence and Aggression. London: Oxford University Press.

Hovland, C.I., Lumsdaine, A.A. and Sheffield, F.D. (1949). Experiments in Mass Communication. Princeton: Princeton University Press.

James, W. (1909). The Meaning of Truth: A Sequel to Pragmatism. New York: Longmans, Green and Co.

James, W. (1955). Pragmatism. New York: Meridian Books, Inc.

James, W. (1956). The Will to Believe and Other Essays in Popular Philosophy. New York: Dover Pub.

Jennings. R.E. (1967). Preference and Choice as Logical Correlates. Mind, 76, 556-567.

Kalin, J. (1970). In Defense of Egoism. Morality and Rational Self-Interest, (ed) D.P. Gauthier. Englewood Cliffs: Prentice-Hall, Inc., 64-87.

Jungermann, H. and G. de Zeeuw. (1977). (ed) Decision-Making and Change in Human Affairs. Dordrecht: D. Reidel Pub. Co.

Kass, L.R. (1971). Death as an Event: A Commentary on Robert Morison. Science, 173, 698-702.

Katona, G. (1953). Rational Behavior and Economic Behavior. Psychological Review, 60, 307-318.

Katz, J. (1972). Altruism and Sympathy: Their History in Philosophy and Some Implications for Psychology. The Journal of Social Issues, 28, 59-69.

Kerr, D.H. (1976). The Logic of 'Policy' and Successful Policies. Policy Sciences, 7, 351-363.

Key, W.B. (1972). Subliminal Seduction. New York: New American Library.

Keynes, J.M. (1921). A Treatise on Probability, London: MacMillan Co.

Kim, J. (1969). Events and Their Descriptions: Some Considerations. Essays in Honor of Carl G. Hempel, (ed) N. Rescher, et al. Dordrecht: D. Reidel, 198-215.

Kneale, W. (1949). Probability and Induction. Oxford: Clarendon Press.

Knight, F.H. (1921). Risk, Uncertainty and Profit. New York: Houghton Mifflin Co.

Kotarbinski, T. (1965). Praxiology: An Introduction to the Science of Efficient Action. Oxford: Pergamon Press.

Kuhn, A. (1963). The Study of Society. Homewood: R.D. Irwin, Inc.

Kuhn, A. (1974). The Logic of Social Systems. San Francisco: Jossey-Bass.

Ladd, J. (1964). The Place of Practical Reason in Judicial Decision, Rational Decision. (ed) C.J. Friedrich. New York: Atherton Press, 126-144.

LaFramboise, J. (1975). A Question of Needs. Ottawa: The Canadian Council on Social Development.

Lakatos, I. (1968). Changes in the Problem of Inductive Logic. The Problem of Induction, (ed) I. Lakatos. Amsterdam: North Holland Pub. Co., 315-417.

LaPlace, P.S. de (1812). Théorie Analytique des Probabilitiés. Paris.

Lasswell, H.D. and Kaplan, A. (1950). Power and Society. New Haven: Yale University Press.

LeBlanc, H. (1962). Statistical and Inductive Probabilities. Englewood Cliffs: Prentice-Hall, Inc.

Lenz, J. (1956). Carnap on Defining 'Degree of Confirmation'. Philosophy of Science, 23, 230-236.

Levi, I. (1966). On Potential Surprise. Ratio, 8, 107-129.

Lewis, C.I. (1946). An Analysis of Knowledge and Valuation. LaSalle: The Open Court Pub. Co.

Lewis, C.I. (1955). The Ground and Nature of the Right. New York: Columbia University Press.

Lewis C.I. (1969). Values and Imperatives, (ed) J. Lange. Stanford: Stanford University Press.

Leys, W.A.R. (1952). Ethics for Policy Decisions. Englewood Cliffs: Prentice-Hall, Inc.

Luce, R.D. and Raiffa, H. (1957). Games and Decisions. New York: John Wiley and Sons, Inc.

Lundberg, C.C. (1962). Administrative Decisions: A Scheme for Analysis. Journal of the Academy of Management, 5, 165-178.

Lundberg, F. (1968). The Rich and the Super Rich. New York: Bantam Books.

Lyons, D. (1965). Forms and Limits of Utilitarianism. Oxford: Clarendon Press.

Lyons, W. (1973). A Note on Wanting to do Some Purposeful Action. Logique et Analyse, 16, 591-594.

MacRae, D. (1968). Utilitarian Ethics and Social Change. Ethics, 78, 188-198.

Majone, G. (1975). The Feasibility of Social Policies. Policy Sciences, 6, 49-69.

Malcolm, N. (1950). The Verification Argument. Philosophical Analysis, (ed) M. Black, Englewood Cliffs: Prentice-Hall,Inc., 244-298.

Manzer, R. (1974). A Socio-Political Report. Toronto: McGraw- Hill Ryerson Ltd.

March, J.G. and Simon, H.A. (1958). Organizations. New York: John Wiley and Sons, Inc.

Marschak, J. (1959). Efficient and Viable Organizational Forms. Modern Organizational Theory, (ed) M. Haire. New York: John Wiley and Sons, Inc., 307-320.

Martin, M. (1970). Religious Commitment and Rational Criticism. The Philosophical Forum, 2, 107-121.

Martin, R.M. (1967). Events and Descritptions of Events. Fact and Existence, (ed) J. Margolis. Oxford: Basil Blackwell, 63-73

Mason, R.O. (1969). A Dialectical Approach to Strategic Planning. Management Science, 15, B403-B414.

McCloskey, H.J. (1976). Human Needs, Rights and Political Values. American Philosophical Quarterly, 13, 1-11.

Merton, R.K. (1936). The Unanticipated Consequences of Purposive Social Action. American Sociological Review, 1, 894-904.

Merton, R.K. (1940). Bureaucratic Structure and Personality. Social Forces. 18, 560-568

Meyer, W.J. (1974). Democracy: Needs over Wants. Political Theory, 2, 197-214.

Michalos, A.C. (1967). Postulates of Rational Preference. Philosophy of Science, 34, 18-22.

Michalos, A.C. (1969). Principles of Logic. Englewood Cliffs: Prentice-Hall, Inc.

Michalos, A.C. (1970a). Improving Your Reasoning. Englewood Cliffs: Prentice-Hall, Inc.

Michalos, A.C. (1970b). Analytic and Other "Dumb" Guides of Life, Analysis, 30, 121-123.

Michalos, A.C. (1970c). Decision-Making in Committees. American Philosophical Quarterly, 7, 95-116.

Michalos, A.C. (1970d). Cost-Benefit versus Expected Utility Acceptance Rules. Theory and Decision, 1, 61-88.

Michalos, A.C. (1971). The Popper-Carnap Controversy. Hague: Martinus Nijhoff.

Michalos, A.C. (1972). Efficiency and Morality. The Journal of Value Inquiry, 6, 137-143.

Michalos, A.C. (1974). Review of "The Primacy of Practice." Dialogue, 13, 623-625.

Michalos, A.C. (1976a). Measuring the Quality of Life, Values and the Quality of Life, (ed). J. King-Farlow and W.R. Shea. New York: Science History Pub.

Michalos, A.C. (1976b). Review of "A Social-Political Report." Canadian Welfare, 52, 28.

Michalos, A.C. (1977). The Loyal Agent's Argument. A Paper Presented at the Conference on Ethics and Economics at the University of Delaware, Newark, Delaware, November 10-12, 1977.

Miller, D.W. and Starr, M.K. (1960). Executive Decisions and Operations Research. Englewood Cliffs: Prentice-Hall, Inc.

Mises, L. Von (1960). Epistemological Problems of Economics. Princeton: Van Nostrand.

Mises, R. Von (1939). Probability Statistics and Truth. New York: MacMillan Co.

Moor, J.H. (1976). Rationality and the Social Sciences. PSA 1976: Volume One, (ed) F. Suppe and P.D. Asquith. East Lansing: Philosophy of Science Association.

Morison, R.S. (1971). Death: Process or Event. Science, 173, 694-698.

Morlock, H. (1967). The Effect of Outcome Desirability on Information Required for Decisions. Behavioral Science, 12, 296-300.

Munsat, S. (1969). What is a Process? American Philosophical Quarterly, 6, 79-83.

Murakami, Y. (1968). Logic and Social Choice. London: Routledge and Kegan Paul, Ltd.

Myers, G.E. (1969). Self: An Introduction to Philosophical Psychology. New York: Western Publishing Co.

Neumann, J. Von and Morgenstern, O. (1944). Theory of Games and Economic Behavior. Princeton: Princeton University Press.

Niebuhr, R. (1932). Moral Man and Immoral Society. New York: C. Scribner's Sons.

Niehans, J. (1959). Reflections on Shackle, Probability, and Our Uncertainty About Uncertainty. Metroeconomica, 11, 74-88.

Niiniluoto, I. and Tuomela, R., (1973). Theoretical Concepts and Hypothetico-Inductive Inference. Dordrecht: D. Reidel Pub. Co.

Norman, R. (1971). Reasons for Actions Oxford: Basil Blackwell.

Norris, S. (1975). The Intelligibility of Practical Reasoning. American Philosophical Quarterly, 12, 77-84.

Nowell-Smith, P.H. (1954). Ethics. Middlesex: Penguin Books, Ltd.

Nowell-Smith, P.H. (1958). Choosing, Deciding and Doing. Analysis, 18, 63-69.

Olson, R.G. (1965). The Morality of Self-Interest. New York: Harcourt, Brace and World, Inc.

Opler, M.E. (1954). Social Aspects of Technical Assistance in Operation. Tensions and Technology Series, Unesco, No. 4, Washington, D.C.

Oppenheim, F.E. (1964). Rational Decisions and Intrinsic Valuations, Rational Decision, (ed) C.J. Friedrich. New York: Atherton Press, 217-220.

Pap, A. (1949). Elements of Analytic Philosophy. New York: MacMillan Co.

Pears, D.F. (1971). Ifs and Cans - I. Canadian Journal of Philosophy. 1, 249-274.

Pears, D.F. (1972). Ifs and Cans - II. Canadian Journal of Philosophy. 1, 369-391.

Pegis, A.C. (1945), (ed). Basic Writings of Saint Thomas Aquinas. New York: Random House.

Penelhum, T. (1956). The Logic of Pleasure. Philosophy and Phenomenological Research, 17, 488-503.

Perry, R.B. (1926). General Theory of Value. Cambridge: Harvard University Press.

Petersen, R. (1977). Small Business: Building a Balanced Economy. Erin: Press Porcepic Ltd.

Popper, K.R. (1945). The Open Society and its Enemies. London: Routledge and Kegan Paul, Ltd.

Popper, K.R. (1957). The Poverty of Historicism. London: Routledge and Kegan Paul.

Popper, K.R. (1959). The Propensity Interpretation of Probability. The British Journal for the Philosophy of Science, 10, 25-42.

Popper, K.R. (1968). Remarks on the Problems of Demarcation and of Rationality. Problems in the Philosophy of Science, (ed) I. Lakatos and A. Musgrave. Amsterdam: North-Holland Pub. Co., 88-102.

Prest, A.R. and Turvey, R., (1965). Cost-Benefit Analysis: A Survey. The Economic Journal, 75, 683-735.

Price, H.H. (1966). Belief and Will. Philosophy of Mind (ed). S. Hampshire. New York: Harper and Row Pub., Inc.

Price, H.H. (1969). Belief. London: George Allen and Unwin Ltd.

Raiffa, H. (1968). Decision Analysis. Reading, Massachusetts: Addison-Wesley Pub. Co.

Ramsey, F.P. (1931). Truth and Probability. The Foundations of Mathematics. (ed) R.B. Braithwaite. London: Routledge and Kegan Paul, Ltd., 156-198.

Rapoport, A. (1966). Laboratory Studies of Conflict and Co-operation. Operational Research and the Social Sciences, (ed) J.R. Lawrence. London: Tavistock Pub., 369-398.

Rapoport, A. (1974). Prisoner's Dilemma - Recollections and Observations. Game Theory as a Theory of Conflict Resolution. (ed). A Rapoport. Dordrecht: D. Reidel Pub. Co.

Rawls, J. (1971). A Theory of Justice. Cambridge: Harvard University Press.

Reddiford, G. (1975). Rationality and Understanding. Philosophy, 50, 19-35.

Reichenbach, H. (1949). The Theory of Probability. Berkeley: University of California Press.

Rescher, N. (1964a). Hypothetical Reasoning. Amsterdam: North-Holland Pub. Co.

Rescher, N. (1964b). Pragmatic Justification: A Cautionary Tale. Philosophy, 39, 346-348.

Rescher, N. (1966a). Notes on Preference, Utility and Cost. Synthese, 16, 327-336.

Rescher, N. (1966b). Distributive Justice. Indianapolis: Bobbs-Merrill Co., Inc.

Rescher, N. (1969a). The Concept of Control. Essays in Philosophical Analysis. (ed) N. Rescher. Pittsburgh: University of Pittsburgh Press, 327-354.

Rescher, N. (1969b). Choice Without Preference: A Study of the History and of the Logic of the Problem of "Buridan's Ass". Essays in Philosophical Analysis. Pittsburgh: Univ. of Pittsburgh Press, 111-158.

Rescher, N. (1969c). Introduction to Value Theory. Englewood Cliffs: Prentice-Hall, Inc.

Rescher, N. (1972).   Welfare. Pittsburgh: University of
Pittsburgh Press.

Rescher, N. (1973a). The Coherence Theory of Truth.
Oxford: Oxford University Press.

Rescher, N. (1973b).   The Primacy of Practice. Oxford:
Basil Blackwell

Rome, B.K. and Rome, S.C.   (1971).   Organizational Growth
Through Decision-Making. New York: American Elsevier Pub.
Co., Inc.

Rorty, R. (1967). (ed)   The Linguistic Turn.   Chicago:
University of Chicago Press.

Rothenberg, J. (1961).   The Measurement of Social Welfare.
Englewood Cliffs: Prentice-Hall, Inc.

Russell, B. (1948). Human Knowledge. New York: Simon   and
Schuster, Inc.

Ryle, G. (1949).   The Concept of Mind. New York: Barnes
and Noble.

Savage, L.J. (1954). The Foundations of Statistics.   New
York: John Wiley and Sons, Inc.

Schelling, T.C. (1963).   The Strategy of Conflict. New
York: Oxford University Press.

Schwartz, T. (1970). On the Possibility of Rational   Policy
Evaluation. Theory and Decision, 1, 89-106.

Scriven, M. (1961).   The Key Property of Physcial Laws –
Inaccuracy. Current Issues in the Philosophy of Science.
(ed) H. Feigl and G. Maxwell. New York: Holt Rinehart and
Winston.

Selznick, P. (1949). TVA and the Grass Roots.   Berkeley:
University of California Press.

Shackle, G.L.S. (1961).   Decision, Order and Time in Human
Affairs. Cambridge: Cambridge University Press.

Shiner, R.A. (1973). The Non-Rationality of Buridan's Ass.
The Southern Journal of Philosophy, 11, 329-335.

Simon, H.A. (1945).   Administrative Behavior. New York:
MacMillan Co.

Simon, H.A. (1957). Models of Man. New York: John Wiley
and Sons, Inc.

Simon, H.A. (1960). The New Science of Management Decision New York: Harper and Brothers.

Singer, M.G. (1961). Generalization in Ethics. New York: Alfred A. Knopf, Inc.

Sobel, J.H. (1967). 'Everyone', Consequences, and Generalization Arguments. Inquiry, 10, 373-404.

Sobel, J.H. (1970). Utilitarianisms: Simple and General. Inquiry, 13, 394-449.

Sparshott, F.E. (1958). An Enquiry Into Goodness. Toronto: University of Toronto Press.

Steffen, A.L. (1973). The Active Tradition: A Convergence of Ideas. Educational Theory, 23, 321-332.

Stein, H. (1952). (ed) Public Administration and Policy Development. New York: Harcourt, Brace and Co.

Stein, H. and Denison, E.F. (1960). High Employment and Growth in the American Economy. Goals for Americans.

President's Commission on National Goals. Englewood Cliffs: Prentice-Hall, Inc., 163-190.

Suchman, E.A. (1967). Evaluative Research. New York: Russell Sage Foundation.

Sumner, L.W. (1968). Value Judgments and Action. Mind, 72, 383-399.

Taylor, R. (1966). Action and Purpose, Englewood Cliffs: Prentice-Hall, Inc.

Taylor, V. (1970). How Much is Good Health Worth? Policy Sciences, 1, 49-72.

Thorsrud, E. and Emery, F.E. (1966). Industrial Conflict and "Industrial Democracy". Operational Research and The Social Sciences, (ed) J.R. Lawrence. London: Tavistock Pub., 439-447.

Tolman, E.C. (1951). A Psychological Model. Toward a General Theory of Action. (ed) T. Parsons and E.A. Shils. Cambridge: Harvard University. Press. 279-364.

Tomas, V. (1957). (ed) Charles S. Peirce. Essays in the Philosophy of Science. New York: The Liberal Arts Press.

Toulmin, S. (1953). The Philosophy of Science. London: Hutchinson and Co., Ltd.

Tukey,   J.W.   (1960).   Conclusions   vs   Decisions.
Technometrics, 2, 423-433.

Vickers, G. (1965). The Art of Judgment. London: Chapman
and Hall.

Wagner, H.M. (1969).   Principles of Operations Research.
Englewood Cliffs: Prentice-Hall, Inc.

Walter,   E.   and   A.   Minton.   (1975).   Soft   Determinism,
Freedom, and Rationality. The Personalist, 56, 364-384.

Walton, D. (1974). Control. Behaviorism, 2, 162-171.

Walton, R.E. and McKersie, R.B. (1966). Behavioral Dilemmas
in Mixed-Motive Decision Making. Behavioral Science. 11,
370-384.

Watkins, J.W.N. (1952).   Ideal   Types   and   Historical
Explanation. The British Journal for the Philosophy of
Science, 3, 22-43.

Watkins, J. (1970). Imperfect Rationality. Explanation in
the Behavioral Sciences, (ed) R. Borger and F. Cioffi.
Cambridge: Cambridge University Press, 167-217.

Wendt, D. and C. Vlek. (1975) (ed). Utility, Probability,
and Human Decision Making Dordrecht: D. Reidel Pub. Co.

Wilensky, H.L. (1970). Intelligence in Industry: The Uses
and Abuses of Experts. The Annals of the American Academy
of Political and Social Science, 388, 46-58.

Wilson, C.Z. and Alexis, M. (1962). Basic Frameworks for
Decisions. Journal of the Academy of Management   5,
151-164.

Wolff, R.P. (1970). Maximization of Expected Utility as A
Criterion of Rationality in Military Strategy and Foreign
Policy. Social Theory and Practice, 1, 99-111.

Zwicky, F. (1967). The Morphological Approach to Discovery,
Invention, Research and Construction. New Methods of
Thought and Procedure. (ed) F. Zwicky and A.G. Wilson. New
York: Springer-Verlag, Inc., 273-297.

Index of Names

Index of Names
prepared by Francis J. Smith

Index of Subjects

Index of Subjects
prepared by Francis J. Smith